I0605056

THE FIRST WITCHES

In Loving Memory of My Mother

1947–2023

THE FIRST WITCHES

Women of Power in the Classical World

Alexis Hannah Prescott

First published in Great Britain in 2025 by
PEN AND SWORD HISTORY
An imprint of
Pen & Sword Books Ltd
Yorkshire – Philadelphia

ISBN 978 1 39903 836 2

A CIP catalogue record for this book is available from the British Library.

Typeset in Times New Roman 11.5/14 by
SJmagic DESIGN SERVICES, India.
Printed and bound in the UK by CPI Group (UK) Ltd.

The Publisher's authorised representative in the EU for product safety is Authorised Rep Compliance Ltd., Ground Floor, 71 Lower Baggot Street, Dublin D02 P593, Ireland.
www.arccompliance.com

For a complete list of Pen & Sword titles please contact
PEN & SWORD BOOKS LIMITED
George House, Units 12 & 13, Beevor Street, Off Pontefract Road,
Barnsley, South Yorkshire, S71 1HN, England
E-mail: enquiries@pen-and-sword.co.uk
Website: www.pen-and-sword.co.uk

or

PEN AND SWORD BOOKS
1950 Lawrence Rd, Havertown, PA 19083, USA
E-mail: uspen-and-sword@casematepublishers.com
Website: www.penandswordbooks.com

Contents

Introduction

What Is a Witch?

Double, double toil and trouble;
Fire burn and cauldron bubble.
Shakespeare, *Macbeth*,
Act 4, Scene 1, lines 10–11.

These infamous lines chanted by Shakespeare's three witches contain some of the most well-known and well-remembered words from the dark, foreboding tragedy of *Macbeth*. Here, the women dance and sing around their cauldron at the approval of Hecate,[1] in much the same fashion as image 1 suggests, as they place unsavoury items into it as part of their potion concoction. In this scene, the witches gather together a collection of severed body parts such as a 'toe of a frog', 'tongue of dog', and a 'lizard's leg', before being interrupted by the appearance of Macbeth who seeks further reaffirmation of his kingship through prophetic means.[2] The three crones in this play form the epitome of the Western view of the type of woman we call a 'witch'. They are old hags, with withered facial features, and hairs sprout from their chins.[3]

In conjunction with their hideous appearance, they also perform acts of dangerous magic that have become synonymous with witchcraft: they foretell the future, albeit in riddles, they control the weather – and are particularly associated with tempestuous storms that blot out the sun –, they are linked to the night, the raven and the screech owl, and worship the goddess of witchcraft, Hecate.[4] But, above all, they can manipulate and destroy men's lives.[5] Indeed, the general consensus during Shakespeare's time was that the witch would be in league with the Devil and the dark arts. The sixteenth-century commentator George Gifford stated that the witch would do 'develish' work for the purpose of 'hurting' others.[6] Likewise, William West referred to the witch during Elizabeth I's reign as a 'hag' who has made a 'pact with the Devil', having full control over 'lightning and thunder' causing 'hail and tempests', and who can even remove 'trees to another place'.[7] The crime against nature was one of their major acts of disruption, alongside the ability to hurt or destroy humans. Witches were often accused of ruining harvests or even preventing farm animals from performing their tasks, such as providing essential milk to the community. Prurience was yet another typical crime with sixty-three women in south-western Germany accused of witchcraft between 1562–1563 due to a devastating hailstorm but also disrupting sexual relations.[8] The word 'witch' itself is thought to derive from the old English 'wicca', meaning sorceress and from the Germanic 'wichelen' which was the ability to bewitch.[9] Sorceresses, therefore, were believed to bewitch by means of destructive spells. In summary, the generic definition for a witch is a woman who can cause harm to others, the environment and essentially destroy communities.[10] This certainly was the view of Shakespeare's audience when *Macbeth* was first performed in 1606 and, indeed, of his patron and monarch of the time, James I, who is said to have spurred on the witch hunts that dominated the first half of the seventeenth century.[11] This view of the witch, however, despite having connections to Old English, was not defined in this era as part of a Christian crusade against the dark agents of the Devil himself. Moreover, despite the dominance that a play like *Macbeth* and the witch hunts themselves may have had upon the Western consciousness regarding the witch and her dark arts, the witch itself, with her elderly and haggard appearance,[12] coupled with her often nightly and ominous pursuits, has a much older origin that is found embedded in ancient Western literature.

Witches in Ancient Greece and Rome

It is a common misconception that the people of the Jacobean era based their representation of the witch upon the Bible, and the King James Bible in particular. Whilst it makes sense that a profoundly puritanical view of the woman as a witch would have its roots in biblical texts, the Bible itself is somewhat quiet on what a witch may look like and, indeed, practice.[13] This does not mean that magic is entirely absent from the Bible. There is some belief that Moses was a magician of sorts who dabbled with magical practices, as stated in Acts 7:22, which claims he was 'taught the whole wisdom of the Egyptians [that is, the magicians from Egypt], and he was powerful in words and deeds', and, as a result, the miracles Moses performed[14] were 'magical in nature',[15] despite Josephus' claim that they prove the divine power of God.[16] The role of the female witch and her extensive use of her craft, however, is decidedly limited in the Bible, other than some brief references. Deuteronomy 18:10–12 speaks of those who observed 'unsanctioned religious practices', such as necromancy, and strongly advised the Levi Tribe against such people.[17] The infamous Witch of Endor encounter by Saul, whereby he called upon a witch to perform a necromantic spell, will be addressed later with the discussion of the Roman witch Erictho.[18] For now, it is sufficient to state that this scene is lacking in exact detail concerning the necromantic practice and, indeed, of any close description of the notorious witch herself. Moreover, whilst Exodus 22:18 contains the Mosaic law which famously states that 'thou shalt not suffer a witch to live',[19] a concise imagery of the witch and her arts is overall limited. For this, we have to turn to the Greek and Roman worlds.

Both ancient Greece and Rome had an abundance of terminology to describe those who practiced magic. These practitioners were real-life women and men who were labelled by the following terms as a means of identifying their magical craft within their societies. In Greece, for instance, we have references to the *agurtes*, who was a wondering beggar priest; the *goetes*, who dealt with spirits and ghosts; the *epodos*, who sang incantations; the *mantis*, who revealed concealed things; the *magos*, which seemed to be a generalised term for someone who specialised in all of the aforementioned aspects of magic; the *pharmakeis* (masculine) and the *pharmarkides* (feminine), who dealt with potions, and finally, the *rhizotomoi*, who were the 'root cutters' specialising in herbs.[20] This vast array of vocabulary for all manner of attributes related to witches, male sorcerers and their occupations suggests that in ancient Greece, magic as a craft was well known.

Likewise, Rome also had a healthy vocabulary when it came to describing witches. Significantly, the list of terms is predominantly feminine, indicating a wider belief that the magical arts were practiced by women. We have references to *cantatrix* or *praecantrix*, referring to a woman who sang prophetic songs; a *vates*, who was a prophetess;

veneficae, who dealt with poison (*venenum*); a *malefica*, who was a sorceress. The *lamiae* and *strigae* tended to be shape shifters who could turn into screech owls and who preyed upon small children. *Saga* was a generalised term attributed to witches, deriving from the Latin *sagacitas* (and so our word *sagacity*); the *sagae* were women who had high levels of prophetic knowledge. Finally, *quaedam anus* was used to specify 'some old woman' when discussing witches in Roman texts.[21] Once again, this abundance of vocabulary for the witch and her practices, suggests that witches were a common entity in this culture.

This does not mean that such practitioners were accepted in society. Quite the contrary. We have a few instances in the historical records that show that magical practitioners were targeted by law. The *Lex Cornelia* of 81 BC made the use of poison (or *veneficium* as it is referred to) a crime and also those *venefici* who penetrated the body with the use of a weapon, such as a dagger.[22] In 331 BC, 170 women were executed for supposedly causing an epidemic in Rome by means of *veneficium*.[23] Further, under Rome's second emperor Tiberius, 'sellers of poison (*venenarii*) and evil-doers (*malefici*) were arrested'.[24] This included forty-five men and eighty-five women who were eventually executed.[25] In 319 AD, Emperor Constantine I forbade those who called themselves diviners from approaching a 'private house' and crossing 'another man's threshold'.[26] We even have references to women being burned at the stake for their witchcraft and many instances of prophetic books being publicly destroyed.[27] According to the historian Suetonius, Augustus, the Roman Empire's first emperor, burnt a staggering 2,000 magical books in 31 BC.[28] Aside from the growing unpopularity regarding witchcraft, we know of renowned writers in Rome who dabbled with 'beneficial' incantations as a way of aiding certain health issues. Cato the Elder records a step-by-step incantation to heal a fractured or dislocated joint. Using a 4- or 5-foot green reed, this is to be split in two and placed on the bone that is causing pain. An incantation must then be read out loud until the reeds that have been halved join together. They must then be bound and attached to the fractured joint with a spell spoken daily until such a time that the fracture is cured.[29] Although this may demonstrate an avid interest in the use of witchcraft, it is more likely a fascination with folkloric remedies similar to our own interest in 'old wives' tales', Cato himself being known to gather much agricultural lore within his own works.[30] Witchcraft itself, or at least the worst kind of it, was generally marginalised. The Greeks, too, viewed practitioners of the craft, who were also assumed to be women, as impious.

What we can establish from these extensive lists of terms and laws are some ideas of what the Greeks and Romans believed these women did. There were some writers, however, who viewed them as frauds. For instance, whilst they believed witches could foretell the future, the more sceptical writers thought many were doing this for the purposes of gaining a profit – this is something which Plato alludes to in his *Republic* when he claims that 'beggar-priests and prophets go to the doors of the rich and persuade them that they have the power, acquired them by the gods by sacrifices and incantations [to aid the rich person]…for a small fee.'[31] Likewise, the view of these practitioners as mere charlatans is displayed in the Hippocratic treatise, 'On Sacred Disease': 'they pretend to be very pious and have special knowledge'. Conversely, the aforementioned lists provide valuable insight into what the overall populace believed these practitioners could do, such as using herbs to make potions and, as an extension, possessing the ability to cast spells. They credited women with the use of poison to harm others. They also believed witches could converse with the spirit world, lending themselves to necromantic practices and exorcism. Rather grotesquely, they also believed that witches could shape-shift and perform cannibalism. Generally, and collectively, such women were viewed as evil wrong doers, hence the term *malefici*.

Moreover, in recent years, there has been an attempt to understand the nature of witchcraft in the Gracco-Roman world through the use of inscriptional evidence as found on gravestones.[32] There are a handful of tombstones that refer to the unexpected death of a relative through sorcery and witchcraft by means of spells and curses that may have been placed upon the individual, resulting in their untimely demise. In the Greek world, there are epitaphs that refer to the specific use of *pharmaka* (so dealing with drugs for the use of potions and poisons) that have been used to destroy the person in question. One such inscription relates the 'terrible' use of '*pharmaka* against my entrails and my life.'[33] Another found in Cilicia was erected for a young, unmarried woman named Hermione, who is described as *pepharmakeumene*, the 'victim of *pharmaka*'[34] The Romans likewise have inscriptional evidence relating similar ills, such as one found in Roman Africa of a 28-year-old woman who died through bewitching: 'by spells, she was lying ill for a long time, as life was forced out from her'.[35] Yet another tells of a freewoman who died a painful death as a result of *veneficae*, sorceresses who dealt with poison.[36] Fritz Graf's study of these inscriptions reflects a society whereby superstition played a major part in influencing close-knit communities, such as within families and the social set up of households, and even within the close community of the imperial household itself, who had its fair share of accusations pertaining to witchcraft,[37] thus supporting the anthropological view that witchcraft persists in small, enclosed groups, especially during times of social stress.[38] However, such a thesis distracts from the publication of literature that was actively encouraged during the rise of Augustan propaganda, whereby the myriad of public titles and roles that were generally attributed to witches and sorcerers at this time meant that the witch was seen as a particular evil entity. It also does not consider the persecution against witches and the laws that were used to outlaw them. If this was indeed a superstitious society where only small households believed in witchcraft, Augustus and other Roman emperors surely would not have taken the extensive measures listed above to rid the city of it. For this current study, whilst the inscriptions provide us with insights as to what families may have believed, they still fall short in supplying detailed descriptions of the witches themselves.

On the whole, however useful the historical records are in helping us understand that witches were feared, they do not provide us with any in-depth detail as to what their practices may have consisted of and why societies felt a need to outlaw them; or, indeed, what a witch herself looked like and how people best avoided having direct contact with one. This is where the literature, namely the poetry, novels and plays of the day, provide us with a rich tapestry of detail relating to these women.

Witches in Greek and Roman Literature

There are many examples of witches mentioned in the literature, some playing minor roles, others having a more dominant appearance. Greek writers generally perceived them to be *pharmarkides* (witches that dealt with potions) and *rhizotomoi* (witches that were 'root-cutters', who dealt with herbs). The Romans, on the other hand, saw them as far more powerful entities who had control over *venenum* (poison) and prophecies. It was believed that they could also shape-shift, perform powerful acts of necromancy and participate in cannibalism. In fact, by the time we reach the Roman world, we are dealing with some of the most vivid portrayals of witches in Western literature. A discussion of witches in the Greek and Roman worlds is, therefore, an analysis of how the modern witch came to be.

The literature also raises questions concerning why some women were written about in this way. The Greek literature tends to be more sympathetic in their portrayal of witches and their craft, but the Romans seem to have had an innate fear of them: for them, most of the major female witches were powerful women who could exert dominance and catastrophe upon their unsuspecting victims, whilst some of the more minor victims were innocent bystanders who sought out witchcraft accidentally. Nevertheless, they were still vilified for doing so. There seems to be a clear element of misogyny in writing of this stock character in literature which will be addressed in the following chapters, but for now, it is safe to say that these women formed significant stereotypes of those females that subverted social norms and acted almost in a perverse manner to the status quo. Such representation of hideous and grotesque witches would hopefully encourage women to maintain social stability by acting as chaste, loyal and good citizens.[39]

What follows are overviews of some popular major and minor witches found in the Greek and Roman texts. These will serve as forerunners for the witches that will be the main focus of this book. You will notice that they share some commonalities: they are powerful; they use elements of witchcraft which you will be familiar with, such as poison, incantations and elements of the night. Above all, their dealings with witchcraft are vividly portrayed as a means to horrify and spark fear.

Medea

Medea is probably one of the most famous women to arise from Classical literature as a powerful witch with connections to Circe and Hecate; she has been labelled as the niece of the former, as well as the daughter of the latter.[40] Through this pedigree, she inherited the use of *pharmaka* (drugs for potions) and Medea is referred to as using this throughout her mythology. She appears quite frequently in the Greek as well as the Roman literature from the fifth century BC. She is the protagonist of Euripides' tragedy *Medea* in 431 BC and is also one of the main characters of Apollonius' *Argonautica* in the third century BC. In addition, she makes an appearance in book IV of Diodorus Siculus' *Bibliotheca historica* composed from 60–30 BC, while also being the subject of Roman writers from Ovid's *Heroides*[41] and *Metamorphoses* in 8 AD and Seneca's tragedy named after her composed in 50 AD. But, the earliest known reference to Medea and her craft comes from Homer's *Iliad*. The Homeric epics, being the most well-known of all the Greek literature, are thought to have been composed around the eighth century BC, but reflect a fantastical society and a heroic age combining the world of the deities, great heroes and traditional Greek folklore. It seems fitting, therefore, that characters like Circe and Medea should be cited within them. In Homer's *Iliad* 11, Nestor relates his past heroic feats and explains how he 'slew the warrior Moulios…he was the son-in-law of Augeias…(whose) eldest daughter Agamede…knew all the drugs (*pharmaka*) that the wide earth bears'.[42] Daniel Ogden convincingly argues that the 'Agamede' referred to is the 'Medea-figure in embryo' as their names share the same root meaning 'clever woman'.[43] Here, we have a woman dealing with drugs and, therefore, concocting potions. But the real vividness of her witchcraft in the literature comes much later when we get a real frisson of fear reading the full extent of what it meant to have contact with her.

Euripides' tragedy *Medea* recounts events after the famous tale of the Argonauts, a tale that is well known. The story focuses upon the hero Jason, who was sent on a quest by his uncle Pelias, who had usurped his father's kingdom. The quest takes Jason to Colchis in the Black Sea region to obtain the Golden Fleece, the sacred and prized possession of Aeetes, the king of the Colchian land. Jason meets Medea, the daughter of the king, who aids Jason in his mission, having fallen in love with him through the intervention of Aphrodite. Aeetes tests Jason's heroism by making him yoke fire-breathing bulls and then sow a deadly furrow, which grows into warriors he has to fight. Medea uses her *pharmaka* to help him with these tasks, as is also alluded to by Euripides in his play.[44] Abandoning her kingdom, she leaves with Jason and kills his uncle Pelias through means of boiling his flesh in a cauldron, again alluded to by Euripides.[45] Banished from Jason's homeland for this murder, the couple arrive in Corinth, where Euripides' play is set. The play covers a few years into their relationship where they now have two sons, but Jason himself wishes to improve his reputation and not be classed as an outsider, has been accepted as the new consort and husband of the king of Corinth's daughter. An outraged Medea seeks deadly vengeance for this betrayal through womanly wiles but also through her witchcraft. The most famous usage of the latter is in her dealings with the princess Jason has married by poisoning a gift of a dress for her which burns her skin to her bones when she adorns it. Whilst Medea herself as a character is ambivalent in this play – she stresses the hardships of the female sex in a predominantly male-dominated society, for instance, which evokes our sympathy for her as a downtrodden, ostracised female – her deadly nature cannot be overlooked as the second half of the play is a whirlwind of madness combined with the use of the dark arts. Medea's madness culminates in her dreadful act of filicide before leaving triumphantly, as image 2 highlights, in a chariot drawn by dragons. The play, overall, demonstrates how deadly a woman can be when she is scorned and hateful and, above all, when she has knowledge of the use of *pharmaka*.

This deadly image of Medea as a witch persists in other accounts of her. By the time we reach 30 BC, Medea's use of *pharmaka* has become formidable. In Diodorus Siculus' *Bibliotheca historica*, Medea's drugs not only have the ability to destroy those that hinder her and Jason, Medea herself can also use them to transform her appearance into that of an old crone and to create an effigy of the goddess Artemis which she uses to hide inside 'all sorts of powerful drugs'.[46] This she does to infiltrate and 'terrify' the population of Pelias' city so that the citizens will take in the effigy, allowing her to trick Pelias with her magic and eventually murder him, enabling her beloved Jason to regain his kingdom.[47]

There are obvious correlations here to the Trojan Horse myth. This, too, was an effigy made to trick the populace of Troy, who take the wooden contraption with no knowledge that there are soldiers inside the horse who will unleash terror upon the city. Medea, therefore, in the imagery of an old crone, coupled with her deadly drugs, has become a destroyer of a nation. The idea of the witch as a crone who can cause terror and destruction will become a popular theme in the later Roman texts.

In the early Roman imperial regime, Ovid's Medea has morphed into the epitome of the witch in the modern sense. In his *Metamorphoses*, for instance, she has the ability to use her magical herbs to rejuvenate the skin of an elderly man and to also trick, beguile and murder through the pretence of magic. In her promise to rejuvenate Jason's feeble father Aeson to the bloom of youth, she leaves 'in the deadly stillness of the night' in order to gather herbs to perform her magic, and in the fullness of the moon, she seeks aid as she stretches her arms to the stars and howls to the Night and her consort, Hecate. As she calls upon the latter, she reveals the full power of her magic: 'With my incantations I force fanged serpents to split their skins; I dislodge the rocks and uproot the trees, shift forests and order the mountains to tremble, the earth to rumble and spirits to rise from their graves. I can draw the moon from the sky'.[48]

Here is a witch who can disrupt nature and effectively dismantle the natural order, who can perform necromancy and pull the moon from the sky. The ability to draw the moon from the sky was a distinct characteristic of witchcraft in Thessaly, an area considered to be the centre of sorcery, magic and witchcraft throughout Antiquity and Medea's association with it here is in keeping with Ovid's overall dark imagery of her.[49] She further uses her magic as a form of trickery so that Pelias, Jason's uncle who usurped his throne, would die. She firstly convinces Pelias' daughters that she has the ability through her arts to make Pelias a youth again by magically restoring a wizened ram to that of a bleating lamb. Convinced of her magic, she tells the daughters to slice their father's throat in the same manner she had done with the ram so that her incantations will work. This is a ruse, however, that results in Pelias' death. This art of manipulation that becomes a stereotypical character trait of the witch is being played out here in gruesome detail.

Medea has evolved throughout the literature from a witch that specialises purely in *pharmaka* to one that can control the environment around her and perform deadly unnatural acts in the darkness of night. Medea is even portrayed in literature as using instruments typically associated with witches, from a cauldron to a curved knife of bronze.[50] The Roman view of her is certainly in keeping with the general idea of the modern interpretation of a witch and, as such, she deserves a place amongst the first witches to arise in the Western world.

Simaetha and Other Minor Witches

Minor witches or women who seek magical powers form a significant element of later Greek and Roman literature. Often these women have

been spurned by the ones they love and desire either to have their lovers restored to them or to have them destroyed. These women do so by seeking the dark arts through direct contact with a witch if they are not one themselves, pouring libations to the spirits of darkness that lurk in the underworld and offering incantations to the full moon or the goddess of witchcraft, Hecate.

Theocritus, a Hellenistic writer living between 300–260 BC, wrote a poem entitled *The Witch* (*Pharmakeutria*) or *The Witches* (*Pharmakeutriai*). Both titles appear to have been passed down.[51] The poem explains how the protagonist, Simaetha, an ordinary young Greek woman, turns to a female magical practitioner to aid her in trying to restore her lost love. This she does by firstly citing a fire spell upon her neglectful lover, the athlete Delphis, amidst a fitting scene of witchcraft with the full moon shining in the background and near the shrine and statue of Hecate. She then burns barley meal, bay leaves, a waxen puppet and some bran upon Hecate's altar. Lastly, she burns the herb hippomanes and a piece of fringe from her lover's cloak, before calling upon the moon and the goddess Hecate to make sure her concoctions have the necessary impact:

> So shine me fair, sweet Moon; for to thee, still Goddess, is my song, to thee and that Hecate infernal who makes e'en the whelps to shiver on her goings to and fro where these tombs be and the red blood lies. All hail to thee, dread and awful Hecate! I prithee so bear me company that this medicine of my making prove potent as any of Circe's or Medea's or Perimed's of the golden hair. (*Idyll*.2.10)

Simaetha then explains that she will give a love philtre to Delphis the next day, the active ingredient of which includes a powdered lizard. Some classic images of witchcraft are being portrayed in this scene like using the night to cast such spells which is a unique feature of the craft. Theocritus also adds iconic items such as the waxen puppet, herbs, parts of animals such as a lizard and part of the lover's clothing as important parts of the spell itself. He even has Simaetha calling upon not just Hecate but also Circe and Medea, women who became increasingly associated with the dark arts. Moreover, Simaetha's words in calling upon the Moon are in keeping with language we associate with those who place curses or make spells upon their unknowing victims. This certainly has an influence in some later Roman pieces of literature and also other pieces of writing in the Western world, including Shakespeare's witches in *Macbeth*, who similarly call upon Hecate and cast a spell in a remarkably same way as Simaetha does here.[52]

In a much more minor role, the Roman poet Vergil subtly includes elements of the dark arts together with references to a witch when he describes the tragic downfall of Dido in his epic poem, *Aeneid*. The *Aeneid* recounts the mythological events leading to the founding of the Roman race. The protagonist Aeneas, forced to leave his burning city Troy, leads those that have survived the destruction to Italy, where he has been told that he will lay the foundations for an almighty empire: Rome. Along the way, his journey is somewhat comparable to that of Odysseus as he similarly encounters the Cyclopes, hears of the dreaded Scylla and Charybdis and also has a love affair with an exotic woman whom he has to abandon. This woman is Dido, a queen in her own right, and someone who has similarly been forced to leave her homeland and lead her people to safety to a new city which they can call home. As a strong-willed woman, she, like her female counterparts Circe and Calypso in Homer's *Odyssey*, is able to seduce and entice Aeneas to her embrace, albeit with the intervention of Venus.[53] Dido even encourages Aeneas to wear the 'Maeonian bonnet' and perfume, thus making him appear more in line with her exotic paradise than that of a man who will be the forefather of the Romans.[54] As Aeneas gradually loses sight of his destiny, the gods act proactively to reinstate his belief in his mission. Mercury is sent as a voice piece of Jupiter to remind him of his task. This results in Aeneas informing Dido of his prompt departure from her shores. With the same reminiscence of the tragedy *Medea*, Dido reacts wildly to his new plans, leaving her to spiral into behaviour that is shocking and disturbing for the Roman audience as she calls upon the one thing that she feels will remedy her hurt and pain: witchcraft. She summons a 'Massylian priestess' who can cast spells and raise the spirits of the dead in order to 'free…the mind of anyone she wishes and to send cruel cares to others'.[55] The priestess advises a pyre to be made to burn Aeneas' possessions that he has left behind and also an effigy of him, whilst she calls in a 'voice of thunder upon the three hundred gods, Erebus, Chaos, triple Hecate', together with using 'potent herbs' and 'milk of black poison'. The priestess also displays her power to override nature and disrupt the natural order as 'the woods and wild waves of ocean has been stilled…silence reigned over field and flock'. The calling upon the priestess is a dramatic ruse to cloak Dido's true intentions which is to throw herself upon the burning pyre as Aeneas' belongings and his effigy are set alight. But the episode demonstrates once again how women are perceived to be drawn to the dark arts in moments of great distress, and pain, especially after being scorned. It is a fearful and terrifying image that is being portrayed in the literature not only of what women can be capable of if they are in such situations but also of the power that can be displayed by female practitioners of witchcraft.

Another further instance of a woman using the means of something deadly to restore what has been lost is seen in the Deianeira story. The story was popularised by the Greek writer Diodorus in 30 BC and later by Ovid in his *Metamorphoses*. Both accounts are similar in their recollection of events: Deianeira, the new bride of the hero Heracles, is almost abducted by the wicked centaur Nessus who is ferrying people across a turbulent river. He offers to take Heracles and his wife safely across the unsettled current, but on seeing Deianeira, Nessus is struck by immediate lust and attempts to whisk her away instead, at which Heracles fights the centaur before finally shooting an arrow at him (see image 3). The arrow happens to be doused in the venomous blood of the hydra, obtained from Heracles' labour in which he successfully slaughtered the creature. Recognising the benefits of using the blood to kill any enemy, he soaked his arrows in it. The arrow thus bleeds its poison into the centaur. Knowing that the weapon is lethal, Nessus quickly seeks vengeance by convincing Deianeira that his blood harbours such potency that it can restore love that had been lost. He advises her to take off his blood-soaked shirt and to offer it as a gift to her loved one when she feels love diminishing. When adorned, he tells her they will love her again. Sometime later, when Deianeira suspects Heracles of having an affair, she sends him the shirt, telling him to adorn it whilst performing a sacrifice. Once he places the garment on his body, the venom of the hydra seeps through his veins, and he dies an agonising and tortuous death.

This myth may not recall the typical characteristics associated with witchcraft, such as seen in the previous sources. However, Daniel Ogden provides a compelling argument as to why Deianeira should still be placed in the category of witchcraft, stating that she serves as an 'archetype for a recurring magical narrative in which a woman attempting to use a love potion to retain the affection of a man accidentally poisons him'.[56] Indeed, we have seen the poison and potion motif in the Simaetha story and, more hauntingly, with Medea who, unlike the others, uses poison with malevolent intent. Interestingly, the Deianeira story has a far-reaching and more devastating impact than the others. The poison of the 'Nessus shirt' and Deianeira's intent on using it and its subsequent devastating impact has become a folkloric tale used in other societies and historically as a means to poison and eradicate races of people. Adrienne Mayor, for instance, postulates that the Nessus shirt of legend forms the basis of germ or biological warfare found later in colonising movements across the globe, most notably by those English settlers who wished to remove the Native Americans when establishing their colony in the eighteenth century.[57] This was achieved by the use of the smallpox blanket, gifted to the natives but infected with the disease, so when placed on the body, the infection would spread widely throughout the community.[58] The obvious correlation to the Nessus shirt story is apparent and demonstrates how the motifs of witchcraft, poison and general nature of destruction associated with such mythology can find themselves being played out in real life, highlighting how these witchcraft folktales can impact our own, more disturbing histories.[59]

Lastly, with the minor witch Canidia, we come the closest, other than Erictho,[60] to what we would call the 'Wicked Witch of the West'. The idea of this type of witch resonates with us from our perceptions of the character of the same name from the book and film *Wizard of Oz*. In the book, the Wicked Witch of the West has pure malevolence, represented in her ability to control wild creatures like wolves and black insects and birds, such as bees and crows. Both the book and film see her in command of an army of winged monkeys and being a general hindrance to Dorothy trying to get home. Even the appearance of the witch is perceived to be an old crone with a hooked nose and a conical hat, much like we see in the film *Wizard of Oz*. But the title 'Wicked Witch of the West' has become synonymous with all evil aspects of witchcraft: she is a witch that can dabble with the dark arts, control nature, wild animals, be linked with nocturnal creatures, perform necromancy and even enjoy cannibalism. We certainly see all these key elements of the wicked witch in the likes of Canidia, a hideous evil woman who is mentioned by Horace in his published *Epodes* of 35 BC. Canidia commits some atrocious crimes in Horace's *Epodes* from kidnapping, murdering, poisoning and torturing, to ripping apart a lamb with her teeth, and horrifyingly, starving to death a child so that she can harvest his organs.[61] The latter forms the basis of Horace's *Epode* 5 in which Canidia the witch strips naked a youthful boy and with 'blunt vipers entangled in her head of dishevelled hair', she performs incantations necessary to starve the boy so as to remove his bone marrow and liver for the purposes of making a love potion:

> [So he] Might die staring at food, brought and taken away
> Two or three times each endless day:
> This so his marrow and liver, extracted, then
> Dried, might form a love potion,
> When his eyeballs, fixed on the meal he was denied,
> Had shrivelled all to nothingness.[62]

Canidia is a powerful witch that warrants much loathing and fear. Her incantations are reminiscent of pure horror and her anti-social attitudes are in line with an archetypal representation of the witch that has gradually emerged in the Classical literature, and one which will have a profound impact on the modern perception of the craft.

Conclusions

It is clear that the woman behind the Greek and Roman witch is powerful. Like Medea, she is often outspoken, knows her own mind and is driven by her emotions. Even the more minor ones are compelled to carry out dramatic and life-changing acts. When they appear in the literature, they do so with imploding impact and the writers demonstrate their tour de force when describing the witch and the enactment of her craft upon others. It is also apparent that the witch is baleful and so should be feared. She can be attractive but also hideous and her incantations are powerful and catastrophic. With an anger that knows no bounds, she is a woman who deserves to be on the periphery of society, like some wild beast you want to keep at bay. The aforementioned witches form only a small element of the stock character of the witch found within the literature but help to demonstrate how this type of woman was handled in the texts from the time.

The following chapters will focus on two collections of witches found within Greek and Roman literature: Hecate, who becomes the Western world's Patron of Witches, and Circe from the ancient Greek world, as well as the Thessalian witches and Erictho from the ancient Roman world. All of these females harbour characteristics that became so significant in identifying what it means to be a witch and so influenced our modern perception of them. Through these witches, we also see a marked change in attitude towards their craft. Hecate and Circe, for instance, are treated with less controversy in their literatures to begin with but as we head towards the fifth century BC, attitudes towards these witches change and both Hecate and Circe become figures to vilify. This change in attitude will be addressed as in the Roman era writers produced some of the most grotesque portrayals of witches to come out of the West, with Erictho, in particular, often classed as Rome's super witch – a clear forerunner for the first ever 'Wicked Witch of the West'.

Chapter One

Hecate: The Goddess of Witches

Hecate ... excelled in her brazen lawlessness ... she was a keen contriver of mixtures of deadly drugs (pharmaka) ... she destroyed her father with a drug and took over his throne ... hence she acquired a name for cruelty.

Diodorus Siculus,
Bibliotheca historia,4.45–46, 48

Writing in the first century BC, Diodorus saw Hecate as a lawless, harmful witch. However, Hecate could not be more of a complexity as she has a stark duality that enables us to admire her on the one hand, as well as abhor her on the other. Throughout her history, she transforms from a goddess of benevolence to a sinister and deadly patron of witches and their craft.

Who is Hecate?

Hecate, like Circe, who will be discussed in Chapter Two, is a divinity. As a goddess, Hecate has many attributes: she is associated with magic and witchcraft, knowledge of the moon, doorways and thresholds, and the underworld.[1] In an animalistic way, she is connected with creatures of the night and barking hellhounds. In fact, she was often given dogs or puppies as sacrifices, as well as offerings of illuminated cakes, because one of her key symbols are burning torches.[2] There are two distinct representations of her in art form. One is of a single-faced goddess and the other, which is more recognisable, is of a three-faced female. The image of her as a single-faced goddess comes from a terracotta figurine accompanied with an inscription of her name, from late sixth-century BC Athens. The classic image of her as a standing triad female (see images 4 and 5) may have been first imagined by the fifth-century BC sculptor Alcamenes as seen on the Athenian Acropolis, c. 425 BC. Indeed, there are no known images depicting her in this way before the fifth century, and from this moment, the triad image prevails.

The three faces relate metaphorically to the sky, earth and underworld and her ability to exert apotropaic power towards three directions. Most of these attributes, aside from her liminal duties, are later bestowments on the goddess after she became an established Greek deity by at least the fifth century BC. References to her witchcraft also begin to emerge at around this time and, later, her knowledge of lunar lore becomes one of her paramount characteristics[3]. Before the fifth century, she was still very much a mystery which, other than a Hesiodic and Homeric reference and very little archaeological evidence pertaining to her cult, makes it difficult to assess exactly where she originated and what her ancient functions truly were.

It is now generally assumed that Hecate is not an original Greek goddess but rather a foreign import, though, as stated, her ancient origin is still a matter of controversy.[4] Up until the twentieth century, she was, in fact, believed to have been purely Greek. L. Farnell, for instance, claims that Hecate was known throughout the Greek world, including the colonies in Italy, Sicily and Asia Minor.[5] He firstly places her origins in Thessaly due to the fact that in later Antiquity, this region gained a reputation for evil and magic.[6] There is, in fact, a Thessalian legend which makes Hecate the daughter of Pheraia, who was exposed at the crossroads at birth, thus highlighting her connection to this important intersection.[7] More specifically, because Diodorus Siculus connects Artemis with Medea and Hecate, Farnell links Pheraia with Artemis, supported by the fact that Artemis was worshipped as a sorceress with evil magic powers in that region.[8] It makes sense to him, therefore, to have Hecate originating there too. However, it is likely that her associations with malevolence, which Thessaly is so renowned for, is a much later attribute. Farnell also refers to Pausanias who draws upon Hesiod's *Catalogue of Women* in which she is transformed by Artemis into Hecate.[9] Equating Hecate with Iphigeneia places her origins in the area of the Chersonese, a Greek colony in modern-day Crimea. His discussion finally positions the establishment of Hecate in Thrace, linking her to the Thracian goddess Bendis, whose worship included orgiastic rites, magic and superstition.[10] The archaeological evidence in this region also comprises a sanctuary of the Great Gods, which includes a rock altar dedicated to her. However, modern scholarship states that her attributes are far too unHellenic, with the majority of scholars stating she is a goddess of Carian origin in ancient Asia Minor/Anatolia or modern-day Turkey.[11] In fact, a 2023 archaeological site has discovered images of her cult as far afield as the Turkish city of Mersin, dating back to the Hellenistic period, indicating at an indigenous spread of her cult. Much older archaeological evidence of the Carian region shows that she had an established cult, predating the Hellenistic period by some considerable years. According to T. Kraus in Lagina in Caria, there was the office of the key-bearer, a position held by a woman who carried a key during an annual festival in honour of Hecate.[12] She was also served by eunuch priests similar to Cybele, another Anatolian goddess. This festival of the key has been argued to represent Hecate's connection to the underworld, with her holding the key between life and death. However, it has been equally linked to her being a liminal deity, a protector of the gateways of the city who used the key for the sole purpose of locking up the city and thereby keeping away dangers, or using the keys to open the city gates to benevolent influences.[13] Whilst the evidence for the key-bearer festival only goes back to the Hellenistic era, Kraus argues that there is evidence of a key-bearer in Babylonian religion as far back as the second millennium BC, thus indicating at a much older use of this symbol which may have impacted the area of Caria before the Hellenistic period.[14] The oldest piece of archaeological evidence for the worship of Hecate is the form of a rock altar dedicated to her in the sanctuary of Apollo Delphinios in Miletus which is on the periphery of Caria. The altar itself is from the seventh century BC. Interestingly, the earliest piece of literary evidence for Hecate is in Hesiod's *Theogony*, dating from the early fifth century BC. It could be that Hecate's cult was on the rise in Anatolia and had travelled over into Greece as early as Hesiod's time. However, given that Hesiod had family connections to Asia Minor, it makes sense that he would have sound knowledge of her.[15]

What we can deduce from the above is that it is universally believed Hecate was an imported goddess. Her connection to crossroads, a key-bearer, eunuch priests and also Artemis and Apollo, who are thought to have a relationship with Asia Minor, points towards an ancient Eastern deity that entered Greece perhaps as early as the eighth century BC. Kraus also attests that her mention in the Homeric *Hymn to Demeter* indicates an early entry into Greece when she fell into the Greek pantheon.[16] Fundamentally, her attributes of the key and crossroads are decidedly beneficial, a necessary protector of doors and entrances in both the public and private domain. Her image in the form of *Hekataia* was placed at entrances as an apotropaic guardian, coupled with titles that we know were bestowed upon her that signified her protective duties: *megiste*, meaning 'greatest' and *soteria*, meaning 'saviour'.[17] Later these functions placed her as a significant chthonic, liminal deity with an affiliation to the underworld symbolising the boundary between life and death; this association, though, will become a dark one, making her the ultimate patron of witches and sorcery, from which a more sinister Hecate will emerge.

Hecate in Hesiod and Homer

Hesiod is a Greek poet composing poetry in the late eighth century BC. He is famous for his *Theogony* in which he provides an extensive overview of the genealogies of the deities in Greek myth. One of these is Hecate, for whom he not only explains her bloodline, but also offers her a hymn in her honour. This was unusual for a minor deity and elevated her above all others. We are first told of her Titan parentage: Asteria and Perses, the latter being referred to as a Titan 'who shone out amongst them all for his wisdom.'[18] This sets up a form of exaltation for Hecate and her lineage. Hecate, we are further told, is 'honoured above all others', as Zeus granted her 'magnificent privileges'.[19] These privileges include a share in power of both earth and the sea, as well as the starry heavens; the ability to grant prosperity upon those who venerate her; rights to sit among kings in times of judgement and for her man of choice to shine among the crowds. Together with these privileges was her overwhelming benevolence that she was to offer to mankind, in the form of the following: aiding men in battle and then the offering of glory once they are victorious; standing by the cavalry and athletes when they are in contest. Hecate also had the power to increase livestock, including cattle, goats, and sheep, with the ability to make 'great out of small'.[20] So renowned was she among the immortals that Zeus 'did not oppress her', even bestowing upon her the title 'fosterer of the young' and making her a nurse and protector of children.[21] All of this is remarkable praise indeed, and a far cry from her later more sinister attributes.

However, there has been much debate regarding this exalting hymn with some suggestions that these words may be interpolations, written much later by a reverent follower of the Hecatean cult and inserted into Hesiod's *Theogony*.[22] The reasons for this postulation arise due to the length of the hymn which appears as an unusual Hesiodic digression and the unlikelihood that Hesiod was aware of a goddess resembling the Hecate he so fervently describes. However, as has already been noted, due to the knowledge that Hesiod may have had of the Anatolian region, and, therefore, of the Hecatean cult, it seems likely that he was aware of her divine status. M.L. West goes one step further claiming that the passage is clearly written by a devotee of the goddess, and that devotee must have been Hesiod.[23] Given that Homer, whose poetry was around the same time as Hesiod, refers to her too, it is more than likely that Hecate was in her early stages of entering the Greek pantheon. Even though her reference in Hesiod has a distinct mystic language pertaining to what the naysayers have dubbed 'devotee' in tone, what Hesiod's passage really demonstrates is that she was indeed a goddess who was honoured, revered and admired. Whilst these attributes will prevail, particularly in Homer and the *Chaldean Oracles*, she will eventually fall prey to a darker and more sinister presentation.

Homer, as has already been referenced, is an almost contemporaneous poet to Hesiod.[24] Hecate appears in his *Hymn to Demeter*, in which his references to her are purely beneficial. However, Homer's Hecate is far more liminal in quality, stressing the attributes for which she is all too familiar. It is also from Homer's account that we see the first instances of her literary beginnings as a torch-bearing deity who has connections to the underworld, which later will be associated with witchcraft. Homer's *Hymns*, of which there are thirty-three in total, are honourable accounts relating the myths and exploits of individual gods. Demeter's hymn focuses upon the loss of Demeter's daughter Persephone who is abducted by Hades as she is gathering flowers, becoming fixated by the splendid narcissus which enables Hades to open up the earth and snatch her. Demeter, when discovering the loss of her daughter, spirals into so great a depression and so great a grief that her powers to control the harvest and nature wane, allowing for a dreaded famine to ensue whereby humans and the gods, who lack the sacrifices and festivities made in their honour, nearly perish and are nearly eradicated. Hermes is sent to the underworld by Zeus as a last resort to save the situation. Hades allows Persephone to return to her mother but having secretly fed her the honey seed berry of the pomegranate fruit, this still ties Persephone to him meaning she would have to spend a third of the year in the depths of the underworld and the rest of the year with her mother on earth.

The hymn has many layers, fundamentally explaining the mythological meaning of the reasons behind seasonal changes, but it also establishes the mystery cult of the Eleusinian Mysteries, stressing the power of Demeter and Persephone as deities in their own right.[25] Hecate appears in the hymn at the beginning and at the end. In the beginning, Hecate hears the painful lamentations of the abducted Persephone as she sits in her cave wearing her bright headband. Moved by Persephone's pleas, Hecate approaches the distraught Demeter 'holding a light ablaze in her hands' and asks her who it was that took Persephone, as she was unable to see the culprit.[26] She reassures Demeter, unlike the other immortals, that she is relating everything truthfully to perhaps ease her heart and remind her that some deities are supporting her. The final time we see Hecate is at the end of the hymn when Persephone emerges from Hades and is reunited with her mother again. Hecate is described as approaching them adorned with her splendid headband and embraces Demeter. Finally, we are told that from that moment, Hecate becomes Persephone's attendant and substitute queen.[27]

Sarah Iles Johnston points out that Hecate's appearance at both the start and the finality of the poem coincide with Persephone's descent into Hades and her subsequent reascension to the upper world, thus demonstrating Hecate as a protector and spiritual guide for Persephone's physical journey.[28] This is reinforced by the Greek words that Homer uses to describe Hecate: πρόπολος, meaning to act before or in front of, and ὀπάων, meaning follower (i.e. following behind) – or, more literally, attendant. In other words, Hecate was both 'behind and in front of Persephone' as her guide and protector on her journey.[29] It is also significant that Hecate lives in a cave, a common liminal symbol in the ancient world, the one place that was seen as a transition between the upper world and the world below.[30]

Moreover, other interpretations of the same myth place Hecate as the initiator of Persephone's yearly journey to Hades and the renewal of her marriage. In Callimachus' *Hymn to Demeter*, Hecate is more proactively involved in Persephone's return.[31] There are also vase paintings that display Hecate in much the same role as the escort and guide. Thus, we have a clear connection of Hecate being related to the underworld. The role of escort in Homer's writing is purely a beneficial one, connected with Hecate's role as a liminal protector of boundaries and transitions, but later literature not only draws upon this connection, but also the torches she is described as branding, defining her as a mistress of souls, a psychopomp and, more maliciously, as a harbinger of dark magic, and unwanted ghostly happenings.

Chaldean Oracles and the Cosmic Soul

It is safe to say that Hecate emerged as a multifaceted deity. She became linked to witchcraft from as early as the fifth century BC and was labelled as a malevolent chthonic entity. However, almost simultaneous to this definition, and certainly from the Hellenistic period, Hecate was seen as a mystic celestial deity, a cosmological female who acted as a communicative entity between god and man, allowing the transcendence of one's soul through ritual, eventually leading to its release. The literary work that portrays Hecate predominately as this beneficent mediator between cosmos and man is in the *Chaldean Oracles.*[32] The oracles were written around the second century AD and mention her specifically as a mediating world soul. The oracles themselves are attributed to 'Julian the Theurgist', a man who had a successful connection with the emperor Marcus Aurelius, using supposed magic to aid him in battles.[33] Julian stated that the divine messages within the oracles were directly handed down by Hecate and Apollo. The messages themselves relate to various ways for the initiate to communicate between the divine and human planes, aided by Hecate who mediated between these realms, commonly referred to as the Sensible and Intelligible spheres. She was, in Platonic terms, associated with the Cosmic Soul, which was a 'transmitter of the ideas and thereby structurer of the physical world'.[34] The oracles further state that she was born 'of the Father, the Supreme God of the Chaldean system' thus through her, it was believed one could communicate directly with this paternal intellect, resulting in ultimate transcendence of the soul.[35]

Why does Hecate have this significant mystical role within these writings, especially considering the fact that she is one of the few Graeco-

Roman deities to appear in this form of mysticism? Clearly her established role as a liminal deity plays some part here. We have seen already that she was considered an intermediary between the upper and lower worlds, with close connections between life and death. But, she was also mundanely connected with crossroads more literally, and also boundaries of cities and homes. Aristophanes in his *Wasps* even states that a *Hekataion*, a statue of Hecate, was placed outside every door in Athens as a means of protecting domestic entrances, in much the same fashion as the *Hermae*.[36] We further know of Hecate being used as a liminal protector at state level whereby her triple form was displayed on top of the Acropolis. However mundane these protective statues may be, they were of paramount importance in the ancient world. The crossing over into a new place or stepping into a place known to you from the outside, like, for example, your home, symbolised a journey, a metaphorical new beginning from the old to the new. It was a transition that had to be closely monitored by the divine in order for your cross-over to be successful.

The Romans especially took this very seriously. They had a special god protecting boundaries called Terminus, who was symbolised by *termini*, boundary markers that signified the boundary of the city as well as the boundaries of farmland between landowners.[37] The annual Terminalia festival assured the Romans that these boundary stones were well protected.[38] The Greeks likewise placed a lot of significance upon these, as we have seen already with Hecate's early Hellenic functions which were actually twofold: she aided men between the boundary of life and death but also throughout daily life, such as walking across the threshold of their own doors.

In addition to being a protector of physical liminal spaces, she was also metaphorically linked to the transitional phase between girlhood and womanhood, guiding the virginal girl towards her role as a married woman. Thus, she was seen as a 'wedding attendant',[39] similar to that of the goddess Artemis. Her role extended further to that of midwifery where she was identified as the goddess who would bring forth babies into the world, passing them over from the womb to life, one of the most significant boundaries. This is represented in the *Chaldean Oracles* where her womb is seen as a metaphor for the source of all life. Even her connection to dogs – which later morphs into frightening hell hounds – had the same beneficial aid in guarding those who were giving birth; the dog itself, in this way, was a protector of his mistress and the newborn baby.[40] As W.H. Roscher points out, one of the dog's ultimate purposes is to look after its master and those they hold dear.[41] Hesiod likewise pinpoints Hecate's role as a 'fosterer of the young', making her a nurse and protector of children, which the Greeks identified as a *kourotrophos.*[42] As a *kourotrophos*, she was the guardian of the young as they transitioned into adulthood, protecting them from extraneous dangers. Visually, we see this represented upon the frieze of the temple at Lagina, the most important centre for her cult, as she is shown protecting the infant Zeus from his cannibalistic father by handing him a stone covered in swathing as the infant Zeus is secretly taken away.[43]

As a result of these key liminal roles, Middle Platonism labelled Hecate the 'mistress of the moon'. This arose from the idea that the moon was a 'limen', a threshold in mysticism between the divine and the earthly plain.[44] In his *De Iside et Osiride*, Plutarch states that the moon was a life-giving entity connected to both Isis and Osiris in Egyptian mysticism, and acted as an intermediary between the heavenly world and the world below.[45] It could be that these ideas influenced the *Chaldean Oracles*, written not long after Plutarch, where the life-giving deities are Apollo and Hecate, with Hecate linked to the cosmic soul, which, for Plutarch, was the key celestial body of the moon. However, aside from the apparent mystical qualities of the moon, the celestial body itself was, for a long time prior to this, thought to embody Hecate as a goddess, as she was both a heavenly and earthly deity, descended from the Titaness Asteria, whose name means 'stars'. Linking Hecate to all this is considered empyreal. Indeed, as we will see, some of the literary invocations of Hecate's name, are often done in the light of the moon because of her close correlations to this entity, and thus predates lunar mysticism and the *Chaldean Oracles*.

Nonetheless, it makes sense that her liminal roles – from life and death, roads and crossroads, doors and city entrances, and the celestial moon – should include a mysticism allowing her to aid initiates in their journey to reach a transcendental plain.[46]

The Invocations of Hecate

The above-mentioned attributes show Hecate as a benignant and, at times, bounteous deity, but she is clearly extremely diverse. Alongside these characteristics of benevolence, she was conversely linked to spells, curses, darkness, daemones and disembodied souls, even becoming the patroness of witches. Similar to the reasons why she became a cosmological deity, her liminal qualities also transformed her into a chthonic goddess. As a consequence, Hecate is, on numerous occasions, called upon by several fictional witches in the literary record. We have already seen in the introduction how some female witches or laypeople dabbling in the dark arts, seek out Hecate in order to make their spells more potent. Theocritus' Simaetha concocts a fire spell upon Hecate's altar amidst a full moon, culminating in her calling aloud to 'Hecate infernal'.[47] During the recitation of her prayer, Simaetha hears dogs barking at the crossroads, a sign that Hecate is approaching. She and her accomplice, her slave girl Thestylis, in their panic at hearing the dread goddess approach, rattle an apotropaic instrument to ward off her evil, but also to ensure that Hecate will bless the love spell and render its potency.[48] Likewise, in Vergil's *Aeneid*, the emotional and abandoned Dido uses the Massylian priestess to create a spell whereby Hecate is called upon for added potency, followed by the use of black poison and potent herbs.[49] Ovid similarly has his Medea invoke Hecate once again in the light of the moon, as she seeks her aid for the famous rejuvenation of Aeson scene.[50] And, finally, our earliest reference to an invocation of Hecate is given by Medea in the famous Euripidean tragedy named after her, where she cries out to 'Queen Hecate' to aid her with the poison that she will use against the princess whom Jason has married. Medea refers to Hecate as a goddess whom she 'venerates' above all others, with her even being portrayed as her consort.[51]

These invocations demonstrate how Hecate was seen to have powers of darkness, with a didactical aid for those who wished to cause harm to others. Moreover, Diodorus Siculus has Hecate as a lawless contriver of witchcraft and deadly drugs which she uses to destroy those around her.[52] For Sarah Iles Johnston, on the other hand, it is Hecate's relationship with daemones and restless, dangerous souls that directly link her to witchcraft.[53] The image of her leading souls in and out of Hades is one that arises early in the literature in her interaction with Persephone, and from this, her ability to call up souls, or prevent them from leaving Hades, becomes a persistent occurrence – in Seneca's *Oedipus* for instance, the seer wishes to call up the shades and knows he will be successful in doing this when he has heard Hecate's dogs bark.[54] In Apuleius' *Metamorphoses*, Hecate is seen to have the ability to keep the ghostly spirits in the confines of the earth.[55] We would automatically identify this role as a beneficial psychopomp, an essential guide for the souls once they have passed. The Greeks placed great importance upon such guides, given that they did have some preoccupation with the afterlife in their society,[56] placing this important position not just in Hecate but also in her male counterpart, Hermes.[57] However, Hecate's role here seems to be twofold, on the one hand, a guide for the soul but at the same time, a necromancer, particularly with the ability to call up dangerous and restless spirits which would cause some potential harm, and it this necromantic power that she exerts in the aforementioned literary examples which will become a typical trope of the witch. Further, because she was seen as both a birth and a death deity, she, therefore, was seen aiding souls on their most profound journeys and, as such, became entwined with daemonic creatures which are perceived to have been liminal entities found in the realm of the thresholds where the souls cross over. Thus, it's natural to see how Hecate became a deity associated with restless ghosts, daemones, dark realms and necromancy.[58] The historical reasoning behind these undesirable qualities of Hecate will be discussed in Chapter Two. For now, it serves to show that she was a goddess with such duplexity that it is difficult to ascertain what image of her prevails in the Greek and Roman world and beyond.

Later Hecates

Hecate's duality certainly persisted in Antiquity. For instance, in ancient Rome, a three-day festival held in honour of the goddess Diana, was also known as the *Hecataen Ides* due to Hecataen symbolism that was used during the event, such as a grove symbolising the link between earth and the underworld, the use of dogs who were presented with a garland, candles and torches which were lit up, and the festival itself was held when the dog-star Sirius shone at night in the northern hemisphere.[59] All these images link to Hecate, and as we have seen, Diana and Hecate were often intertwined. Moreover, inscriptions from the area state that Hecate was 'the benevolent goddess of Rome'.[60] Further, it is even noted that Hecate was a desirable apotropaic goddess. During the reign of Tiberius, the much-loved Germanicus, father of the notorious Caligula, was supposedly poisoned by Piso the governor of Syria and his wife

Plancina, after he came into conflict with them. Leading up to the poison, he was plagued with witchcraft and so scared was he by the portents he saw that he took to keeping a jade figurehead of Hecate close by him in the hope of warding off unwanted dark magic.[61]

Notwithstanding these positive affirmations, it is actually the Hecate as patroness of witches and their craft that still prevails throughout the centuries after the fall of Rome. She is used in the form of invocations in more modern literature, and is often portrayed in her triple form with symbolic imagery pertaining to the night in artwork. In Shakespeare's *Macbeth*, she is invoked by the three witches in their incantations but also by Macbeth himself: just before Macbeth enters the king's chamber in Act 2, Scene 1 to kill King Duncan, he calls upon the supernatural to give him the strength to carry out the murder with references to witches, blood, wolves and ghosts in his monologue as he recalls his encounter with the three witches he had earlier, and exclaims: 'witchcraft celebrates Pale Hecate's off'rings, and wither'd murder, Alarum'd by his sentinel, the wolf, whose howl's his watch' (Act 2, Scene 1, 51–54) Here he envisions the witches making offerings to Hecate, with the personified Murder and his sentinel, the 'wolf', who have been unleashed to offer assistance to Macbeth so that he can commit regicide.

Later in Act 3 Scene 5,[62] Hecate herself appears as the queen of the witches. She chastises the three crones for not consulting her over their dealings with Macbeth explaining that that this is an insult as she is 'the mistress of [their] charms' and 'close contriver of all harms'. She insists that they meet her at the pit of Acheron, one of the rivers of Hades, after she has invoked the moon to spread her malign influence upon her herbs. Two scenes later, the witches are busy working alongside Hecate as they chant the famous 'Double, double toil and trouble, fire burn, and cauldron bubble', whilst tossing innards and parts of animals into their pot to create a spell with which Hecate proclaims 'well done! I commend your pains'. Hecate is seen as the commanding force behind the witchcraft in *Macbeth*. She actively invokes the moon, has strong ties with the underworld, and encourages pain and harm towards others, thus demonstrating the negative imagery of her as a dark, manipulative witch whose very spells can disrupt the natural order.

Modern artwork similarly continues the theme of Hecate and her relationship to witchcraft. In 1795, William Blake produced a piece of artwork entitled 'The Triple Hecate', see image 6.

The figure in the artwork relates to a character that features in his own mythology, but who is based upon, and thought to represent Hecate with similar attributes.[63] The artwork itself shows Hecate in her triple form, two images of which are represented as a boy and a girl hiding their heads behind Hecate, who takes centre stage in the triad, possibly showing her powers of oppression. She has her hand placed upon a book of black magic as she stretches out her left foot, the left being considered more sinister and malevolent.[64] The animals that accompany her are all classic images in magical symbology: an owl, a cat-headed bat, a donkey eating a thistle and the head of a crocodile.[65] The scene is one of nightmares and is, again, demonstrative of her prevailing negativity.

It is only in more recent times that Hecate, the benevolent goddess of old, has been finally restored to her former glory. With the rise of Neopaganism or the religion Wicca, which advocates a desire to use white magic and nature as part of its doctrines, places great emphasis upon a range of deities from Celtic ones found upon the British Isles, including a primordial Great Mother, but also a triple goddess which is more than likely based upon Hecate. The latter in Neopagan circles represents the stages of womanhood from Maiden, Mother and Crone. The goddess also acts according to the waxing and waning moon, something which, as we have seen was Hecate's key connection in antiquity, and further represented in the third-century AD philosophical work *On Images*:

> The moon is Hekate, the symbol of her varying phases and of her power dependent on these phases. Wherefore her power appears in three forms, having as symbol of the new moon the figure in the white robe and golden sandals, and torches lighted.[66]

Neopaganism effectively draws upon this more gracious appearance of the goddess from the ancient world helping to revive her more positive attributes. Finally, Robert Graves, in his extensive work *The White Goddess*, refers to Hecate as the original and most dominant triple goddess with equally more accommodating and considerate traits.[67]

Hecate's history is a long and, at times, arduous one. Her many beneficial attributes were slowly eroded through a persistent and prevailing misogyny which will be discussed further in the following chapter. Thankfully, though, as we have seen, her liminal concerns and elements of white magic have been restored in the last few decades.[68] Her history is not too dissimilar to that of her relative Circe, who was, according to some sources, perceived to be her daughter.[69] Whatever their genealogical link, both Hecate and Circe, as will be discussed, were deities well versed in the use of *pharmaka*, had an ancient heritage where they were both considered initially beneficial, but then later morphed into the archetypal manipulative dark witch before having their benevolence reinstated.

Chapter Two

Circe: The First Western Witch

Who is Circe?

In due course we came to the island of Aeaea, the home of the beautiful Circe, a formidable goddess, with a mortal woman's voice...

Homer's *Odyssey*, book X.135–37

Homer's description introduces us to Circe, the oldest reference to this female in Western literature. Circe is indeed formidable, and her tale weaves a rich tapestry in the Greek and Roman texts. Her stories are often adventurous with heroic exploits, and, in places, sometimes horrific. She serves, like her other female companion, Medea, to highlight the progression of a witch with a godlike past to a Machiavellian temptress and dark female who will have no qualms in wielding her witchcraft and dabbling in deadly drugs aimed at those who dare to stand in her way. Circe is herself a minor deity and a beautiful one at that. She is described by Homer as being the daughter of the god of the Sun, Helios and sea nymph, Perse.[1] She is also the sister of Aeetes, the father of Medea, thus having close familial ties with another powerful female witch. But, fundamentally, Circe is divine and attractive. It is for this reason that much debate has arisen as to whether Circe can be seen as a witch at all. Firstly, for Ronald Hutton, she is simply not human, when witches are meant to be mortal, wielding malevolent powers they happen upon or manage to conjure up.[2] Secondly, whilst she uses transformative powers and the archetypal instrument of a witch – a wand –, Hutton believes the classical texts are far too ambivalent in discerning whether she can be seen as a witch as defined so far in this book.[3] Matthew Dickie supports this view by emphasising that the idea of magic and witchcraft were not terms widely defined or indeed used until the late fifth century BC, sometime after the composition of the *Odyssey*.[4] Circe, therefore, should not be defined as a witch and any mention of magic that may be attributed to her should be very loosely applied and associated more with her divine powers.[5] Judith Yarnall also does not regard Homer's Circe as a witch but as a long-lost primordial goddess who has been misunderstood within the Homeric tradition. For her, Circe is a goddess of 'prodigious powers' reflecting an ancient tradition of goddess worship that stems back in time thousands of years before the first recital of Homer's *Odyssey*.[6] Her appearance in the *Odyssey* marks a pivotal moment in the primordial goddess' history when her powers give way to the rise of patriarchal supremacy in the Mediterranean.[7]

There may well be some truth in this. We have long assumed that prior to the rise of Western civilisation, as we know it, matriarchies in the Palaeolithic and Neolithic eras were commonplace. The evidence suggests that during these respective eras, worship of a mother goddess was prevalent. She took many forms from being zoomorphic, often represented in a raptorial manner or as a female surrounded by animals, bulls or felines. These figurines have been found in the Levant region, and also Anatolia, and as far afield as Willendorf in Austria. Jacques Cauvin's extensive study of these figurines and statues examines the power of the female at the archaeological site of Catalhoyuk and especially the representation of a female dominating the wall of a domestic sanctuary in which a woman is seen to be giving birth to a bull.[8] She is also flanked by vultures; a raptorial image associated with death.[9] One of the most famous statuettes to have been found at this site (image 7) shows an obese goddess, giving birth, seated on panthers that serve as her throne.

All these symbols are thought to have fertility connections as the woman's voluptuous appearance is seen to be a symbol of fruitfulness and abundance. She was linked to the life force of the culture she was worshipped in as she had the ability to give birth, but she was also concerned with death, hence the raptorial vultures that surrounded the goddess at Catalhoyuk. Maybe she acted as a psychopomp of sorts, but it has been suggested that she was a juxtaposed goddess, one who could give life and nurture it but also destroy it at will.[10] What is apparent is that she harboured the necessary components that signalled the circle of life. Daniel Ogden discusses the Near-Eastern female deities as a potential connection to Circe.[11] This, he believes, is due to their common title of 'Mistress of Animals'.[12]

One goddess in particular that has close correlations to Circe is Ishtar from the epic *Gilgamesh*. She is a powerful transformative goddess who, when her advances towards Gilgamesh are rejected, resorts to transforming her shepherd into a wolf to hunt down Gilgamesh's herdsmen.[13] Whilst Circe does not seek this particular style of vengeance in the Homeric world, she does have a penchant for transforming men who potentially could try to seduce her. There is a connection here to some of the Olympian goddesses such as Artemis who has often been thought of as an 'import' goddess; that is, a goddess adopted by the ancient Greeks who has a far older and more primordial origin. These goddesses changed their heritages as they shifted between matriarchy and patriarchy, but still held onto some of their strong independent female attributes. Circe, similarly, can be linked to the same heritage. Her name 'Kirke' means hawk, thus connecting her to the idea of the raptor that these goddesses are associated with.[14] Even the name of her island – Aeaea – is thought to be a Semitic word for eagle.[15] She is also a goddess who is often accompanied by felines, so Homer has mountain lions roaming her house. And, as we shall see, she has the ability to be nurturer as well as destroyer, with a close connection to the underworld. Furthermore, these ancient goddesses were considered to be practitioners of 'white magic', that is, a type of magic that would have been deemed as beneficial to the tribe or village such as the bringing forth of crops, a healthy birth, and the healing of the leader.[16] These elements fit the argument that Circe is a goddess with a strong ancient heritage, someone who can wield great power, both good and bad. However, there is no solid evidence to suggest this may be the case, no figurine or inscriptional evidence that we can safely say represents the Homeric Circe that existed many thousands of years in our own prehistory.[17] She may well be the original imaginings of Homer who perhaps reshaped images of an ancient goddess he was aware of or morphed her into his own rendering. What we do know is her first appearance is in the *Odyssey*. Whilst Hutton, Dickie and Yarnall may dismiss her witch-like qualities in this epic poem, on closer reading, those stereotypical attributes of the witch are there, albeit in a more benevolent and divine light. Indeed, if we apply Stith Thompson's *Motif-Index of Folk Literature*, in which he categorises the main motifs linked to witches, Circe does indeed fall into the category of the classic witch from controlling animals, transforming and enchanting their victim, raising winds, enticing men, calling upon the spirits of the dead and having powers compromised by the use of steel.[18] In order for us to examine these, we have to first take a closer look at her story in the Homeric poem.

Homer's *Odyssey*

An odyssey describes a long and exciting journey and essentially Homer's epic poem, from which this word derives, focuses upon Odysseus' arduous but adventurous voyage home to Ithaca after fighting in the Trojan war. These adventures, though, are sandwiched between two other major events: the *Telemachy* which covers the first four books of the twenty-four-book poem exploring the exploits of Odysseus' son as he searches for news of his father, and Odysseus' return to Ithaca, from Books 13–24. Metaphorically these books can also be described as a journey insofar as Telemachus makes a personal journey of growth and maturation, and Odysseus journeys psychologically through Ithaca and his palace in order to reestablish his authority there. But the interim books are often seen as standalone adventures which take the audience to another world, set apart from the rest of the epic. They are fantastical and contain characters and creatures from ancient Greek folklore such as the Cyclopes and Scylla.

Odysseus and his crew who survived the Trojan war navigate themselves through each of these encounters sometimes with trepidation but other times with gusto and heroism: both Odysseus and his crew, for instance, are often full of fortitude as they eagerly venture out to discover what each island they land upon may offer them, but often their hopes turn to fear and agony when they realise the dangers that the inhabitants may bring them. Each episode serves as an opportunity for Odysseus to display his talents but also his pitfalls as a hero and protagonist of the epic: he especially demonstrates his skills of *metis* (cunning/guile) when he outwits Polyphemus the cyclops by calling himself 'Nobody', a perfect ruse so that when the injured Polyphemus calls out to the other Cyclopes to come to his aid, he will exclaim that it was 'Nobody's treachery…that is doing me to death,'[19] to which the other cyclopes will assume he is alone, thus enabling the swift escape of Odysseus and his men. This ingenuity, however, is quickly forgotten after Odysseus foolishly reveals his true identity as an arrogant means of showing the cyclops that it was he who dared to wound and escape from so mighty a giant. This only results in a curse placed upon him and his men as Polyphemus calls upon his father, the god Poseidon, to make sure that they suffer accordingly for their injustice against him. It is among these adventures that Circe appears. She falls exactly halfway through the adventures and also half-way through the entire epic. This can be seen as deliberate on the part of Homer as it can indicate a heightened moment in the story, placing Circe as a crucial and vital encounter for the intrepid adventurer Odysseus.

The Encounter with Circe in Books 10–12

Book 10 sees Odysseus and his men at their lowest ebb: they have been drugged by the Lotus Eaters; witnessed the consumption of some of their comrades whilst trapped in the Cyclops' cave; driven off course from Ithaca after foolishly opening a bag of disruptive winds which had been removed and gathered up and gifted to them by the god Aeolus; and seen the loss of further comrades at the hands of the man-eating giants, the Laestrygonians. Arriving on Circe's island leads them to grieve heavily and feel despondent about their future. But the forever intrepid adventurer, Odysseus, insists on an exploring party being sent out after seeing smoke rising from a forest of trees. This party is led by Eurylochus, a man who has grown weary of the adventures and Odysseus' leadership. Making their way through the forest, they stumble upon a house of polished stone surrounded by tamed wild beasts that have been enchanted by the magic of Circe. Inside they hear an enticing woman's voice singing as she sits at her loom. Eurylochus suspects a trap and remains hidden from the entrance of the house but the others believing her to be hospitable like any other woman could be, knock at her door. She welcomes them and provides them with much-needed food and wine. But the wine has been intoxicated with a drug which leads them to forget their native land. She then uses a wand to tap each of them, transforming then into pigs but with their 'minds…as human as before'.[20] They are then led weeping to their sties.

Eurylochus, distraught at witnessing the transformative powers of Circe, rushes back to inform Odysseus of his comrades' fate. Full of disgust at what he has heard, Odysseus quickly and valiantly takes his sword to confront Circe but on his way to the forest in which she dwells, he is accosted by the messenger god, Hermes. Hermes informs Odysseus of Circe's wiles and how she will try to intoxicate him, so the god gives Odysseus 'moly', a herb that can serve as an antidote against her potion. Odysseus must then, Hermes insists, boldly confront her, drawing out his sword and getting her to swear an oath that she will do no harm. She will willingly agree to his wishes and turn his men from swine to humans again, but not before she leads him to her bed. The events are carried out as Hermes prophesies and Circe transforms from someone who could threaten and hinder to a hospitable lover, and later valuable guide. Indeed, such is Circe's hospitality that Odysseus and his men spend a whole year with her 'feasting on lavish quantities of meat and mellow wine', before realising their true destiny is to return home.[21] Circe does not hinder their departure but provides guidance in how to achieve their homecoming: she tells Odysseus that he must descend to the land of the dead, Hades and whilst Odysseus despairs for his life at having to embark on such a venture, Circe informs him of the precise location he has to go to, the necromantic practices he has to perform in order to consult with the ghostly prophet Teiresias who alone can tell him the safe passageways to take to Ithaca.

Book 11 details Odysseus' descent to Hades, where he carries out exactly what Circe has guided him to do. Having succeeded in this task and consulted with the prophet, and other confidants such as his mother and the leader of the Greek army during the Trojan war, Agamemnon, he ascends to the earthly plains and revisits Circe. This visitation takes place at the start of Book 12, where Circe, once again, guides Odysseus with her valuable advice as to how to safely sail the passageway to his homeland. He is told that he will first sail past the Sirens with their enchanting voices that lure men to their deaths. To avoid this fate, Odysseus is told to place beeswax into the ears of his crew but to tie himself tightly to the mast of the ship should he wish to enjoy their tones.[22] Next, he is told of two passageways to take: one leading to the Wandering Rocks where no ship remains intact, or past the area where Scylla 'the creature with the dreadful bark' and Charybdis the whirlpool 'that sucks the dark waters down' reside.[23] Scylla and Charybdis are the best option to sail past, with the ship heading more towards Scylla as they pass through. Finally, Circe warns him of the island they will take rest upon – Thrinacie – the isle of the sun god whose cattle must be left untouched.

Once again, the last appearance of Circe is as a 'formidable goddess with the beautiful hair and a woman's voice', but rather than acting malevolently by using her transformative powers, she offers them a 'friendly escort of a favourable wind'.[24]

What are we to make of Circe's appearance in the *Odyssey*? She is clearly divine, albeit a minor deity, with an important divine ancestry. Her transformative powers are also similar to other deities who can do the same – note that Athene in the *Odyssey* can also transform herself at will into a bird.[25] Homer, although he may have been influenced by an Anatolian heritage of goddess worship,[26] has morphed her for his own plot to harbour characteristics that will become the typical attributes of later witches, and indeed of Circe herself. If we consider her role as a witch in the *Odyssey* then she is, on the whole, juxtaposed: she is both good witch and bad witch combined. When Eurylochus and the other men first come across her house, it has an almost modern-day fairytale feel with the finding of an isolated witch's house in the middle of thick forest reminding us of similar settings in stories such as Hansel and Gretel. Whilst this is not a Hansel and Gretel-style cottage but a polished stone palace, the isolation of Circe and her house tucked away in the forest which creates an air of uneasiness will become a trope typically associated with witches. The tame animals flanking her house help us to visualise her already mentioned formidable nature: this woman can cast spells, powerful enough to tame the wild. She is also seductive as she lures the men to her with her voice, not too dissimilar to the Sirens in Book 12 who Circe incidentally refers to as creatures that can bewitch by their song, and anyone who encounters them will have 'no homecoming'.[27] This is somewhat reminiscent of Circe's own dealings with the men when she lured them and drugged them so that they would have no knowledge of Ithaca. And unsurprisingly, when the men enter her home, they are manipulated and beguiled by her hospitality as she uses her wand, *ῥάβδος*, to transform them into pigs. This last act is the most malevolent – she has changed them to an animal that we consider sordid, uncouth and carnal. Not only that, but she has imprisoned them in this form with their human minds intact so that they can know and understand what state they have been placed in, a tortuous form of suffering placed upon the victim. Daniel Ogden goes one step further with regard to Circe's transformative powers, suggesting that her desire to transform men can be found elsewhere on her island and is not just centred around pig sties.[28] The 'tame' mountain wolves and lions that fawn around her palace are also, he suggests, men.[29] This would even mean that the meat that Odysseus and his men were fed by Circe, or indeed the stag that was initially killed before they encountered her, was that of mankind, showing that the witch has tricked them into cannibalism, a common motif that arises within the witch tale but also within the fantastical world that Odysseus travels through as a way of juxtaposing this world to the safety and more civilised one that he desires to return to. So, Circe certainly appears to have some attributes of witchcraft: she's an isolated woman, potentially cruel in her dealings with humans, who can manipulate and seduce, has knowledge of *pharmaka lurga* – significantly the Greek text refers to them as 'baleful drugs' –, and possesses a wand that can cause a horrifying and cruel metamorphosis. Moreover, as the *Motif-Index of Folk Literature* suggests, she is also a witch who is compromised by the use of steal as she significantly bows down to Odysseus' sword when he reveals it to her.[30]

Some arguments of positivity have been levelled at the aforementioned analysis. It has been postulated, for example, that the transformative powers of Circe and especially her penchant to change men to pigs is actually a positive zoomorphism and in line with religious practices. This arises from the fact the pig was considered a symbol of purification in ancient Greek religion: its blood was used as a cleansing process and as a key sacrifice during the rites of the Mysteries of Eleusis and the Thesmophoria festival.[31] Gabriel Germain even states that Circe performs this transformation as a way of initiating the men into an ancient goddess cult by allowing their true natures to die in the transformative process and for them to be rekindled and reborn through the power of the pig into a more enlightened and younger self.[32] But this loses sight of Eurylochus' fear and Odysseus' horror and anger when hearing of their fate. It also misunderstands the intervention of Hermes and his helpful tip of taking the moly, a herb that has been seen as acting as a talismanic element against Circe's dark arts and magic.[33] It has similarly been argued that Circe's stick was not a magic wand per se but merely a driver's stick, not too dissimilar to those used in farming, and that the real potency of her power lies with the toxic drug she provides.[34] The 'wand', it seems, if we follow this line of argument, becomes a puissant phallic symbol that she can wield against men, a way of her exerting her matriarchal influence upon those she wishes to dominate. But this does not seem to be the view of the ancient Greek audience who were familiar with this story. As image 8 demonstrates, the rod/wand/stick of Circe was seen as a significant instrument of power: the visuals on the vase show a dominant Circe wielding her wand against one of the men, with the wand itself taking centre stage.

There is no doubt that Circe does have some key moments of benevolence within the Homeric epic. This arises from her own personal transformation after the encounter with Odysseus whereby she acts as the perfect example of hostess, but most significantly as Odysseus' valuable guide. As a guide, she provides him, as we have seen with remarkable details on how he can achieve his homecoming, *nostos*. This involves a journey to the depths of Hades which serves as a pivotal moment within the epic enabling Odysseus to explore his own katabasis. The Greek term 'Katabasis' (*καταβασις*) is a word which amalgamates two Greek words, *κατά* meaning 'down' and *βαίνω*, meaning 'go'. It often relates to a trip to the underworld in the epic cycle of poetry in the classical world. A trip to the underworld was a rite of passage for the hero. It was a way for them to descend to the unknown depths, have their heroism tested, perhaps even experience an enlightened moment and then reappear on earth, renewed and reborn into a greater hero.

Circe aids Odysseus with this rebirth by telling him precisely who to seek – the shade of the dead Teiresias – and sharing with him the necromantic procedures and incantations he has to perform in order for his spirit to appear. As Teiresias' spirit arises, so do others who Odysseus has valuable contact with, each one enlightening him even more with information relating to his homecoming and future. Teiresias informs him of the enmity of Poseidon and how best to appease him when he's home in Ithaca, and Odysseus is also emphatically told that when he and his crew land on Thrinacie, the isle of the sun god, to leave the cattle of this god untouched to avoid further suffering. His mother, Anticleia, reassures Odysseus of his wife's patience and tears as she awaits his return and how his father has become a recluse in the absence of his son, so encouraging him to reestablish his filial bond with him. His encounter with Agamemnon, the leader during the Trojan war, provides the most troubling information for Odysseus.

Agamemnon relates how he was murdered on his return to his palace at the hands of his wife, Clytemnestra and her new lover, Aegisthus; he warns Odysseus to be wary of Penelope and to take a more secret approach as he returns to Ithaca. This appeals to Odysseus' propensity for cunning ruses and no doubt has some bearing upon his playacting when he eventually arrives home, allowing him to effectively rid his palace of the suitors who had long outstayed their welcome. The descent to Hades is, therefore, essential in allowing the whole plot of the epic to evolve towards its climactic end. Notably, it is Odysseus' ability to survive this trip into the dark depths that places him alongside great heroes of old and empowers him with a rebirth that makes him a braver, and more hardened man. As Circe exclaims when Odysseus returns, 'What audacity…other men die once; you will now die twice.'[35] Circe is the mastermind behind his rebirth, and even though she was not present during the process, she is certainly his spiritual guide that enabled his success.[36] We are meant to see Circe, therefore, as a key turning point in his whole tale. Through her, Odysseus, now bolder and wiser, is able to survive Scylla and the wrath of the sun god when his men foolishly devour his cattle, and, even though he is imprisoned with Calypso, he will once again tap into his reborn strength as he washes ashore to the very people – the Phaeacians – that provide him with a vessel that will eventually see him achieve his homecoming, *nostos*.

Homer's Circe: A Summary

The aforementioned demonstrates Circe is a witch with power that can both destroy and torment, but also bring necessary salvation. She is, more than any other character in the adventure books of the *Odyssey*, the most important for Odysseus' development. Even Calypso, the nymph that Odysseus resides with for seven years is more beguiling and dangerous than Circe, despite the fact that Calypso is not too dissimilar to her female counterpart: she provides hospitality to Odysseus just like Circe by staying with her and sleeping in her bed, and she helps him with his homecoming, similar to Circe, by lending him the necessary tools he needs in order to make a raft to leave her island. Yet, Calypso is the ultimate hindrance, she keeps him imprisoned in a cave for years and simply does not want him to depart from her shores so she tries to entrap him with the offer of immortality. Circe does none of these things, she gives Odysseus and his men full rein of her palace and helps, guides and willingly allows Odysseus to achieve his long-awaited return to Ithaca. She is the witch that can offer the perfect gifts to our protagonist – aid and enlightenment.

Whilst she may not be a witch that brings continual fear and terror, her duality is all too apparent in the Homeric text, and we do certainly begin to see elements of her dark witchlike qualities in the *Odyssey*, albeit subtly: her use of the wand, *pharmaka lugra*, destructive transformative powers and also in her necromantic knowledge. Indeed, her knowledge of the latter is extraordinary. Necromancy is the ability to call up the dead, converse with them, often for prophetic means. It is a practice that we typically connect with the witch and one which will become darker and more sinister when we look at other witches in the classical world. For Circe, she tells Odysseus to perform this important necromantic incantation, so that he may successfully commune with Teiresias, allowing him to embark on his personal katabasis. The details of the necromancy are concise and show that Circe has a sound understanding of them: Odysseus is to dig a pit, a bothros (*βόθρος*), and offer a libation which is poured into this of milk and honey, sweet wine and water, sprinkled with barley meal.[37] He is to make vows[38] and then perform a sacrifice: one ram and one black ewe, with their heads turned towards Erebos, whilst he, the sacrificer looks the other way. Lastly, he is to pray to Hades and Persephone. The scene that arises from this perfectly crafted necromancy is a terrifying one as Odysseus sits with sword in hand, reminding us of his previous exclamations of fear at having to endure such a task which is perfectly encapsulated in Füssli's painting in image 9 showing a trepidatious Odysseus looking up in fear as the spirit of Tiresias appears before him. But whilst Circe's necromantic powers here are for the greater good, this relationship with the underworld, and the spilling of blood combined with necromantic chanting, will serve only to define the dark arts that the witch herself is to become so connected with.

Circe does, indeed, transform into a supreme dark witch. From her first mention in the Homeric fantastical world of adventures and heroes, she gradually becomes more dangerous and perverse, especially when we reach the Roman era.

Circe's Transformation into Witch Extraordinaire

We have seen already that misogyny dominates literature in the Roman era and representations of Circe are certainly affected by this. The reasons for this prejudice will be addressed later in this chapter, but for now, we will examine how Circe is described during the Roman period. There are three references to Circe from the first century BC and AD that are worth addressing. The first is in Diodorus Siculus' *Bibliotheca historia*. Diodorus was a Greek historian born in Sicily who wrote his *Bibliotheca* between 60–30 BC, at a time when the Roman Empire was growing and the Republic with its civil wars was in full swing. He certainly would have been influenced by Roman culture and values, and also the general disturbance that this period provided. Diodorus' major concern is Medea and her dark arts, but Circe gets a mention as her sister and daughter of Hecate. The transformation of Circe in his twelve-line assessment of her from the almost benevolent helpful witch of the *Odyssey* to the dark murderous manipulator that Diodorus sees her as is quite remarkable.

For Diodorus, Circe, like her mother Hecate, is skilled in 'deadly drugs'.[39] She marries a Scythian man and exerts so much 'cruel violence' upon him and her subjects that she is exiled from her queenship and forced to occupy a deserted island where she continues to practice her cruelty upon those who dare to come near her home.[40] Diodorus' description of Circe is brief but telling: she is a witch who needs to be on the periphery of society, clearly the best place for her as she is cruel, violent and wild. She marries into a tribe that is typically associated with the wilderness – the Scythians were thought to wander the Eurasian steppes as nomads. Yet, even her cruelty can surpass nomadic wildness. She is fittingly skilled in drugs that are described as deadly, violent and cruel. This is not a woman who can have any form of benevolence about her, or who will offer aid to heroes seeking their fatherland. She is so far removed from the Circe in the *Odyssey* that she is terrifying, unwelcoming and lethal. Unfortunately, this description of Circe becomes all too commonplace, and we see a similar representation of her in Vergil's *Aeneid*.

Vergil's epic is a tour de force of composition, taking almost ten years to write from 29–19 BC, with some belief that the poem is not completed in its entirety as Vergil himself died before he could close the poem in an effective manner. It was composed at a time of great political change with Augustus establishing himself as the first Roman emperor after a period of upheaval that saw the downfall of the Republic. On the one hand, the *Aeneid* is a poem that helps to extol the virtues of the newly appointed emperor as the one man who can restore peace and posterity and improve much-needed morality in a city that had lost its familial and moral ethics. But as Vergil lived through the latter years of the republic, he was greatly influenced by the turmoil of the civil wars that were a marked feature of this period. He cleverly embeds many fears within his writings regarding war, and the men that wield it, including more subtle worries concerning Augustus himself and his ability to solely lead such a vast empire.[41]

It is for this reason that the latter half of the epic is often seen as his *Iliad*,[42] detailing the many battles, sometimes in gruesome and poignant fashion, that ensue when Aeneas lands in Italy and tries to establish himself there. Conversely, the first part of the epic is classed as his version of the *Odyssey* as Aeneas travels and navigates his way across seas in the hope of finding his destined land. It is when Aeneas is just about to arrive in Italy at the start of the second part of the epic that we meet Circe in a few brief lines in the opening of Book 7. This book falls after Aeneas' descent into the underworld. Like Odysseus, Aeneas needs to travel to the dark depths as a necessary expedition to help enlighten him of his destiny and future fatherland. He is guided with this venture by the priestess of Apollo, the Sibyl, who informs him, like Circe in the *Odyssey*, of the essential procedures he needs to conduct in order to enter Hades safely: he must first pluck the golden bough found in a grove that is sacred to Proserpina; he and his comrades should then bury the dead comrade, Misenus, who had fallen to his death whilst at sea but had not had a proper burial, his body is to be honoured and buried to prevent any pollution. Lastly, Aeneas, similar to Odysseus, should gather black cattle in order to perform sacrifices of their bodies and use their blood for purification.

With these procedures carried out, Aeneas enters the underworld with the sibyl by his side acting as his spiritual guidance. She aids him through the empty halls of Dis, the boiling whirlpools that form the topography of the darkest part of Orcus and even encourages a disgruntled Charon to take Aeneas across the river Styx. Aeneas succeeds in reaching his destination: the isles of the blessed where his father Anchises dwells. Here, he is given a golden vision of the future souls that will rise up from the underworld to be reborn into the greatest Roman men, from

Romulus to Augustus. The vision reassures Aeneas of the significance of his future bloodline, and he leaves the underworld through the Gate of Ivory.[43]

Straight after these events, at the very start of Book 7, we have our reference to Circe. Vergil has chosen not to have Circe as his underworld guide, the role she had played so excellently in the *Odyssey*, but instead portrays her as a sinister threat that could potentially destroy Aeneas' Roman mission. She is introduced to us in the same fashion as Homer, by referring to her as the daughter of Helios, the god of the sun, and that her home lies in 'untrodden groves', from which you can hear her pleasant 'never-ending singing' as she sits at her loom.[44] But the niceties end here as Vergil adds a more menacing tone: lions, boars, bears and wolves that live within her land growl and howl out of anger 'late into the night'.[45] These beasts, we are told, were once men who Circe has completely imprisoned, and penned up, leaving them angry at what has become of their lives.[46] They are a far cry from the tamed beasts of Homer's *Odyssey* who could wander freely outside Circe's house of polished stone. Vergil's Circe, therefore, is frightening. She is further described as 'dangerous', her shores 'deadly' and so threatening is she that Neptune has to arise from the seas to prevent Aeneas and his men from landing on her island.

Circe has no key role in the *Aeneid*. She is, like most other women of the epic, savage and vicious, driven by the one characteristic that Vergil highlights as the downfall of all those that harbour it: *furor*, meaning anger and rage, and women, he seems to argue, have more of a propensity for this than their male counterparts. Suffice it to say, it is of no surprise that Book 7 has other examples of females that are equally unparalleled in their actions. Juno, the queen of the gods, who despises Aeneas most of all, seeks to disrupt his mission at any given opportunity and is outraged to witness that Aeneas has been welcomed by the king of the Latins, Latinus, and that Latinus, believing Aeneas to be the fulfilment of an ancient prophecy whereby a stranger from a foreign land will marry into his family, offers Lavinia, his daughter, to Aeneas in marriage. So infuriated is Juno at this newfound alliance that would mean Aeneas and his men settling in their new homeland, that she seeks the fury Allecto 'from her infernal darkness of her home', the bringer of grief, war, and treachery.[47] Allecto is ordered to 'shatter [the] peace they [Aeneas and Latinus] have agreed between them', and to create war.[48] This Allecto does by visiting Turnus, the original man once betrothed to Lavinia, and encourages his lust for fighting by throwing a firebrand deep within his chest. She also spurs on Amata, the wife of Latinus, who had long desired Turnus as the husband of Lavinia and not Aeneas. She drives her into a wild possessed state, comparable to a maenad who runs through the streets calling upon all mothers to join in her frenzy against the new foreigners that have landed on their shores.

What is Vergil's message here? Book 7 is dominated by crazed females who will disrupt Aeneas' founding of his new kingdom in Italy. Circe finds her place amongst these characters. She is not the guide, or the benefactor that she has been in the past. Instead, she is clumped together with misery, grief and *furor*. Vergil uses the Sibyl in Book 6 as Aeneas' underworld guide, purely because she is the voice piece of the male god Apollo, a god who was incidentally greatly honoured by Augustus. There is, therefore, no need to have misogyny levelled at the Sibyl as she stands as a humble servant of her god. Circe, on the other hand, has no such connection and her transformative powers are utterly deadly, with her isolation so strong that it matches those of other witches in Roman literature, such as Erictho, who similarly lurks on the outside of society. Circe is even placed alongside the personification of grief itself, Allecto, and like most females in the Roman literary world, she has a dangerous tendency for anger and rage that can destroy those that allow it to dominate their psyche. It is typical of Vergil's *Aeneid* that women are viewed in this way, they are the harbingers of doom, especially ones that are strong-willed and driven by emotion, as we have already seen, even the empathetic Dido destroys herself because of her excessive anger.

The *Aeneid* is fundamentally a man's poem, honouring patriarchy, and the ultimate masculine titles in the Roman world of the *paterfamilias* and *pater patriae*,[49] it is the men that rule, govern and control, not the women. Circe is meant to be seen in this misogynistic light and is one of the reasons why witches play such marked roles in the literature of this time. Their grotesque nature helps to usher in fear for the male audience, enough to make sure that strong and powerful women are kept as far afield as Circe is on her isolated deadly shores. But this is not the whole story. Aeneas, the protagonist of the epic, is not the great Messianic man we are initially meant to view him as. He, too, is driven by *furor*. In fact, his anger is so great, that it dominates and drives him to commit catastrophic acts in Books 10–12. Mostly this is due to the loss of Pallas, the boy he is meant to protect and loses to Turnus. But Aeneas is meant to be the bringer of *Pax Romana*, the key peace that marked the reign of the historical Augustus, and to stand by clemency and diplomacy, marked features also of Augustan propaganda. Yet Aeneas gives into *furor* as he mercilessly kills Turnus after his supplication at the very end of Book 12. If *furor* is meant to just dominate females, why is it allowed to take over the one man who is supposed to be our saviour? So much has been debated over this from R.D. Williams' view of Aeneas as merely a reinvention of the hero who has human qualities about him that we, the reader, can simply relate to and, therefore, forgive.[50] Other interpretations arise in relation to Vergil's anti-war message and that furor is a characteristic that is a terrible marked feature of war, and that during such times of battle, even the most pious of men like Aeneas are driven by blood lust.

But one section in Book 7 has had little discussion among scholars. It involves the giving of gifts by Latinus to Aeneas as part of their alliance. Latinus gifts Aeneas a war chariot driven by fire-breathing horses, horses that have been bred by Circe no less. Could it be that Aeneas may have been bewitched by these horses during battle, or even, like Allecto, fired up by their ability to breathe flames? Is this then Circe's subtle gift to the protagonist? Unlike the beneficial gifts of Homer's Circe, these ones destroy him and single him out as the most troubled of all heroes. This may well be a stretch, but the gift is highly unusual and as we have seen, any gift from a witch, particularly in literature written after Homer, can have dire consequences. So perhaps her role in this epic is more prominent than we first imagined, albeit a more lethal and much more deadly one.

Ovid is another poet writing in the Augustan era who is far more complex than Vergil. This is seen in the type of poetry that Ovid chose to write with his topics often classed as burlesque, lacking convention and set apart from the general Augustan propaganda that was so dominant at this time. Essentially, Ovid was a love poet, enjoying the parody of this emotion as evident in his *Amores* and *Ars Amatoria*. This parody was sometimes risqué: the voyeuristic tone of *Amores* 1.5 being a classic example in which the poet invites his reader to witness the tearing off of the tunic of his lover, Corinna, proceeding to describe her naked body from her shoulders to her thighs. The poem becomes even more indecorous when we consider that Corinna is in fact his mistress, a married woman who he is having an ardent and torrid affair with. This lacked the dignified convention that Augustus himself was hoping to restore in his newly formed regime as Ovid seemed to flout the marriage laws Augustus had established, which encouraged men and women to marry and have children, advocating the belief in the nuclear family which would restore the loss of morals that signified indecent behaviour of the late republic. It is safe to say that Ovid pushed the boundaries in his writings, with other works like *Ars Amatoria* which encourages adulterous affairs, and his *Heroides* which gives voice to downtrodden mythological women in a world that is heavily patriarchal. Ovid is eventually exiled by Augustus in 8 AD. The reasons for the exile remain unclear, except for this illusive phrase in relation to his exile by Ovid himself, where he explains that he was driven from Rome due to a 'carmen et error', 'a poem and a mistake'.[51] Maybe his poetry was becoming too insulting for Augustus. It has been postulated that *Ars Amatoria* was the work that drove Augustus to make such a drastic decision.[52] It was during the first year of his exile that his magnum opus, *Metamorphoses*, was published in which Circe significantly plays a key role in Book 14.

The *Metamorphoses* is a comprehensive handbook of mythology detailing the creation myth, the rise of the Olympians and humans and culminating in the mythological founding of Rome. But Ovid enjoys playing around with the mythological tradition, he likes to draw his audience from the mythical world into thinking about our own contemporary situations and how myth is in some way reflecting what is happening now. Book 1 is the most obvious example of this. He takes us on a trip to see the gods on Mount Olympus, a mountain which is compared to the Palatine Hill in Rome where the most important people lived. The most important gods are comparable to the most important people in Rome. This sets up an important theme for the *Metamorphoses* – how the gods can use and abuse their power. Jupiter is synonymous with Augustus and whilst this doesn't mean Augustus raped women which is the main crime of Jupiter but the using and abusing of power and elevating yourself above others is the clear message of autocracy.

Ovidian poetry, though, is notoriously difficult to analyse. His messages are generally humorous but have a serious and disturbing undertone. The *Metamorphoses* is no exception. His retelling of the famous myths that focus upon various forms of bestial and natural transformations highlights disturbing messages of male dominance over the female. Ovid's version of the Pan and Syrinx myth fits this mould. Syrinx is described as a 'remarkable naiad' who is pursed by Pan, god of the wild, but avoids his lustful advances by calling upon her sister nymphs who transform her into 'marsh reeds'.[53] However, Pan sees an opportunity to always have her in his clutches and 'bound' the reeds into a set of pipes – the pan pipes – which he triumphantly claims 'will enable us always to talk together'.[54] Ovid is a master at highlighting oppression and suppression of liberation in this epic, perhaps as an unsettling message about the Augustan regime which he lived under and, as we have seen, eventually exiled from. He is also seen as a writer endorsing protofeminism: his women in the *Ars Amatoria* are encouraged to choose their own sexual pleasures, whilst in this epic their suppression is haunting and disturbing which enables us to sympathise wholly with them. But Ovid's Circe is not like these women. Instead, she is the quintessential femme fatale, the scorned witch who can exert tremendous and devastating curses upon those who cross her path.

There are three stories concerning Circe that Ovid weaves into his narrative in Book 14. The first involves her dealings with the river god Glaucus and his love for the nymph Scylla. Desperate to win the affections of the nymph, Glaucus visits Circe knowing that she can cast spells and knows of a herb powerful enough that Scylla will return his passions. But Circe desires Glaucus for herself, desires that are quickly rejected by Glaucus who claims he could love no other whilst Scylla still lives. So incensed is she by this rejection that she seeks through 'the spells of her witchcraft' to transform Scylla from beautiful nymph to wretched fiend.[55] Ovid employs his great poetic skills to describe the hideous metamorphosis: after discovering a pool of water where Scylla takes a noonday rest, Circe sprinkles her 'monster-producing poisons' within it so that when Scylla immerses herself, her limbs and loins morph into barking creatures and gaping hell-hounds.[56] She becomes the Scylla so familiar to us in the Odyssean epic, a creature so potent that it will gobble up frightened sailors.

Our next Circean encounter is with Ulysses which is told to Aeneas when on his travels to Italy. This is the tale from the *Odyssey* that Ovid keeps remarkably the same: Ulysses' men land on her island and a party is sent out to investigate; they find Circe's palace with her wolves, lionesses and she-bears wondering outside; she invites the men in and laces their wine with her potion and taps them with her wand at which they transform into pigs. The part of this story that Ovid focuses upon the most is the metamorphosis of the men to pigs, with their noses growing long into snouts and their hands making hoof prints as the change fully took over them. The description is vivid and dramatic like all of Ovid's metamorphoses, not least because this is the central theme of his epic, but the vividness also adds to the vigour of Circe's transformative abilities. Quite fittingly for Ovid's Circe, like Vergil's *Aeneid* who Ovid tries to emulate in this book, her help as a guide is completely omitted.

The final Circean story covers her dealings with Picus and Canens, also told to Aeneas. Picus was the son of the god Saturn. In Roman myth, Saturn represents a golden age of peace and prosperity, and instantly this means we should view Picus as the sorrowful victim. While Picus is hunting one day, Circe catches sight of him and according to Ovid 'her breath was completely taken away' by his beauty.[57] Using her witchcraft, she 'conjured up an illusion', a phantom boar to lure Picus deeper into the woods in order to entrap him.[58] She also 'darkened' the heavens so his attendants lose their way and give her time to 'ambush him'.[59] To her dismay, once ambushed, Picus 'firmly rejected' Circe's advances, claiming that he is devoted to his wife, Canens.[60] Circe as 'an injured woman in love', strikes Picus with her magical wand three times and to his surprise 'wings had sprung from his body' and 'he pecked at the wild trees'.[61] Picus becomes a woodpecker.[62] Circe's wrath continues, using a noxious substance and summoning Hecate, the goddess of witchcraft, she turns his attendants into monstrous beasts. Leaving Canens heartbroken, she prostrates herself by the banks of the river Tiber and eventually fades away.

Ovid's Circe is clearly a very powerful witch. At certain moments he refers to her as a sorceress, witch and even Titaness, perhaps as a way of reminding his audience of her primordial origins and power. She enjoys wielding her poisoned wand, and like most witches in the classical world, her powers are enlivened by the act of being spurned. She becomes utterly lethal, a witch of lust, that Aeneas must, make sure that he keeps well away from, just as in Vergil's epic. But if Ovid is to be seen as this radical writer, following a protofeminism narrative in the Roman world, why has he portrayed Circe in this way?

Prima facie, Ovid seems to enjoy the use of magic in the *Metamorphoses*. As already noted, Circe is not the only sorceress that Ovid re-articulates in his epic. He also focuses on Medea. It has been argued that the play on the Latin noun *carmina* meaning 'songs' (i.e. poems) and *carmina* as (witches') spells were well established in Latin poetry.[63] So, Medea's and Circe's use of magic reflects an aspect of Ovid's poetic ability, his imaginative power to re-imagine, reinvent and refashion inherited tales.[64] But Ovid's fascination with witchcraft is more prosaic than this: he simply does not like the practice of it and finds it degrading and generally dangerous. These thoughts may well be a reflection of his own contemporaneous society whereby magic was sidelined and, in some instances, outlawed.[65] The most obvious example of his dislike arises emphatically in his *Amores* 1.8. This poem's protagonist is the old bawd called Dipsas who Ovid claims is a witch. Bawds in Roman times were described as selling their services for profit and one such service was to introduce women to men. This poem explores Ovid's dismay at the advice given to a girl who is told by Dipsas to seek the love of the man who has riches rather than the man who writes her poems. Ovid begins his poem by describing the bawd's deep-rooted witchcraft with poetic flare:

> She knows the magic arts and the spells of Aeaea…by her art she turns back the flowing waters…[she] threads which move with the whirling wheel…when she wills it clouds gather over the whole sky, the day shines bright. I have seen the stars dripping with blood…[and] the moon was red with blood…she flies through the shadow of the night in changed form…covered with feathers…she summons [souls] from ancient tombs..and splits open the solid earth with long incantation.

Dipsas harbours all the witch-like characteristics that have been under close examination: she can disrupt the natural order, perform necromancy, has strong transformative powers, and notably is linked to Circe with knowledge of the spells from Aeaea, Circe's homeland. The reference to the whirling wheel is an instrument used in love spells, found elsewhere in the Roman world. Although it has been pointed out that Ovid is drawing upon a stock character that is typically found in love poetry.[66] Propertius and Tibullus also write about witchcraft in their love elegies in similar terms, but unconnected to bawds. It is apparent that Ovid writes here of a profound, albeit fantastical, knowledge of the craft itself and the general views that people had of it at the time. Dipsas' attributes are not too dissimilar to those of Circe. She, too, can control nature and has potent transformative powers, all of which arise when her emotions are impacted by love. So rather than empathising with her and allowing her to have her voice, she is vilified like the bawd, darkened and morphed even more into the definition of the witch that we are so familiar with. Moreover, it is Ovid's Circe, more than any of the others, that influences future depictions of her, until we reach the twentieth century.

Circe: From Greece to Rome

From Homer to Ovid, the role of Circe changes dramatically. The fairer representation of her in Homeric poetry displays a witch who can be tamed and use her connections with the afterlife for guidance and aid, singling her out as the most significant and beneficial of all of the encounters along Odysseus' journey. However, the Roman writers morph Circe into a femme fatale, a witch driven by lust who will use her dark arts in a malignant and catastrophic way. Why does this change occur?

As has been already mentioned, patriarchies dominated the Mediterranean during the classical era and beyond. Whilst the Greek world, in particular Athens, was certainly male-dominated, Rome was overwhelmingly male and was sometimes even overbearing in its portrayal of masculinity. Despite this, it has been suggested by Marilyn Arthur that Roman Republican women were somewhat more liberated than those in the imperial era, having a more active role within city life as evidenced in their extra marital affairs, but also politically.[67] One famous incident that highlights women partaking in political affairs is recounted by Livy. During the Second Punic War between Rome and Carthage, a law was passed to suppress the luxuries of the women, ordering them to give up their valuables to aid Rome's poor finances. The law extended beyond the end of the Punic War and twenty years later, the women took to the streets, filled the Capitoline Hill, and blockaded all entrance ways to the forum as a dramatic sign of protest against the harshness of the legislation that had now lasted well into peacetime.[68] It was one of the most dramatic images of a protest for female liberation in the ancient sources. Nonetheless, the evidence supports the fact that the female voice and her image were dramatically oppressed, particularly in the late republic and early imperial era. As K.B. Stratton argues, the Romans were concerned with the sexual licence of women and their luxury during this time as they longed to reinstate the power of female chastity as a symbol of social stability. This, Stratton believes, is the reason why the witch plays such grotesque roles within the literature, the image being used as a way of regulating female behaviour. Any man with access to such literature would be scared into ensuring that his wife knows her place.[69]

Stratton further argues that Rome was led by a strong corporal ideology that infiltrated every aspect of their society and notably their literature. This ideology related to the integrity found within the physical body of the male.[70] Such traits as 'courage, grace, and self-hierarchy' resided within the body from birth and enabled men to grow into the leading males of the state.[71] Any tampering with these traits would mean a breakdown of these key attributes, and, therefore, a pollution that would threaten the stability of the empire. It is for this reason, Stratton claims, that witches are portrayed in Roman literature as vile creatures who have the power to disrupt the physiology of the male: stories of body mutilation, transformation, and even infanticide are all apparent in the texts; frightening mechanisms that would encourage better control of the female sex. Circe, of course, falls within this category – she can transform men at will from human to animal, thus rendering them powerless, unintelligible beings.

Contrastingly, Judith Yarnall claims that the transition of Circe's goodness to pure malevolence actually stems from the origins of allegory and the rise of the so-called allegorists who are responsible for much of the way that women were portrayed from the sixth century BC onwards.[72] Allegory, by definition, means the use of an art form, like a narrative or artwork, to examine hidden meanings, whether they be political or moralistic, within the representation of a particular character. For Yarnall, the allegorists decided to strip Circe of all goodness, and make her, instead, the 'personification of passion and vice', and it is at this moment that her career as a witch begins.[73] Later Roman allegorists, Yarnall continues, distrusted women for their passions and rages, so that with the development of the stoic movement, by which certainly Vergil and other Augustan poets were influenced, we have further darkened images of the female in the texts; women with immense power who can manipulate their environments and those within it as a result of their burning, fiery and uncontrollable lascivious desires.[74]

What all these interpretations suggest is that fundamentally, misogyny was rife in the literature, certainly from after the Homeric period and beyond, dominating the way men wrote about women, and particularly Circe, for almost two millennia.

Modern-day Circe

Misogynistic representations of Circe as a dark lustful and dangerous witch persisted beyond the Roman era and well into modern history. Artists and writers alike continue to enjoy using her as an example of corrupt power, and the danger of coming into contact with a lustful whore. Modern artists' portrayals of Circe tended to display her wielding her dark magic, in much the same fashion as the images we have on Greek vases. The famous *Circe Invidiosa* by John William Waterhouse, painted in the late nineteenth century, visualises Ovid's Circe at the moment she pours her monstrous inducing drugs into the pool that the unsuspecting nymph Scylla will immerse herself in, transforming her into an unrelenting hideous fiend (image 10).

The dark hues of the painting, coupled with the emerald green of her poison help to encapsulate her hideous power. Whilst Chris Woods argues that the painting helps to demonstrate the tragedy of Circe, claiming her passions have driven her to an act that she cannot control and will later regret,[75] the eyes of Circe, however, reveal to the onlooker a different woman, one bent on premeditated maliciousness, with clear evil in her heart, regardless of the consequences.

Written accounts of Circe have been equally unforgiving. Yarnall draws upon the epic poem *The Faerie Queen*, written by Edmund Spencer in the late sixteenth century.[76] The poem explores the adventures of knights as they tackle many obstacles on their way to prove their virtuous attributes and worthiness in being a knight of the realm. The poem is emphatically influenced by the virtues of the contemporary world of the Elizabethans and by the ruler Elizabeth I herself. Nonetheless, characters within the poem are influenced by the ancient mythological world. One such character is the witch Acrasia who is clearly modelled upon the Homeric Circe: she lives upon an isolated island called the

Bower of Bliss, a land that is, in fact, the antithesis of its name as she lures men to her, seduces them and turns them into beasts. Incidentally, Acrasia's name means a lack of self-discipline, stressing a woman who is easily driven by her uncontrollable lust.

This persistence since the Roman era of presenting a misogynistic Circe has slowly eroded over the twentieth and twenty-first centuries with the rise of the feminist writer Margaret Atwood. Atwood is well known for her sometimes haunting renditions of tales that either allow women to speak or place women in a world in which the female sex is forever oppressed as a way of reminding us of their long-berated history. Her *Peneliopiad*, for instance, gives a much-needed voice to the often quiet and tearful Penelope of Homer's *Odyssey*, whilst her *Handmaid's Tale* takes us into a dystopian period dominated by female oppression where the only role of the handmaid is to breed, leading to any form of mistreatment should they step out of line. Atwood forever allows us to see a world that can be bleak when personal freedoms, like for so many women throughout history, have been obliterated. As readers, we are always on the side of the female.

Circe, of course, is a part of Atwood's literary imagination. In the early 1970s, Atwood composed her own epic poem in which Circe takes centre stage. Her retelling of the Circe story appears in a collection of poems entitled 'You Are Happy', under the subheading 'Circe/Mud Poems', published in 1974. Notably, the environment in which Circe lives in these poems is not one of lushness, but bleak, barren and charred, possibly as a metaphor for centuries of female oppression. When Odysseus arrives on her island, she shows little interest in his heroic exploits simply telling him that there must be more he can do with his life. Here is the marked change in her character, a woman who has minimal awe in male heroic exploits, unlike the Odyssean Circe who marvels at him, this is one step forward for the female sex exerting their own personal exploits which can be seen as greater or even surpassing those of men. Circe expresses fears of her own sex and the act of sex itself, raising modern issues of women being taken advantage of and simply used only for the pleasurable act of intercourse: she recalls a story told to her by a passing traveller who related an episode where he and his friend constructed a life-size headless female model out of mud whom they repeatedly raped. Circe fears that her dealings with Odysseus are similar to this story and that she, too, is simply a sexual object.[77] This is a modernised Circe reflecting upon contemporaneous fears of sex and relationships in a world where women were beginning to have some autonomy.

Atwood's Circe was contrived during a time of great social change for women in what has been called the second feminist movement of the twentieth century – the first starting in the late nineteenth century and culminating in female enfranchisement. The movement that Atwood lived through saw more equal opportunities for the female sex in both the workplace and education. No doubt, this is as an influencer for her Circe. Although the role of women has changed dramatically from the staid patriarchal days of yesteryear, it is still always attracting debate. Female empowerment does, after all, have centuries of oppression to shake off. In our current world, we are seeing an increasing array of traditional male-dominated stories being rewritten from a very female standpoint. For instance, in Angela Carter's rather dark retelling of classic fairytales, her aim in her anthology, *The Bloody Chamber* is to allow the woman to be the protagonist throughout her collection which effectively dismantles the power of the male, who for centuries has pulled the strings. Other writers such as Natalie Haynes is renowned for rewriting female versions of Greek myths such as her recent rendering of Medusa in *Stone Blind*.

Madeleine Miller similarly wrote her own retelling of the Circe story, written entirely from Circe's viewpoint. Miller cleverly uses all the popular stories associated with Circe from Homer to Ovid, even drawing upon the lesser-known epic poem the *Telegony* that explores the story of Circe's son, Telegonus, whom she had with Odysseus.[78] Miller's Circe is still a complex character. She is a witch that can use drugs, powerful enough to be detrimental but the feminist touches given to her narrative allow us to empathise with Circe from the moment she is born to the moment she desires mortality at the end of the novel. Miller's Circe is kind and understanding from a young age, we see this first when she is the only one within the halls of her father's palace who provides much-needed nectar to a beaten and bruised Prometheus who has been dragged before the other immortals as they debate his punishment for his transgression against Zeus.[79] Even though Circe uses her baleful drugs to transform Scylla, in line with Ovid's version, Circe is driven to do so by the arrogance of Glaucus whom she had changed into a god and who, afterwards, callously ignores her. We have, here, the classic modern interpretation of the man giving the woman the cold shoulder after he has mercilessly led her on. Whilst this cold rejection leads Circe to transform Scylla, she is full of remorse for her actions and is subsequently ostracised to Aeaea.

On the isolated island, Circe delves more into her magical arts, becoming a powerful witch in her own right. One scene that displays her confidence with her own magic is when she effectively brews a potion on top of the highest peaks of the island, sprinkling the concoction in the full light of the moon as she sings her incantations.[80] Her singing brings forth a wild animal of the island, the lioness having been tamed by the magic and who Circe befriends and plays with like we would our own pet. This is certainly a new Circe on display here. She is no longer the dark, malicious woman of the past but a white witch who can use her magic to befriend the animals and protect her own skin. Indeed, for Miller, Circe's transformative powers are not used because she wishes to emasculate the male arrivals to her island, but because she must do so out of necessity due to the one man who raped her after she had offered him hospitality.[81] Her magic and porcine metamorphoses become an essential protection for her own body. At the end of the novel, following the lesser-known epic of *Telegony*, Circe falls in love with Telemachus. This ensues after her son Telegonus leaves his mother to seek his father, Odysseus, only to accidentally kill him when Odysseus attacks him after he arrives at his palace. Forlorn, Telegonus returns to his mother with Penelope and Telemachus. The novel closes with her drinking a potion so she can seek mortality and live out her days with her beloved Telemachus. With Miller's Circe, we have come full circle. Her novel takes us back to where Circe first appears. Circe is at last the benevolent witch of Homer's imaginings. One who can still cast spells and create some potent transformations, but who also has a heart that can love, help and understand. Circe's own voice, after centuries of misogynistic oppression, is at last loud and clear. Significantly, her mortality at the end fittingly strips her of her witchcraft, the very thing that had plagued her representations for over two millennia. Perhaps if we were to strip away the magical dark arts from all the other females that we have so far encountered, it would enable us to see, and understand, the real woman behind the potions.

Circe and Hecate, as we have seen, have been allowed to be cleansed of their dark arts. But this will not be the case for the following witches, who are vilified to such a degree by the Romans that even in our own world of female liberation and empowerment, they still lurk in the deep, dark woods and in our worst nightmares.

Chapter Three

Thessalian Witches

As soon as she'd mounted and stroked the bridled necks of her serpents, she gave a shake to the slender reins and was swept to the sky, from where she looked down on Thessalian Tempe and steered her dragons to places she knew would provide her with herbs...

Ovid, *Metamorphoses*,
Book 7.220–24[1]

Thessaly: The Witches' Playground

Witches, as we have seen, were generally considered to live remotely, on the edge of civilisation and in a desolate wild and unexplored environment: Circe, for instance, resides on her own isolated island, whilst Medea's homeland is Colchis, which, for the Greeks, was at the furthest edge of their world by the Black Sea, an area itself thought to be barbaric and dangerous. Indeed, the idea of Colchian barbarism is accentuated in later renditions of the Euripidean tragedy of *Medea*. Pasolini's 1969 film adaptation of the tragedy introduces us to Medea's Colchis, a primitive tribal community who perform ritualised human sacrifice as a way of ensuring the fertility of their landscape.

In a graphic scene reminiscent of a bloody horror film, the Colchians eagerly await the butchering and dismembering of a young man. His blood is drunk as part of the ritual. This grim scene foreshadows Medea's own act of dismemberment that will come later in her story when she butchers her brother as she escapes from her country. Pasolini plays upon the idea of *sparagmos*, a Dionysiac ritualistic sacrifice whereby the victim is torn limb by limb and their flesh is consumed. The *sparagmos* itself marks the climatic end of another Greek tragedy – Euripides' *Bacchae* – but this, too, is a scene of shock and horror. Pasolini's aim in portraying the Colchians in this way, whilst providing a shocking element to his film, is to stress the barbarity of Colchis, an area primaeval and otherworldly and very much in contrast to the civilised Greek city-states. Such a representation firmly places Medea alongside savagery and cannibalism.[2]

Other witches such as Ovid's Dipsas lurk in unsavoury parts of the city in areas where the upper echelons would not dare to set foot[3] and, although Hecate, as a goddess of witches, was more ubiquitous, she was associated with those dark, untouched boundaries where only restless spirits loiter. Witches, therefore, were not meant to be seen in the built-up, populous areas of the cities. Their dangerous natures were, like their foreign counterparts, seen as uncultured, savage and were best placed in areas where they could do no harm.[4] Thessaly was one such area.

Thessaly was situated in north-eastern ancient Greece, a mountainous region endowed with a variety of plants which were traditionally used for potions and poisons according to the literary tradition. The reasoning for this interconnection between the geographical location of Thessaly and the use of plants in incantations may well have arisen due to Thessaly's lack of intercourse with the rest of Greece historically. It has been stated that Thessaly was too far north to have immediate contact with contemporary Greek city-states from as early as the Dark Ages when there was an impetus for the city-states to seek overseas colonisation and improve economic statuses.[5] Thessaly did not take part in these ventures further secluding itself and becoming increasingly backwards in its outlook as it did not have direct contact with other metal-using districts. Politically, Thessaly did not fare any better, becoming an almost negligible state by the sixth century due to internal social unrest and instability amongst aristocratic families.[6] It is of no surprise that a negative reputation arose concerning Thessaly, labelling it as barbaric in contrast to the sophisticated, civilised south. The region quickly became a wilderness, primitive and uncivilised within the literary tradition. Indeed, in Greek myth, it was the area where the centaurs resided, who were generally seen as barbaric and savage.[7] Placing witches alongside these creatures, similarly, classed them as a band of disenfranchised entities.

Topographically, the forestry and mountains of the area have led to much debate as to why these geographical elements became a symbol of primitiveness. Richard Buxton explains that mountains especially are outside and, therefore, wild; they indicate 'humanity's place of first inhabitation' and are considered a boundary, beyond which lies wilderness.[8] Forests likewise reflect the same ideology. This, therefore, seems a fitting place for witches to make their potions, perform their incantations and even necromantic practices. Not only do witches reside in Thessaly according to the literature but there are many instances of various visitations to the area for the purposes of obtaining plants for specific potions and incantations. In Ovid's *Metamorphoses*, Medea heads towards this region in order to find the necessary herbage for use in her deadly potion to rejuvenate Aeson.[9] Richard Gordon states that the area, even though part of the Greek world, was decidedly non-Greek and Medea's appearance here in the literature further demonstrates a xenophobic and prejudiced attitude towards the region and the women that lived within it.[10] This could be another reason why Thessaly gained a reputation for the evil arts, together with its remote geographical setting. The Roman poet Lucan similarly describes the richness of the soil in the 'highlands' and the copious herbs that are available for the magical practitioners:

> Thessaly's soil, moreover, produces up in the highlands noxious herbs and magical stones that respond to the deadly configurations and spells of the wizards. Poisons found there strong enough even to master the gods; Medea from Colchis brought no foreign drugs; and she found there all that she needed.[11]

Coupled with the abundance of poisonous plants and herbs, witches who resided in or visited Thessaly could also draw down the moon, an ability to make the night darker or to rid the world of daytime. This they did by using a spinning wheel. In this respect, the pulling down of the moon was a form of a lunar eclipse, perhaps as a way of using the darkness to disguise the witch's spelling making. It was a common practice in love spells as well, the belief being that by pulling down the moon, the witch could use the magical ingredients that it provides for her love potions.[12] This feat became known as the Thessalian trick and is mentioned in classical literature as old as the fifth century BC. In Aristophanes' *Clouds*, for example, the character Strepsiades who is attending Socrates' school is beginning to doubt the sophistic methods he is being taught and exclaims, 'What if I buy a Thessalian witch... make the moon go down and put her in a box...and I keep an eye on her.' This he does so that he can make the months disappear in the hopes his monthly educational bills do as well.[13]

Thessaly and its witchcraft association were clearly known to the Greeks and to Hellenistic writers. One such occurrence of this is seen in the poem *Pharmakeutriai* (*The Witches*) composed around 270 BC by the Hellenistic poet Theocritus. It relates the woeful desires of Simaetha who is desperate to regain the affection of her former lover Delphis.[14] She seeks out old women who have the knowledge of dealing with love spells that can reignite love that has been lost. Part of these spells involves the use of the magic spinning wheel and the process of calling down the moon, two classic features of Thessalian witchcraft which Theocritus, no doubt, acquired from contemporary knowledge of sorcery within the area. But it was during the Roman period that Thessaly reached its zenith as an area prevalent in the dark arts. To understand why this is the case, we have to examine the role of the witch in Roman literature.

Witches in the Roman Literary Tradition

It would certainly seem that Theocritus' Simaetha had some impact on the development of the witch in the Roman world. This is evident in Vergil's *Eclogue* 8, c. 39 BC, where a woman is described as seeking the reemergence of love from a man called Daphnis. Various rites are referred to as the woman partakes in a love spell which contains such things as the drawing down of the moon, and the use of voodoo dolls that are placed in flames.[15] However, the overall development of the witch in the Roman literary world takes an overall malignant turn.

Throughout the first century BC we have an unprecedented emergence of nefarious women in Roman literature that engage in all manner of evilness that makes them, as Ronald Hutton proclaims, 'characters that have no parallel in Greek literature'.[16] They have a profound knowledge of hideous poisonous herbs and incantatory rites that can raise nocturnal entities and ghosts, sometimes for the sole purpose of destruction; they use all manner of ingredients to enact their spells and curses from venomous herbs, body parts that have been scattered in cemeteries, feathers from the screech owl – parts of animals that have been ripped apart by the witch herself –, and most grotesquely of all, they enjoy participating in the capturing and murdering of young children. Together with these disturbing acts, they are shown to be more potent in their ability to control nature from demonstrating a powerful sway over tempestuous forces to being able to bring about nighttime during the height of the day and even melt mountains and make the planet stationary. Moreover, the Roman witch became a hag with grey hair, had a Thessalian connection and was a capable shapeshifter, often choosing to metamorphose into nocturnal animals and ones found in the wild, such as the wolf.[17] These characteristics are indeed the forerunners of our 'modern Western Halloween-style witch'.[18]

Some of the most infamous Roman hag-witches include Horace's Canidia, Petronius' night hags and the Thessalian witches in Apuleius' *Golden Ass*. In the introduction, Horace's Canidia was assessed as being a witch of the most loathsome kind with her desire to starve a young boy to death in order to harvest his organs as part of a spell. There are actually six Horatian poems which feature Canidia but only one in which she takes centre stage as the antagonist in *Satire* 1.8: Canidia in the Gardens of Maecenas. The poem is written from the point of view of the statue Priapus who has been newly erected in the Gardens of Maecenas.[19] Priapic statues were recognisable by their over-large phalluses and, like the *Hermae*,[20] served as apotropaic talismans who would ward off unwanted entities. In this case, the statue acts almost like a scarecrow figure who is meant to frighten away birds and also thieves from entering the gardens and causing mischief. This he does with his right hand, a symbol of righteousness to deter thieves[21] while the reeds sticking out from his head would scare away birds. More pruriently, the phallus also served as a threat of buggery for those thieves that dared to cross over into the gardens. The gardens themselves have been built in an area that was once used as a paupers' graveyard and still has remnants of the 'whitened bones'[22] that were strewn across the ground as the bodies were unceremoniously thrown down. The area used to be a hotbed for unsavoury characters to lurk in the night such as the aforementioned thieves. However, despite the presence of Priapus and all his talismanic grandeur, his appearance does not ward off the witch Canidia and her entourage from entering the gardens in the thick of night in order to conduct spells, perform necromancy, and steal the bones that still lay about.

The description of Canidia is a particularly vivid one. She has come to the gardens in order to disturb the spirits of the dead with her spells and drugs; she wears black cloth, her feet bare, and hair down. She is described as shrieking, scratching the earth with her bare nails and ripping apart a black lamb with her teeth; the lamb's blood and gore poured into a ditch so that she can perform necromancy, calling upon ghosts to consult with. Canidia and her witches are lastly seen handling dolls, one of wax, the other of wool, thought to be used for the purpose of an erotic spell. Before they are disturbed, they call upon Hecate and the fury Tisiphone, and chant incantations which help to manifest hell hounds and snakes. They are finally disturbed in their act of spell-making and necromancy when Priapus lets out a large fart, scaring them to such an extent that even Canidia's false teeth fall out.

Canidia is the ultimate intruder in this poem, coming to an area that has recently been revamped to allow the people of Rome to promenade during the day. It is not perceived to be a cemetery anymore, yet her intrusion reduces the newly formed area to one that can only be seen as unsavoury, uncivilised and unwelcoming. Canidia, as is fitting for her witch status, has been dehumanised by Horace. She is seen as animalistic and bestial when she scratches at the earth and tears the lamb apart with her teeth.[23] She dresses in a wild manner by having her feet bare and hair down and shrieks like a wild bird. Horace employs effective use of language to convey her wild presence: he uses the Latin word 'horrendus' to entice the reader to see her appearance as uncouth, whilst our word 'horrendous' derives from this, here it has a more profound impact, translated as 'dreadful'. He also refers to the sound that Canidia and the other witches make as 'ululantem', other translators interpret this word as 'shrieking' perhaps in line with the idea of the screech owl with which the night hags were associated, but alternatively it can mean 'howling', another fitting word to personify them as creatures of the night.

Canidia is, in these descriptions, completely on the edge of humanity. Her actions are highly inappropriate and are seen as someone who needs to be removed from civilisation.[24] Whilst it can be argued that the poem is humorous in a purely satirical sense, especially if we consider the way Priapus acts in a scatological manner,[25] nonetheless, Horace draws upon images of witches from other well-known works such as Homer, Vergil and Theocritus, using the already established stereotype to morph her into what will become the typical Roman hag-witch.[26] Indeed, it has been argued that Canidia is Rome's first literary witch and her gothic cruel nature mentioned here will become a precedent in other Roman literary texts, a frightening emblem of the wild, uncouth and powerful female.[27]

Petronius, writing almost a century later, similarly uses the same hag-witch stereotype within his famous *Satyricon*. Petronius' *Satyricon* is a Roman novel so a step away from the poetry that has been so far analysed but it employs the same poetic stereotypes. Much of Petronius' novel has only survived in fragments, the episode concerning the extravagant dinner party hosted by Trimalchio being the only full episode available. Trimalchio is a freedman who enjoys flaunting his newly acquired wealth in a pompous and overbearing manner. He invites other fellow freedmen to dinner where they are exposed to extravagances such as wall paintings depicting himself amongst various Olympian deities, and the giving of gifts which are theatrically lowered through a coffered ceiling. Whilst at dinner, a guest called Niceros relates a story that he experienced involving a supernatural encounter. This is followed by another supernatural storytelling by the host Trimalchio.[28]

The first story concerns Niceros who, when still a slave, makes a journey to see the woman he loves called Melissa. Her husband has recently passed away and Niceros seizes his opportunity to seek her out. Niceros' master had left for Capua leaving enough time for Niceros to leave the house himself, asking, one of the guests in his house to accompany him on the journey. This man is a soldier which Niceros considered a fitting travelling companion due to his bravery. Along the road and in the thick of night when the full moon is shining, they take a break near a set of gravestones. Niceros leaves his companion to relieve himself and when he returns, the solider has stripped naked and miraculously turned into a wolf, with his clothes morphed into stone. The wolf man runs off amongst the gravestones. Petrified by this sight, Niceros makes his way to Melissa who tells him that she and the slave had just been attacked by a wild wolf and that her slave had hit him in the neck with a spear. The next day, Niceros makes his way back to the place where he witnessed the metamorphosis, only to find no trace of the solidified clothes and only remnants of blood. Making his way back home, he finds his soldier companion with his neck all bloodied and being seen to by a doctor. It was then that Niceros realised that the soldier was indeed a shapeshifter – a *versipellis*, literally meaning 'pelt-changer'.

This story is clearly focused upon a werewolf, and, alongside the ancient Greek myth concerning Lycaon, relates one of the oldest versions of this mythological creature in the Western world.[29] However, the Romans often classed those who possessed this form of transformative power as shapeshifters with witches and sorcerers who were both capable of performing at will, and the very fact that Petronius' werewolf heads towards the cemetery, shows that he had a strong affiliation with ghosts, another close relationship that witches also have.[30] There is, however, a more direct relationship between the witch and the wolf in Vergil's *Eclogue* 8 which recounts the events of a young woman, sung by the herdsman Alphesiboeus, who makes a magic spell to reignite lost love in the heart of her former lover, Daphnis. She approaches a sorceress called Moeris who she explains is adept in the use of 'poisonous plants' and has the power to 'become a wolf' at will, hiding herself in woods and 'deep graves'.[31]

In the *Satyricon*, Trimalchio tells of his own supernatural encounter with hag-witches. When he was still a slave, his master's favourite boy slave died and his mother, together with the rest of the household, was stricken with grief. As the mother poured her lamentations upon her dead son, witches could be heard howling outside. Another slave described as a brave, tall Cappadocian chap, rushed outside to ward off the witches with his sword drawn and managed to stab one of the witches in the stomach. When he returned, his whole body was covered in black and blue marks as if he had been flogged. He had, according to Trimalchio, been touched by the evil hand. The mother meanwhile returned to her dead son only to find that the body had been snatched by the witches and a straw baby had been put in its place. This story is more in line with the classic imagery of the malignant Roman hag-witch, who sought out bodies of children and snatched them away in the middle of the night for their own grotesque satisfactions. The imagery is also similar to the Roman belief in the type of female demonic witch called the 'strix'.

The female demonesses, the *strigae*, were thought to be night witches who enjoyed seeking out infants and children, often killing them and devouring them. This belief crosses many cultures and is a far more ancient one than that of the Romans. The Greeks had their own child-killing female demon called the *lamia*,[32] but it is thought that these demonesses can be found in ancient Mesopotamia as well.[33] However, the killing of children was not exclusively a female preoccupation as there are instances of males in the mythology devouring infants too: the classic example being Cronus, the Titan father of the Olympian gods, who ate his own children out of fear that they would usurp his power or out of fear that he would be castrated by them, the latter crime he had so committed upon his own father, Uranus.[34] The act of castration was a symbolic removal of male potency.

Indeed, there are some sources that state that the consuming of children became a form of child sacrifice, held in honour of Cronus, in some ancient communities, namely in Carthage – perhaps as a macabre way of ensuring the god's commitment to protection, with him reciprocating sacrifice with essential sustenance needed during the dead of winter.[35] Cronus, though, like most deities, was a juxtaposition as he could also symbolise a golden age when as Diodorus of Sicily claims, he 'cause[d] all men who were his subjects to change from a rude way of living to civilised life'.[36] Even the idea of sacrificing to Cronus was considered by classical writers to be an act of the direst cruelty performed only by the likes of Carthaginians and not by the Greeks and Romans. In *Minos*, for instance, Plato refers to human sacrifice as 'not legal, but unholy, whereas the Carthaginians perform it as a thing they account holy and legal…some of them sacrifice even their own sons to Cronus'.[37]

Carthaginians aside, the male preoccupation with child killing was, nonetheless, historically performed in the classical civilisations of Greece and Rome through the legalised 'exposure' of infants. Whilst this practice was not a sacrifice per se or an act of cruel consumption, it was a form of removing an unwanted child by 'exposing' them to the outside world. It was the ultimate decision of the male in charge of the household for a newborn child to be removed from the family. The practice generally involved leaving the child in specific areas. Juvenal refers to the *lactoria columna* or the *spurci lacus*,[38] places that may have ensured the unwanted child's survival, as someone wanting to adopt a child would generally look in these parts of the city. Sometimes, however, a child could be left in places where it was more likely to die, being cast out into the wilderness naked or injured which would often lead to its demise. Suetonius mentions that Emperor Claudius insisted the daughter of his wife Urgulanilla by a freed slave be 'cast out naked'[39] so reducing its chances of survival.[40]

Notwithstanding the above, the act of taking the life of an innocent, particularly your own blood or even of the life of another child, even if this was part of a sacrificial act for a deity, was still the ultimate taboo in the classical era, as Sophocles' *Andromeda* is quick to point out: this act of killing is itself inhuman, and one which only barbarians would partake in.[41] It is for this reason that the killing of infants and children became a pastime of the Roman witches, it helped to further highlight their uncivilised, barbaric and intimidating natures. The Romans uniquely believed that a demoness could morph into a screech owl which enabled her to freely move from one place to another. This seems an appropriate metamorphosis as the owl itself is often associated with witchcraft: it is nocturnal, unusual in its ability to rotate its head, has claws resembling something otherworldly, is predatory by nature and can screech in the night.[42] All these attributes marry well with the Roman idea of a witch. The witch-cum-owl would fly to the child at night and feast on its blood and internal organs.

A few Roman writers provide some disturbing accounts of this type of witch. Ovid, as we saw with his dealings with the witch Dipsas, hints that this was her desired nocturnal activity in his *Amores* 1.8 when he claims that she would fly through the night covered in feathers. He also provides a much more vivid account of these creatures in his *Fasti*, an extensive poem published in 8 AD which details the many origins of Roman festivals and their customs:

> *They are birds of prey...*
> *They have huge heads, goggling eyes, beaks carved for plunder;*
> *Their feathers are cast with grey, their claws hooked.*
> *They fly at night and target children still unweaned,*
> *Snatch them from their crib and defile their bodies.*
> *They are said to gorge on milk-fed flesh with their beaks*
> *And to cram their throats with gulps of blood.*
> *Screech-owl is their name; and the cause of the name*
> *Is their hideous screeching at night...*
> *Either they are born birds or become so by magic,*
> *Turned...from crones to birds.*[43]

Interestingly Ovid equates these vampiric *strigae* with the festival of Cardea, the goddess of door hinges, held at the beginning of June in ancient Rome. As Cardea was a liminal goddess who needed to be observed to ensure protection of the household, certain charms were attached to the doors at this time to ward off entry from the *strigae*. Moreover, Ovid links Cardea with an older goddess called Carna, linked to the Latin word 'caro, carnis' meaning flesh, probably due to the *strigae* and their cannibalistic tendencies.[44] Ovid's description of the *strigae* is a particularly repulsive one but certainly is in keeping with the overall image of the Roman witch thus far explained: like Canidia, they enjoy nocturnal gatherings and prey on the innocent; and they are also typically considered to be hags/crones with powerful transformative powers.[45] Sextus Pompeius Festus later refers to the strigae as 'flying women',[46] further showcasing how the Romans set forth the development for the Halloween-style witch, the witch of Halloween is often associated as flying on her broomstick of course. Indeed, it would appear that the 'strix' had somewhat of a profound impact upon other more modern cultures, most notably the *strzygi* which was a female demoness from Slavic folklore who often had vampiric attributes. They were perceived to be ghoulish, with animalistic features such as clawed hands and feet and vampiric-style teeth. Their general countenance and behaviour resemble that of the Roman *strigae*, and even their name is clearly a derivation from the Latin 'strix', as Aleksander Bruckner asserts.[47]

Aside from the literature, there is also epigraphic evidence that suggests that the Roman populace were firm believers that witches were responsible for the theft of infants. An epitaph records the death of a child who was snatched by witches in the dead of night: 'As I was approaching my fourth birthday I was seized and put in the ground, when I could have been sweet to my mother and father. A magic hand [saga manus – that is, the hand of a witch] stole me away, everywhere cruel. While she is on earth, she can also harm you and your children; guard them, parents, lest sorrow be driven into your hearts.'[48] Superstition no doubt played a part in the parents' belief. However, this serves to demonstrate the strong beliefs in witches at this time which were spurred on by the publication of the above-referenced Ovidian literature and other writers of the early imperial era.

The Romans certainly set in stone the classic image of our modern perception of the witch and triggered an overall fear for this type of woman within their culture and beyond. But while they have witches visiting Rome or even residing within it, Thessaly was still perceived to be the witches' playground. The most famous instances of Thessalian witches to be found in the Roman literary world are those referenced by Apuleius in his *Golden Ass*.

Apuleius' *Golden Ass* or *Metamorphoses*

Apuleius was a second-century AD Roman writer born in the Roman province of Numidia. He was an ardent traveller and student, studying extensively in both Carthage and Athens and becoming well-read in philosophy and rhetoric. He was profoundly interested in mystery cults, particularly the Isiac religion and made a journey to Egypt to study this cult further. En route to Egypt, he fell unwell and stayed with his fellow friend Pontianus in Oea, modern-day Tripoli.[49] Apuleius grew close to Pontianus' widowed mother whilst in residence with the family, eventually marrying her, but the situation took a turn for the worse when Pontianus' new father-in-law convinced his uncle, brother of his mother's dead husband, to indict Apuleius on a charge of magic.[50] He was accused of placing love spells upon Pontianus' widowed mother to entice her to marry him so he could gain access to her fortune. He was additionally accused of murder as Pontianus suddenly passed away.

Apuleius defended himself against the charges with his remarkable grasp of rhetoric in his *Apologia*.[51] Having been acquitted, Apuleius made his way to Carthage desiring to reside there permanently. He wrote some of his most profound literary pieces in this city, including published lectures and speeches under the title *Florida*, and a treatise entitled *De deo Socratis*, *On the God of Socrates*, that explores the existence of demons and helps to catalogue them from those who reside within the human body; those that had left the human form and those with special powers and no connection to humans.[52] It has been noted that Apuleius' writings, and especially his examination of philosophy, had a significant impact on the continuation of the study of Middle Platonism from his own time and into the medieval era.[53]

His most well-known piece of work is his *Golden Ass*, also known as *Metamorphoses*. This work is remarkable not least due to its composition but also because it is the only novel from the Roman world to survive in its entirety. The title *Metamorphoses* primarily refers to the main character's change from human form to that of an ass, but there are also other metamorphoses present in the story hence the use of the plural. As Apuleius states in his preface, his work focuses upon 'transformations of men's shapes and destines into alien forms'.[54] This title is also in keeping with Apuleius' overall desire to acknowledge great writers before him or emulate them. He pays homage to Ovid's *Metamorphoses* and, indeed, the many metamorphoses within Apuleius' work remind the audience of the great bestial transformations in Ovid's own epic: Apuleius includes transformations into weasels, owls, asses, and even divine transmutations.[55]

The dating of the novel is controversial, some believing it was written in his early life as the text has a youthful exuberance to it, whilst others recognise a more mature philosophising to the text.[56] Indeed, there is some belief that the novel reflects Apuleius' own life and that the protagonist, Lucius, is meant to be Apuleius himself.[57] There are many autobiographical elements in the text from the insertion of magic, which as we have seen impacted his life quite dramatically, a trial that reflects Apuleius' own legal battle, and the mention of a statue that is offered to Lucius, much like the one historically erected for Apuleius when he spent his later years in Carthage.

Apuleius' Novel

The story of the *Golden Ass* focuses upon Lucius who, at the beginning of the novel, travels to Thessaly on business. On his journey, he meets a man called Aristomenes who relates a fantastical, magical tale involving the power of a witch named Meroë. From this moment, Lucius becomes fascinated with the idea of magic and witchcraft. When he reaches his destination in Thessaly, he stays with his friend Milo, his wife Pamphile and a slave girl called Photis. He visits his aunt who happens to live in the area, and she warns Lucius that Pamphile is an evil witch who he needs to be wary of. His aunt's friend Thelyphron tells Lucius of another magical tale about the evilness of witchcraft, but Lucius ignores the warnings wanting, by this time, to become a witch himself. Having witnessed Pamphile morphing into a bird, Lucius begs the slave girl Photis, who has had much exposure to the witchcraft in the house, to transform him.[58] She accidentally changes him into an ass.

From this moment, the story changes focus and explores the many adventures that Lucius has whilst being an ass: he is captured by thieves and placed alongside another prisoner of theirs called Charite. Whilst in a cave with Charite, an old woman working with the thieves relates the love story of Cupid and Psyche which results in its own transformation when Psyche becomes a goddess. Lucius manages to escape from the thieves but has further adventures from being tormented by a boy, nearly publicly executed, and then sold to many professionals from a miller to a farmer. The story culminates with Lucius' initiation into the cult of Isis when he is eventually transformed back into human form. It is the references to witchcraft and specific witches in the first half of the novel, and one later tale in the latter half that are of most significance for the current study.

Apuleius' Witches

The first reference to witchcraft comes from Aristomenes' story which he relates to Lucius concerning the witch Meroë. Aristomenes stumbles upon his friend Socrates who appears to be down and out and he explains to Aristomenes how he has become so unrecognisable to him: he was robbed by bandits whilst travelling through Thessaly and found an inn for refuge; the inn was run by Meroë who although was 'getting on in years',[59] was still attractive and they ended up in bed together. Socrates claims his misery began then as he was made to surrender himself to her as she was a powerful witch. Socrates vividly describes the powers that Meroë possessed: 'She's a witch…with supernatural powers. She can bring down the sky, raise the earth, freeze running waters, melt mountains, dispatch gods to the world below, black out the stars, and light up hell itself.'[60]

Socrates further explains that Meroë's main obsession was making men fall in love with her and when they spurned her advances or wished to end their liaison, she unleashed her magic upon them with catastrophic consequences, often demonstrating her transformative powers. She transformed one man who chose another woman over her into a beaver as it is believed that beavers escape their pursuers by biting off their own genitals;[61] a pain she wished to inflict upon her former lover. She was also inspired to perform her witchcraft against those that affected her business as Socrates explains that she changed a neighbouring innkeeper who was competing for her custom into a frog. Meroë even took her magic out on those women directly linked to her male lovers. She cursed the heavily pregnant wife of one of her lovers with an indefinite pregnancy as she was heard to mock Meroë. The woman was forced to carry the unborn baby for eight years leading her to look severely misshapen.

In the end, Meroë was condemned to death by stoning by her community, but she used her necromantic powers to call upon spirits to haunt the inhabitants in their homes and removed the house of the man who had called the public outrage against her and placed the house precariously upon the tip of a rugged mountain.

After Socrates relates these terrors to Aristomenes, they retreat to bed in Aristomenes' inn and, nervous that the witch may appear in the night, Aristomenes barricades the door. The witch does, indeed, appear in the middle of the night, flinging open the barricaded door with ease, accompanied by her sister Panthia. Aristomenes cowers under the bed but despite being struck with fear, he humorously compares himself to a tortoise. Meroë plunges her sword right down to the handle on the left side of the sleeping Socrates' neck. She collects the blood that spurts out into a leather bottle and then sticks her hand deep into the wound and pulls out his heart. Her sister Panthia stops the wound with a sponge whilst inciting an incantation and finally cuts his throat before leaving the room. Both sisters urinate over Aristomenes' face. Remarkably, Socrates survives the gruesome attack, startling Aristomenes who was considering suicide as he believed he would be blamed for his death. Both men decide to make a hasty retreat from Thessaly. On their journey from the area, and after growing weary, they take a break by a river where Socrates tucks into his food only to grow increasingly pale and thirsty. As he bends over the river for a drink, the sponge that had been placed by Panthia into his wound pops out and Socrates immediately falls over dead into the water.

There are many things to note from this story. Firstly, Meroë is described as both aged and beautiful which combines a Greek and Roman perspective concerning witches: Greek witches were typically attractive whilst Roman ones were often an 'anus', old woman or hag. Apuleius combines the two as Meroë's perceived attractiveness highlights her manipulative ability over her many lovers.[62] The reference to her age, though, is a reminder that Roman witches are always somewhat older, a common archetype that is adopted in the modern world. Her attractiveness also adds an Odyssean quality to the tale: like Odysseus with Circe, Socrates is bound to Meroë after his sexual encounter with her. Although Odysseus eventually is released from the grasp of his witch encounter, this Roman one is far more potent as Socrates eventually dies. Other similar witch encounters in the *Golden Ass* end the same way, not necessarily with death but with a desire not to return home: Thelyphron, as we shall see, completely abandons his homecoming altogether and Lucius, after being transformed by a spell cast by Photis, does not go home but ultimately initiates himself into the Isiac cult. Homecoming, or *nostos*, as the Greeks referred to it, is of utmost importance in Homer's *Odyssey* as it enables Odysseus to reclaim his kingdom and status. The idea of a man being in charge of his own domestic sphere was a significant part of the male reputation in both the Greek and Roman worlds. The fact that witches are seen to threaten, disrupt or prevent this from happening makes them particularly nefarious.[63]

Meroë's punishments that she inflicts upon her former lovers and those who are related to them, show aspects of her vitriol and malice. These punishments are in keeping with the general belief that such women had transformative powers, tracing connections back to Circe. But Apuleius attributes other, more heinous powers to Meroë which we see in more modern history relating to witches and their craft. Meroë can control pregnancy for malignant purposes, this power is interestingly seen in the witches of the Mandari who reside in East Africa.[64] Moreover, the attack upon Socrates and his ability to still appear to be alive despite the removal of his heart is a practice seen with the Vele of Guadalcanal and the Vada of south-eastern New Guinea where witches similarly daze their victims, remove their hearts, and keep them alive before allowing them to die shortly afterwards.[65] There is even a belief that Apuleius has Meroë and her sister taking part in more modern-style vampiric practices as they attack their victims at night and delight in collecting the blood of Socrates. However, they do not appear to be suckers of his blood.[66] Overall, Meroë is a typical Thessalian witch as she performs necromancy, and is described using the Thessalian characteristic of pulling down the moon.[67] On the whole, her traits are particularly odious and continue the theme of the Petronian style of witch we saw earlier.[68] They also appear to have a profound impact on our own perceptions of witches.

The Story of Thelyphron

Lucius is exposed to another gruesome yet fantastical tale concerning Thessalian witches. This is told by Thelyphron, a friend of his aunt, when he attends a dinner party. The storytelling setting and the tale itself have a significant Petronian, but also very Roman feel to it. Thelyphron begins his tale by explaining that he was travelling through Greece to see the Olympic Games but by the time he reached Larissa in Thessaly, he had run short of finances. He happened to hear a man in the forum advertising for a guardian of a dead body who was to be handsomely paid. Curious, Thelyphron asked a passer-by the meaning of the advertisement and he was told that in Thessaly it was common practice for witches to seek out corpses at night when they lay in wait before burial, so they can remove parts of the corpse's face for magical purposes. A guardian was, therefore, essential to ensuring that a body remained intact for the official funeral. If the guardian moved his gaze, it was possible for a witch to transform into various creatures to carry out their task, such as a dog, mouse or fly.

Dismissive of this superstition, Thelyphron decided to take on the role. He was led by the widow of the dead man to where the corpse lay. The widow performed an inventory of the body to make sure all parts were intact before Thelyphron took up his guardianship. After demanding a lamp, he began his nightly watch. A weasel who fixed him with a piercing stare suddenly interrupted his guardianship. After chasing the creature away, Thelyphron was immediately overcome by heavy drowsiness and fell asleep. He woke in a panic, worried that in his sleep witches may have come and taken parts from the corpse. But the corpse appeared intact. Pleased with his service, the widow paid Thelyphron, the corpse was removed from the room and taken into the forum in order for the funerary rites to commence.

Whilst in the forum, a man approached the corpse and accused the widow of poisoning the young man to please her adulterous lover and lay claim to his inheritance. The man demanded that an Egyptian prophet called Zatchlas be summoned to bring the body back to life, to tell the truth of what happened. The prophet arrived, placed a herb in the corpse's mouth, and another on his heart, and addressed the rising sun. The corpse was reanimated and told the truth of his demise: he was indeed poisoned by his new bride. Some members of the crowd doubted his words as 'no credence should be lent to the lying words of a corpse'.[69] To prove his truth, he told the crowd that he would recount the events of the night before and show them proof of his words. He then pointed out Thelyphron from the crowd and explained that in the middle of the night, some aged witches attempted to get at his corpse by transforming themselves several times and calling upon him to come towards them. But because his limbs were weak through death, he was not able to fully rise. It just so happened that his guardian's name was the same as his and when his guard fell into a deep slumber, he rose at the call of his name and the witches quickly went to work on his face, removing his nose and ears and replacing them with wax prosthetics to cover up the work they had done. Thelyphron was terrified on hearing these words and as he frantically touched his face, his nose and ears quickly fell away. He then realised that the weasel he had seen was, in fact, a transformed witch who had put him to sleep and that he had, indeed, been attacked by the witches in the thick of night. Due to his mutilated appearance, he refused to return to his ancestral home and instead wondered the land with his hair grown to conceal his disfigurement.

Here again, we have a classic Roman witchcraft tale that contains transformative powers, and the snatching of body parts for magical means. The story also has a male sorcerer who performs necromancy, although it should be noted that his role is far more benign within the overall story.[70] The impact of the witchcraft – in this instance, facial mutilation – is again so immense that it leads Thelyphron to abandon his homecoming. Daniel Ogden even points out that the reference to the poisoning in the story, a classic witchcraft weapon, implies that the widow may indeed be the witch;[71] she is interestingly referred to as attractive, yet another feature of Apuleius' witches, but as to whether she is actually behind the nightly crimes remains inconclusive.

Pamphile, the Miller's Wife and the Witch

There are two further instances of witchcraft in Apuleius' work. The witch Pamphile forms an ongoing background story in the first few books of the novel whilst the other tales are related to Lucius. Pamphile is the wife of Milo, the man Lucius is residing with in Thessaly. He is warned by his aunt, Byrrhena, that Pamphile is a powerful witch: she is a specialist in all forms of necromancy; she only needs to breathe on twigs and pebbles before plunging the light of day into the lowest depths of Tartarus. Like other Apuleius' witches, Pamphile is attracted to young men who she dominates and imprisons with eternal love and if they reject her, she will transform them into stones or cattle.[72] Later on, we learn that Pamphile has prophetic powers, peering into her lamp,[73] which she uses in one instance to foretell the coming of a storm and in another instance to aid her with her metamorphosis.[74]

It is her metamorphosis that is the most remarkable and detailed part of her craft, one which Lucius witnesses, spurring him on for his own transformation into the ass. Pamphile's ritual for her transformation involves the removal of her clothes, and application of unguents to her body before using her lamp and flapping her arms and legs. Feathers then sprout upon her limbs as her arms morph into wings and her nose curves and nails grow into talons.[75] She eventually changes into an owl which, as we have seen, was an important bird associated with witchcraft in ancient Rome.

The last tale referred to by Apuleius comes towards the end of the novel in Book 9 when Lucius has been a fully formed ass for some time and has been sold to a miller. The miller's wife has been having an adulterous affair discovered by her husband. She calls upon a witch to help reanimate the miller's love for her and if this fails, she tells the witch to kill him instead. Firstly, the witch uses love spells which do not work upon the husband, so she resorts to necromancy and conjures up the ghost of an old woman who is described as dishevelled with greying hair blackened by ashes and with bare, unshod feet.[76] This woman enters the mill and asks to converse with the miller in private to which he agrees. When he enters his private room with her, he is not seen for some time until the other workers, growing suspicious, enter his room only to find him hanging from a noose and the old woman found nowhere.

Once again, these two references to witchcraft harbour the same characteristics of the Roman witch we have been dealing with. In the case of Pamphile, she is very much the Thessalian witch who can blot out the daylight, transform herself and others at will and act purely out of vengeance and malice. The last witch again deals with love spells, but her ultimate power lies in murderous necromancy where she has the ability to command ghosts to do her evil bidding. It is also noteworthy that the latter witch is commanded to do such malign deeds by a woman, so following the Roman belief that women can be devious murderers, adulterers, poisoners and dabblers with witchcraft.

Conclusions

Thessaly was clearly a hub of witchcraft for the Roman literary world and one that is emphatically brought to light by Apuleius. Indeed, Apuleius, along with other Roman writers like Horace and Petronius, cement the stereotype of the night hag-witch, a woman capable of creating catastrophe through various modes of spell binding, necromancy, transformation, and general maliciousness. Whilst Apuleius portrays his witches, except for the witches in Thelyphron's tale, as old but attractive, their general behaviour is hideous; on the other hand, Petronian and Horatian witches are ugly in both facial features and behaviour. This is significant as it is this perception of the old ugly hag that prevails beyond the Roman era and becomes a marked feature of modern perceptions of the witch and her appearance. We can safely say that this perception starts with Roman literature. Moreover, the isolated Thessaly with its wooded and mountainous topography is the perfect place to have the witch dabbling with her magic, on the periphery of the civilised world and out in the wild, it is again this type of environment that perpetuates in modern fairy tales and other such narratives that focus upon the evil hag.

We must also consider why there was such a marked change in the Roman world regarding the witch. It has already been noted that Greek witches were far more beneficial and that their representations, albeit discredited at certain moments, are fully restored in our modern eyes. But the Roman witches do not have this same treatment. They still live among us in the malignant Weird Sisters of Shakespeare's *Macbeth*; in the classic Wicked Witch of the West from *The Wizard of Oz*; and, in more recent popular culture in the Sanderson Sisters of the film *Hocus Pocus* – witches who, incidentally, live off the life force of children. More importantly, why exactly did this perception of the evil hag-witch emerge during the Roman era?

It was argued in Chapter Two that one reason why the Romans adopted a more sinister portrayal of witches by morphing them into malicious females was to ensure the status quo of the male corporal ideology.[77] Returning to this argument with analysis of Apuleius' witches, we can see a deeper and more persistent fear that arose in the Roman world between the first century BC and the second century AD which is when the most grotesque images of witches appeared in literature. These centuries were a period of great social and political change within Rome when the republic moved to an imperial regime dominated by the Julio-Claudian family and later by the Flavian dynasty and then the Nerva-Antonine dynasty.

It was the Julio-Claudian period especially that saw a change in attitude towards the female sex. Whilst it can be argued that women acted more freely and liberally during the republican era,[78] it has been postulated that women during the imperial regime were dominant, outspoken, politically proactive behind the scenes, wielding influential but also dangerous power.[79] Tacitus' *Annals* is a good place to see the danger of upper-class women – wives of governors, senators and even the wives of emperors – who seemingly manipulate the roles of men, for the purpose of removing an enemy, competing against a rival faction or to ensure that a particular man is chosen as heir to the emperor.[80] It is for these reasons that many women during this period were accused of using *artes magicae*, that is, the art of magic. According to Elizabeth Ann Pollard, *artes magicae* make up almost a third of the criminal trials referred to in Tacitus' *Annals*.[81] Historically during the first century AD especially, women could be accused of being a *saga* (witch), whose practices included the use of *venena*, *poculum amoris*, *Medeides herbae*, *philtra* – all commonly translated as the use of potions, or poison.

Tacitus offers examples of women delving into witchcraft, using poison as a way of ridding themselves of certain rivals. Munatia Plancina, for instance, a woman with an infamous knowledge of poisonings, apparently aided Piso, the governor of Syria and his wife Plancina in the murder of Germanicus, a popular and well-loved member of the Julio-Claudian family. Tacitus portrays Plancina as the mastermind behind the use of magic to bring on Germanicus' death.[82] Coupled with this power play that women wielded in politics, literary works emerged that harboured a distinct misogynistic bent. Juvenal's *Satire VI*, written around 100 AD, lists women who committed a series of misdemeanours as a way of warding off male readers from marriage. These misdemeanours include adultery leading to abandonment of the family home and women taking on male pursuits such as athletics. The emperor Claudius' wife Messalina even gets a mention as a debauched whore whose sexual appetite led her to take part in a sexual contest with various members of the imperial court and with other lower-class customers. Women, therefore, were seen as a threat. A threat that could disrupt the natural order of male politics, their bloodline, and essentially bring chaos to well-established reputable families.

Cautionary tales needed to circulate in the Roman Empire as a way of making sure these types of women did not continue to act in such impious ways. Thus, we have the insertion into the literature of the hag-witch, a powerful entity with immense supernatural powers that brought chaos and impiety upon any man who dared to deal with her. This was a way of encouraging men to stay clear of any powerful women, or better still, to keep women well within their range of the domestic sphere.

Kimberly Stratton argues that the witch was a symbol of female independence and the dangers that came with this.[83] Barbette Stanley Spaeth elaborates upon this argument, pointing out that as the hag-witch stories were predominately aimed at a male audience there was a key 'focus on male concerns over their appropriate sexual and social roles and on their fears of emasculation/feminisation and its concomitant loss of social status'.[84] In other words, a Roman man was meant to display masculinity through active dominance over women who were perceived to be the passive sex. This assertion was displayed politically where the man was in charge of the state whilst the woman stayed at home, and in relationships where the man was a symbol of virility, the active penetrator of the female who brought forth their heir who took claim of his name and fortune. In consequence of this social set up, Roman men had an innate fear of effeminacy, *mollitia*, and any form of emasculation. The night hag-witch stories display a disruption to this natural order as they show men being overpowered by actively dominant women: the hag-witch attacks at night by metaphorically penetrating the man and, therefore, rendering him effeminate as she physically bursts into his house, an area he was meant to dominate and control.[85] The hag-witch violates the man by wounding him or by using magic to make him a figure of derision, thus effectively emasculating him.

All these elements are clearly seen, as Barbette Stanley Spaeth suggests, in Apuleius' witches.[86] Socrates had been dominated by Meroë, being overpowered by her once he slept with her. He was further emasculated when Meroë easily burst into the room where he lay, removing his heart and threatening to castrate his friend Aristomenes. Likewise, Thelyphron was hired as a guardian, a job typically carried out by men due to their strong and able physique. Yet Thelyphron, like the men in the previous story, is dominated and emasculated by a witch who is able to remove his nose and ears and make a public mockery of his guardianship.

From this analysis of the Roman witch, it is clear that Roman men feared any inversion to their natural order. They believed that a witch could destroy manhood, reduce masculine reputation and make men outcasts in their own cities.[87] To sum up with Barbette Stanley Spaeth's words, these hag-witch stories show that 'the natural order must be preserved, in which men through their association with culture are dominant over women and nature'.[88] This is certainly a valid argument if we consider other such stories where men fall prey to dominant women: Aeneas in Vergil's *Aeneid* is dominated by Queen Dido of Carthage. Wearing female clothing and perfume, a form of emasculation, prompts Jupiter to send Mercury to remind Aeneas of his destiny, one that involves martial valour and control of his own mighty kingdom, and not the current parading he was doing with a queen who outdoes him in rank and power.[89] Moreover, Euripides' tragedy *Medea*, similarly portrays an outspoken woman who is able to dominate and manipulate the men around her: Medea successfully manipulates King Creon to allow her to stay an extra day in Corinth; she is able to persuade Aegeus to offer her refuge in Athens; and finally, she is able to convince Jason that she is accepting of his new marriage. These examples of dominance over men allow Medea to successfully carry out her heinous crimes of burning the new bride through a poisoned dress, together with the new bride's father Creon, and finally to commit filicide, knowing that she will have a place of refuge in Athens once her crimes have been committed. Like the Roman witches, Medea offers an example of how powerful women can be when allowed to be independent and free speaking, it can lead to catastrophe. This fear of female dominance is combined with the outright misogyny and patriarchy of Roman society (and Athenian culture).

In addition to the above arguments, Pauline Ripat examined the nature of historical cases involving women of high social standing who were accused of witchcraft in the imperial era.[90] She believes that the threat to the disruption of the social hierarchy and the ideals attached to this were a prominent factor for why Roman women were seen as witches.[91] Roman women of high social standing were expected to take on an obedient uxorial position within the household, accepting the dominance of the husband. In return, the husband was meant to display equal respect towards his wife, recognising her as the *matrona* of the household, who had important responsibilities such as overlooking the household cult, and publicly overseeing the functioning of such festivals as the *Matralia*, a festival held in honour of the goddess Juno, honouring her association with childbirth, the key role of the wife herself.[92] This balance in the relationship, between husband and wife, was regarded as the perfect sense of harmony within the household set-up, or what the Romans would have referred to it as, *concordia*.[93] However, destabilisation of this *concordia* could occur and frequently happened when there was a rival within the domestic sphere in the form of a slave girl who may catch the husband's attention.

Plautus humorously indicates in his plays that a slave girl may well appeal to the husband due to her compliant ways as the wife will all too often become the stereotype of the nagging woman, thus placing the blame for the disruption of the *concordia* firmly upon the female.[94] But if a wife saw a slave girl as a potential rival, then this would seriously impact her social standing and respect within the home. As Ripat explains, wives might well 'find themselves bereft of the markers of their identity; cheated of the respect and protection their position was supposed to afford'.[95] The wife may also feel that her social standing will be publicly impacted as well due to the nature of the sexual liaison between the husband and the slave girl that would bring shame upon the household and family name. It is for this reason that wives of high social standing who found themselves in such uncompromising positions would resort to witchcraft. Ripat believes that this was often in the form of curses that were used to hinder the household rival, enough to frighten them to step away from any form of relationship with the master of the house.[96] These curses were enough to create, as Artemidorus claims, 'countless evils' upon the rival, driving them to have fitful dreams and disturbed nights.[97] For Ripat, the use of witchcraft was a result of real problems that women faced historically and was essentially a product of self-preservation in a society that upheld reputation at all costs. The literature that attempts to demonise wives fails to recognise the immense difficulties that a lot of these types of women were facing daily and from this, a stereotype of a 'jealous, lust-crazed… power-hungry female' emerges in the form of a witch.[98]

Fritz Graf builds upon this argument.[99] He believes that in both ancient Greece and Rome, the household and its defined roles played a huge part in the world of witchcraft. For the *oikos* in ancient Greece,[100] the patriarch was all-powerful and often wives and their mothers were seen as the intruders in this heavy patrilineal environment.[101] If the master of the house should fall ill, often the wife or her mother was the target of suspicion, relating to some use of witchcraft. In the Roman world, as we have seen, women could use witchcraft within their domestic sphere as a means of maintaining their position if a rival should threaten it. Graf also claims that freedmen were sometimes targeted as sorcerers given that they had ambivalent social positions within the house as they were no longer slaves nor full citizens, suspicion would naturally fall upon them if something untoward was to take place.[102] Pliny the Elder, for instance, relates the story of a freedman who was accused of removing a neighbour's crops into his field through the process of magic.[103] Graf relates his overall argument to the anthropological model which argues that close-knit communities, like the household in this instance, will often fall prey to witchcraft due to their restricted relations to the outside world and will, therefore, create a hotbed of superstition.[104] This may well increase when there are elements of social stress such as a potential rival that may threaten the stability of the power game within the home. Power politics no doubt played a part but Graf fails to take into account the nature and publication of the literature, including the public persecution of the witches in combination with the laws that were set up to hinder the craft.[105]

In sum, the stereotype of the witch may well have been set in stone during the imperial era for a myriad of reasons. Notably, the image arose out of fear relating to women becoming too powerful, and a need to frighten men into controlling them further, or from men feeling a sense of volatility in the presence of a powerful witch-like woman who may strip him of his masculinity. On the other hand, women may have been accused of witchcraft historically due to their need to protect their reputation and social standing when they took desperate measures in the form of curses and spells to maintain their reputable state. This filtered into the literature as the ultimate stereotype of the power-hungry witch. Essentially, though, these reasonings indicate a raging misogyny that allowed women to be seen in this manner.

Apuleius' novel with his Thessalian witches no doubt had a profound impact on our Western views of the witch. It is also noteworthy that his novel impacted not only folklore in Italy but also the emergence of the popular story 'Pinocchio' by Italian writer Carlo Collodi of Florence.[106] Pinocchio is somewhat like Apuleius' protagonist Lucius, who naively wonders into the world seeking adventure and is drawn towards 'naughty' behaviour, much like Lucius' obsession with witchcraft, which leads to Pinocchio's own transformation into an ass before finding redemption and satisfaction in becoming a real boy, similar to Lucius' transformation into a devotee of Isis. Notwithstanding these influences, it is Apuleius' night hag-witches that permeate the narrative as a reminder of what powerful women can do to men, their masculinity and the overall patriarchal world around them, which is probably why the Roman literary hag has had such a tenacious hold in the West throughout the patriarchal centuries that followed Rome's demise.

Finally, there is one more Thessalian witch who is richly portrayed by the Roman writer Lucan that needs attention. She is Rome's super witch, predating Apuleius' witches by a few decades and no doubt profoundly influencing his work. Furthermore, it can be argued that she is the forerunner for our very own Wicked Witch of the West. This witch is the persistently cruel and wicked Erictho.

Chapter Four

Erictho: The First Wicked Witch of the West

Who is the Wicked Witch of the West?

Now the Wicked Witch of the West had but one eye, yet that was as powerful as a telescope and could see everywhere. So, as she sat at the door of her castle, she happened to look around and saw Dorothy lying asleep, with her friends all about her. They were a long distance off, but the Wicked Witch was angry to find them in her country; so she blew upon a silver whistle that hung around her neck.

At once there came running to her from all directions a pack of great wolves. They had long legs and fierce eyes and sharp teeth.

'Go to those people,' said the Witch, 'and tear them to pieces.'

'Are you not going to make them your slaves?' asked the leader of the wolves.

'No,' she answered, 'one is of tin, and one of straw; one is a girl and another a Lion. None of them is fit to work, so you may tear them into small pieces...'

Chapter 12, 'The Search for the Wicked Witch',
from *The Wonderful Wizard of Oz*,
L. Frank Baum.

In 1995, writer Gregory Maguire published his reimagining of Baum's classic representation of the Wicked Witch of the West,[1] since transformed

into the popular musical, *Wicked*. Maguire gave his protagonist the name Elphaba and explored her origins and how she came to be known as a wicked witch.[2] He made his reader empathise with Elphaba who was born with green skin and sharp teeth; a girl ostracised not just by her family who finds it difficult to come to terms with her appearance but also by the world she grew up in. Maguire's book is heavily politicised, raising issues relating to animal rights, a positive cause that his wicked witch advocates. In contrast, he portrays the Wizard of Oz as running an oppressive regime in Emerald City, forcing Elphaba to become an active freedom fighter against him. Despite humanising her, it is her interest in sorcery that leads to her acquiring the title of 'Wicked Witch'. But ultimately, we the reader, see her as a troubled woman living in a troubled world, making her a product of the tyrannical society she has been born in.

This is, of course, a far cry from Baum's Wicked Witch of the West who is, at best, described as a malevolent woman, who lacks any form of human empathy, wishing to cause as much harm to both Dorothy and the Wizard as she can. As we can see in the above lines, Baum's Wicked Witch of the West is the one that became immortalised in the 1939 film 'The Wizard of Oz', and in most children's imaginations as the green witch, with hooked nose, and black conical hat who has the power to command wild animals to do her evil bidding against Dorothy and her companions – sending wild wolves, crows, bees, and even her winged monkeys, the latter of whom are able to capture Dorothy, making her the witch's slave.[3] Dorothy is able to escape the witch by pouring water over her, resulting in the witch melting away, perhaps an allusion to holy water being thrown upon an evil entity. Baum's Wicked Witch of the West is portrayed not too differently to the ancient witches that have so far been examined: she is hostile, lives in a castle that makes her isolated from others, is surrounded by wild animals – typically the crow and wolf, animals linked to witch iconography – and who is innately wicked by nature in her aim to inflict pain and harm.

Baum draws upon the stereotypical hag-witch image reminiscent of the Horatian, Petronian and Apuleian witches examined in Chapter Three. However, there is one more Roman witch that has not yet been discussed, one who has a longer narrative dedicated to her, which is far more potent and horrifying than the likes of Canidia, Meroë, Pamphile et al. This is Lucan's Erictho, who should be seen as the very first Wicked Witch of the West.

Life and Times of Lucan the Poet

Lucan was a popular poet living under the regime of the emperor Nero. He lived a privileged life and was exposed to a rigorous education becoming adept in literature, rhetoric and philosophy. Moreover, being the nephew of the stoic philosopher Seneca, a man who had a profound influence on Nero's early years, enabled Lucan to become a close friend of the emperor, possibly even being educated alongside him.[4] Lucan quickly flourished with his poetic skill, outdoing Nero's own literary ambitions. Even though Nero awarded him a victory crown for his recitals, the emperor quickly turned against him, seeing him as a rival. According to Suetonius, Lucan was banned from further poetic recitals and using his rhetoric in law courts.[5] The emperor's tyranny from this moment is famously discussed by both Suetonius and Tacitus who describe him as paranoid and ruthless, leading to the catastrophic fire of AD 64 which raged through five of Rome's city's districts.[6]

Nero was a target of arson rumours especially as he used the rebuilding after the fire as an opportunity to build himself the Golden Palace, *domus aurea*. Realising the growing resentment against him, he accused the Christians of starting the fire who were systematically put to death. From 64–65, there was growing unrest towards Nero among ranks of nobles, including the senatorial and equestrian classes.[7] This led to a conspiracy plot aimed at assassinating Nero, led by Gaius Calpurnius Piso, and commonly referred to as the Pisonian Conspiracy. Lucan was part of this conspiracy and indeed has been labelled as a ringleader for it.[8] The plot was soon discovered leading Nero to enact a series of bloody proscriptions against the conspirators including Lucan who cut his veins on 30 April, 65 AD at just 25 years old.[9] In little over three years later, Nero's reign, and with him the Julio-Claudian regime, was over.[10]

Lucan's Epic Poem 'Bellum Civille', Also Known as 'Pharsalia'

Lucan composed his 'Bellum Civille' amidst the aforementioned chaos of Nero's later years and the epic is a reflection of this dark, disturbing and foreboding time. Essentially the epic focuses upon the civil war between Julius Caesar and Pompey during the republican era which reached its climax at the battle of Pharsalus in 48 BC. Lucan's epic is decidedly anti-Caesarean, viewing the ruler as a bloody dictator whose only basis of leadership was brought about by civil war which was perceived to be a moral collapse driven by *furor*. Caesar's career can, indeed, be viewed as a paradox. Whilst he demonstrated military skill and valour, and added an essential extension to the empire through his conquering of Gaul, he was, at times, unconstitutional – as seen in the forced removal of his rival Bibulus from the Senate House so as to have his measures passed during his first consulship;[11] the crossing of the Rubicon which resulted in the civil war that Lucan focuses upon; and finally his consecutive consulships that led to him declaring himself 'dictator perpetuo'. These events led to his assassination in 44 BC driven by what Lucan would only refer to as freedom fighters.[12]

Lucan wishes his audience to sympathise with Pompey and his allies, and, despite the inevitable success of Julius Caesar, we are not meant to view the victory as a roaring triumph for the *res publica* but, rather, as a 'tragic death of Roman *libertas*'.[13] Even though Lucan's epic emulates the likes of Vergilian, Horatian and Ovidian poetry, the subject matter is entirely different. The latter poets wrote during a golden age of poetry revival when Augustus had declared himself sole ruler over the Roman world and brought an end to the violence of the republic. These poets, therefore, were obliged to integrate as much propagandist material as they could muster. To be sure, there are times when Vergil is decidedly anti-Augustan and Ovid, too, is far too satirical and boorish to ever acknowledge Augustus in Messianic tones. Their poetry, though, certainly exudes divine Roman glorification at times.[14]

Lucan has no such sense of glorification. Instead, he notably breaks with epic tradition by dispensing with the divine intervention altogether. However, the supernatural still plays a key part within the epic in helping to endorse the overall gloom of civil war and the impact upon those that partake within it, so there are passages provided that cover dreams, visions, portents, prophecies, and consultations with supernatural forces.[15] The dreams offer little consolation to Pompey whose failure in this war is foreshadowed from the outset. In Book 3, he is visited by the 'dreadful, dire image' of his former wife Julia who claims she has seen 'the boatman of Acheron..preparing countless rafts',[16] meaning many will lose their lives and will have to traverse the river of the underworld. The portents seen on the eve of the decisive battle at Pharsalus are equally inauspicious: the sky is described as being covered with torches of comets and columns of colossal fire, in combination with tempestuous weather with severe thunder and lightning that melts even the swords of the army.[17] Amongst these dark, ominous dreams and forewarnings of doom, Lucan inserts a vivid and grotesque portrayal of the witch Erictho.

Lucan's Erictho

Erictho has much of Book 6 of Lucan's epic dedicated to her. This is no coincidence. Not only does her ghastly and foreboding appearance coincide with the eve before Pompey's disastrous defeat at Pharsalus in Thessaly, it also corresponds to Book 6 of Vergil's *Aeneid*. Whilst Vergil's book 6 is dedicated to Aeneas performing his *katabasis*, guided by the Sibyl, and culminating in him seeing the grandeur of the Roman world that descends from his own family line, Lucan's is the antithesis of this. We are exposed to all the ghastly and dreaded imagery that the underworld can offer. It climaxes not with the glorification of a royal line but with a deadly necromantic shade that foretells Pompey's doom and the absolute destruction of his bloodline. Erictho herself is similarly an inversion of the Sibyl, the latter guiding, protecting and even enhancing the character of Aeneas,[18]; the former so hideous and menacing that she only adds to Pompey's total demise.

Lucan separates his description of Erictho into three distinct parts: the topography of Thessaly where Erictho resides; the description of Thessalian witches in general and how Erictho outdoes these with her impiety and finally, Sextus Pompeius' consultation with the witch. Lucan's geographical setting of Thessaly is somewhat reminiscent of the mountainous and wooded environment we encountered in the last chapter. But Lucan adds an extra element of darkness to his topography by emphasising how the mountains and forests deliberately resist any form of light, even repelling rays of the sun:

> 'When deepening summer draws Phoebus to the heights of heaven, Pelion's shadows resist his newborn rays... the solstitial head...[is] repelled by wooded Othrys...'.[19]
> In addition to this resistance to light, he stresses how the valleys, once full of lushness and fields, are now 'hidden

> under endless swamps'.[20] What is more, it is a land which not only gave residence to the barbaric centaurs but also 'the monstrous serpent Python', and the impious Aloeus who dared to war against the gods.[21] These added elements help to enhance Thessaly as an anathematised land, but the added element of darkness transforms the area into an almost liminal territory as if it is a place on the threshold to something far more dangerous and otherworldly. As Lucan himself states, it is a 'fate-damned land'.[22]

The women that reside in this territory are the Thessalian witches we encountered in Chapter Three. But Lucan makes them even more terrifying and inverse to the way females are meant to act at this time. He vividly describes their control over nature: the world can stand still when it hears their spells; they can cause mighty tempests with their charmed voices, soaking everything with the rain they cause to fall, and raising the waves within the sea when the wind appears to be calm; they have the power to stop the flow of waterfalls; reduce the sheer size of mountains; melt snow in the deepest winter; their chanting can even prevent the oceans ebbing and flowing and thus they thwart the power of the moon upon the pull of the seas; and all this they can do by deceiving Jupiter himself who is oblivious as to how nature can be so controlled.[23] Finally, Lucan relates their relationship with fierce, wild animals: 'Bloodthirsty tigers and the infamous wrath of lions fawn on them with licking tongues; for them the adder spreads his chilly coils…'.[24] If this was not deadly enough, Lucan's Thessalian witches harbour venomous human breath that can 'blast' wild animals and any other creature that dare to disobey them.[25]

The Thessalian witches described here are utterly deadly and petrifying. However, Erictho is said to be worse than these female counterparts as their 'wicked rites and crimes' are far too pious for the likes of her savagery.[26] Erictho is, in every sense, the wicked witch: her desired place to dwell is among graves in a dark cave, so she enjoys loitering in the boundary between life and death; the deities she holds dear are the ones of Erebus and not the ones in the heavens and as such, she knows nothing of the religious and pious practices that most humans partake in; her appearance is filthy, ugly, unkempt and generally disgusting, combined with matted hair; she emerges from the threshold of death only when the earth is shrouded in black storms and this is when she will perform her most heinous of crimes. Most of her vile offences concern souls, dead bodies and infants. She has the power to bury good souls still trapped in their bodies when fate still owes them years; she can perform necromancy seamlessly; she can rip away the marrow from a rotting body, as well as digging out its eyes and nails, this she does through the action of gnawing. Sometimes she waits to snatch innards from the thirsty jaws of wolves. Finally, in her hunger for fresh blood, she'll happily entrap a pregnant woman and snatch the foetus from her womb to hungrily drain it of its life force.[27] Lucan portrays Erictho as a wild savage beast that ravenously seeks carrion, a cannibalistic, yet inhuman creature that gnaws at the marrow of the innocent.

It is Pompey's son, Sextus, who seeks out Erictho. While Lucan sees Pompey in grandiose terms, a necessary freedom fighter with the epithet of 'great', his son is in juxtaposition to him as 'unworthy', 'worthless',[28] and dishonourable who will, post-civil war, resort to piracy, becoming embroiled in yet another civil war leading to his execution after being classed as an outlaw. Everything that Sextus involves himself in is meant to be seen in contrast to Pompey, so he is the fitting man to believe in and exult in Erictho's powers. Sextus, together with his servants who are 'used to crime', actively search for her. [29] This they do in order for them to discover the future outcome of the war, believing in her prophetic potency. When they catch sight of her seated among the grave mounds, she is crafting a spell to ensure the continuation of the war so that she can mutilate the slaughtered carcasses and their bones and to 'own so many souls'.[30] Sextus demands her to reveal the fortunes of the war, which Erictho claims can only be done by lifting a newly slain body from the fields who can 'speak with full voice'.[31] She wanders the battlefield strewn with corpses and makes even the ravenous wolves and birds of prey disperse at her presence with her head shrouded in 'squalid mist'.[32] She chooses a corpse with its throat cut and drags it to her cave to perform her necromancy. The necromancy itself is, as Daniel Ogden points out, 'the most elaborate account of a necromantic rite to come down to us from ancient literature'.[33]

It is certainly vividly grotesque which has had some profound influences on modern literature.[34] She firstly makes fresh wounds in the corpse into which she pours menstrual blood together with an elaborate mixture containing a myriad of ingredients: poison from the moon, mixed with the froth of dogs, guts of lynx, the joint of a hyaena, marrow of a stag, *echenais* – a type of fish which was believed to hinder ships, eyeballs of dragons, stones warmed by a pregnant eagle, flying serpents from Arabia, vipers from the Red Sea, the skin of a horned snake and finally, the ashes of a phoenix. She then starts her incantation to the ghosts below by calling in a voice that contains: 'the bark of dogs and howl of wolves, the fearsome eagle owl's and nocturnal tawny owl's laments, the shrieks and cries of beasts, the serpent hiss'.[35]

She proceeds to call upon all the entities of the underworld from the Furies to the personifications of Chaos and Death and lastly the ferryman, Charon, himself. Whilst the body remains lifeless, she whips it with living serpents and angrily resorts to threats in order to reanimate the corpse by calling upon the Furies Tisiphone and Megaera, claiming she will hunt them just as they hunt others; she tells Hecate that her face is pallid and rotten and that she will reveal her true pale form which she disguises when she visits the gods of heaven.[36] The worst threat of all is releasing a creature that resides lower than that of Tartarus, a creature so powerful and horrific that it can even look upon the Gorgon's face.[37] With these last threats, the corpse becomes reanimated and still pale and stiff he reveals the outcome of the battle.

The prophecy is, inevitably, a dark one, as the corpse informs Sextus that the underworld soon awaits Pompey and his line but also that of other leaders including Julius Caesar. Interestingly after the corpse has given his prophecy, Erictho sets a pyre for the young soldier and allows him to burn, a fitting burial that will enable his shade to enter the depths below. This is an anomaly given the sinister steps that Erictho used in order to reanimate him, but as she had previously explained to the corpse that she would burn him if he foretold the future, she may be keeping her word so that she will be in favour with the deities and powers of the underworld when she performs this phenomenon again. Book 6 closes with Erictho leading Sextus in the thick of night as she orders the darkness to keep the day at bay.

Erictho: An Analysis

There is no doubt that Lucan's Erictho has some resemblance to Canidia, the literary construct of Horace, predating Lucan by a few decades.[38] As we saw with Canidia, she too, had a penchant for wondering among

1. A wood engraving displaying the moment Macbeth meets the three witches, c. nineteenth century

2. A krater vase showing Medea flying in a chariot drawn by dragons, c. 480 BC

3. Statue of Hercules and Nessus by Giambologna, c. 1599. Found in the Loggia dei Lanzi in Florence, Italy

4. A Roman copy of Hecate found in the Museo Chiaramonti

5. Relief of Triple Hecate displaying common tropes associated with the goddess, including torches. Found in Kinsky Palace, Prague

6. William Blake's painting entitled 'The Night of Enitharmon's Joy' or 'The Triple Hecate', c. 1795

7. Female Goddess found in Catalhoyuk. Displayed in the Museum of Anatolian Civilisations

8. Circe portrayed on a lekythos, c. 490–480 BC

9. Depiction of Tiresias appearing before Odysseus as found in Book 11 of Homer's *Odyssey*, by Johann Heinrich Fussli, c. 1780–1785

10. Circe Invidiosa by John William Waterhouse, c. 1892

11. The Vale of the Tempe, a gorge that cuts through the mountains of Thessaly with evidence of waters and forests

12. A Strzyga by Filip Gutowski, c. 2017

13. Invidia by Albrecht Durer, c. 1501–1502

14. Invidia by Zacharias Dolendo, c. 1596–1597

15. John Hamilton Mortimer's depiction of Sextus meeting the witch Erictho, c. eighteenth century

16. Sextus, the son of Pompey, seeking Erictho in order to know the fate of the battle of Pharsalia (Wikimedia Commons)

17. Baba Yaga by Ivan Bilibin, an illustration from *Vasilisa the Beautiful*, c. 1900

18. A woodcut displaying Bluebeard being slain, by Walter Crane, c. 1875

19. Illustration of Hansel and Gretel, by Arthur Rackman, c. 1909

20. The Evil Queen with her magic cauldron during 'Fantasmic!' - Performed in Disneyland.

human bones, rousing the dead, tearing at animals with her (false) teeth, and generally appearing as bestial in both appearance and manner. Horace's Canidia, though, was satirically constructed. Indeed, we even chuckle at her disturbance during her spell-making when the statue Priapus decides to pass wind, terrifying Canidia so much that her false teeth fall out. There is no such chuckling at Lucan's Erictho. Instead, his account, although at times grandiloquent,[39] conjures up so much horror that we would be mistaken for reading a proto-gothic literary genre, designed deliberately to make us feel a true sense of disgust and unease. She is the true harridan-witch, the very personification of inverted order.

We see this first when we meet her roaming around a cemetery dishevelled, in a permanent state of *fūnestātus* (polluted, disgraced, dishonoured). This juxtaposes the traditional Roman matron who would be typically veiled, clean and tidy. Whilst a Roman woman would partake in funerary arrangements and provide lamentation when necessary, this was only at extreme times of mourning, and they certainly would not exult in such a lugubrious environment.[40] Moreover, it appears that Erictho is childless, living alone in a liminal world, so furthering the inversion of how a typical Roman woman should behave, the latter expected to procreate. Erictho is impious and does not acknowledge or participate in the general daily pious activity of her female counterparts, such as prayer and sacrifice. Her rituals are decidedly against Roman religious rites, performed at night, and involving stolen funeral fires and body parts. Coupled with this are her sacrificial practices that are an inversion of traditional animalistic type as she wantonly performs human ones instead.[41]

Indeed, her use of Roman sacrificial *exta* (the bowels or entrails of animals) is quivering human internal parts. Rather than making use of animal *exta* for the purposes of divination, she uses animal innards for her potions. She is also bestial, competing with carrion wildlife as she tears at human parts. Her divination and prophetic powers involve an enhanced form of necromancy that, as we saw, was vividly portrayed. This again is an inversion to traditional Roman diviners that typically used the practice of augury.[42] The reanimation of the corpse appears to be a further inversion, this time it is as if she is performing a surgical procedure as a pariah, making wounds in the body and pouring in her noxious potion as adept as any educated surgical practice, but not to save life, only to forcibly bring the dead man to life for a few brief sinister moments before sending him to his death again. Finally, Erictho's realm is a deep, dark cave surrounded by an equally shadowy forest, a dark liminal environment, a final added inversion of the traditional Roman values, as an altar was normally used for divination purposes, which was situated in front of a temple.

Lucan, it would appear, has followed the hag-witch stereotype which became commonplace in the first century AD and beyond. His evocative description brings to life the stark idea of female inversion, and, following Kimberley B. Stratton and Barbette Stanley Spaeth's arguments discussed in the last chapter, Lucan has perfectly embodied the type of woman who played upon all men's fears.[43] However, this may not have been Lucan's main aim in including her in his poem. Given the subject matter of Lucan's overall epic, the use of the supernatural in Book 6 enhances the bleak negativity of war. Erictho is, therefore, seen as a harbinger of doom for Pompey and his bloodline, a fitting addition to an epic poem that is, on the whole, a piercing tale of savage tyranny. Ironically, though, it is Lucan's Erictho, more than any others that have been analysed, that has such a wide impact upon future negative representations of the witch.

Later Ericthos

Erictho certainly lived on beyond the Roman era. During the medieval era and through to the Jacobean period, it can be argued that Lucan's witch, and indeed other Roman literary constructs, laid down a precedent for the Western world to perceive childless, older women, in their post-reproductive years who lived remotely as malignant witches. During this timeframe, these types of women were malefic: they desired to cause harm through the sin of envy, as a result of their jealousy for younger more attractive females. Their various powers included the ability to cause tempestuous weather and to pride themselves in debauched activities, particularly during sabbaths,[44] where witches would meet and take part in orgies, dance and perform sexual acts with demons and worship the Devil himself with whom they had signed a sexual pact with.[45] They generally were thought to attack pregnancy, consuming infants or using their fat as a flying potion, causing a threat to the stability of family life.[46] Their appearances were always hideous and a complete inversion of the stereotype of a woman. Hags would be seen to have hanging, almost phallic-style breasts with hardened nipples to give the impression of a woman so far removed from her reproductive years and almost harbouring masculine qualities which contributes to the idea that the witch disrupts the natural order.[47]

We see these beliefs in the portrayal of Erictho: she is hideous, living alone in a liminal environment, she actively removes infants from the womb and devours them, and she is decidedly anti-fertile. Erictho's removal of infants could well be inferred to as a termination, therefore, she is an abortionist, which in some instances was frowned upon in ancient Rome.[48] Lucan, therefore, sees the act of abortion as malevolent, as she wishes to remove the infant for the purposes of consumption. This idea is elaborated upon after the fall of Rome when midwives were sometimes perceived to be worshipers of evil, who would remove the infant and offer it to the Devil. The profoundly influential fifteenth-century work concerning witches and their practices, the *Malleus Maleficarum*, composed between 1486–1487, specifically refers to witches as baby-sacrificers.[49] Moreover, the *Malleus* gives details of witches desiring to obstruct the family home through the process of miscarriage and causing impotency in men.[50]

This ideology of the witch is reflected in modern literary works where, once again, we see clear echoes of Lucan's Erictho. Most notably, the descriptions of the weird sisters in Shakespeare's *Macbeth* have an uncanny resemblance to her. In Act 1, Scene 3, Banquo remarks upon the unusual, and hideous appearance of the witches when he states that they have 'choppy fingers', 'skinny lips', and 'beards'. The choppiness and skinniness of their complexions highlight their hag-like, elderly nature and their beards add a masculine quality to their faces, making them the juxtaposition of a female. Moreover, later in Act 4, Scene 1, during the witches' recital of the famous 'Double, double toil and trouble' incantation, the innards they use in their cauldron have a clear resemblance to the animal parts so used by Erictho: eye of newt, toe of frog, Adder's fork, blind-worm's sting, lizard's leg, howlet's wing, scale of dragon, tooth of wolf and so on; including a reference to 'slips of yew, silver'd in the moon's eclipse', a link to the classic tradition of 'pulling down the moon'.

Like Erictho, the Weird Sisters of *Macbeth* are wicked, ugly hags that encourage and enhance our disgust. Over two centuries prior to Shakespeare's publication of *Macbeth*, fourteenth-century writer Dante Alighieri wrote his *Divine Comedy* within which he makes a specific reference to Erictho. The epic poem explores Dante's own journey to Hell, guided by Vergil, the Roman poet. Given the impasse at the entrance to Dis, Dante understandably wants to know if anyone has previously made the journey from upper hell, down to lower hell. Vergil responds that he himself has made a previous journey at the bequest of Erictho to fetch a soul in the lowest circle of hell as part of her necromantic ceremony.[51] The story itself is an invention of Dante but is likely based upon Lucan's elaborate necromantic scene. It further shows that it was believed Erictho could summon messengers to carry out her commands, and thus make them fall victim to her sorcery as in the case of Vergil.[52]

Later works of literature will also pay homage to her, particularly in the height of the romantic movement, that fused elements of the gothic. Mary Shelley's *Frankenstein* for instance, is long considered to harbour vestiges of Lucan's Erictho. This stems from an understanding that Mary Shelley's husband, Percy, admired the poetry of Lucan, and so imbued Mary with an equal fascination with his writing. The most obvious connection can be seen with the actual reanimation of the monster that correlates to Erictho returning life to the corpse. However, as Ogden postulates, the closest connection between the two works is more likely with Victor Frankenstein himself.[53] The novel's namesake is so impassioned by his idea of 'creating' a human that his explorations into this pseudo-science lead him to not only act selfishly by disconnecting himself from family members but also to act in a perverse way against Christianity. This is evident in his nocturnal visitations to graves, charnel-houses, dissecting rooms and slaughterhouses to eagerly obtain the body parts he uses to make his human being.[54] This is an act that is against divine nature as it was believed God created all men. His nocturnal exploits also harbour elements of the grotesque and portray him disrupting burials and resting places of the deceased. Victor Frankenstein, therefore, is an emulation of Erictho, the night graveyard wonderer who acts impiously.

The subversive nature of witches also persisted during these centuries in the form of what can only be described as grotesque artwork. The images produced conjure up not only the eldritch imaginings of these women but even hark back to classical renderings of them, in particular, once again, Lucan's Erictho comes to mind when we observe them. Albrecht Dürer's reimagining of an earlier witch engraving portraying the personification of the Christian sin Envy, *invidia*, demonstrates the type of iconography that dominated this period (image 13).

In image 13, the naked old woman sits astride a goat with herself riding him opposite to the direction he is facing, thus reinforcing the unnaturalness of the witch. Her long hair streams behind her allowing us to observe the grotesque nature of her body which exudes masculine muscles, and skinny breasts which typically hang with no evidence of fullness as would be expected of younger females. She clasps a broomstick in her hand, the symbol of the witch at this time, and has four cherubs surrounding her that brandish symbols of witchcraft, such as an alchemist's pot. The picture starkly demonstrates the monstrous image of the witch who has the power to control the weather, the use of the broomstick was thought to do this, and evidence of this power is seen in the top left corner of the image which shows the coming of a tempest. The goat was the emblem of the Devil so she is league with him, and the hag-like appearance of her is the complete antithesis of how a woman was meant to be. As Malcolm Gaskill proclaims she is 'naked, unabashed, licentious – a stylised negation of idealised womanhood'.[55]

We are indeed reminded of Lucan's vivid portrayal of Erictho who similarly 'negated' the perception of the Roman *matrona* with her unkempt appearance which made even carrion animals run from their ravenous consumption of cadavers. Dürer had a profound influence upon the depiction of witches in art and inspired later artwork of them, including Zacharias Dolendo's sixteenth-century imagery of Envy (image 14) which shows an old hag, again hideous in appearance, with snakes for hair, clutching live vipers in her hand and devouring her own heart, showing her lack of compassion, as she walks almost triumphantly at having created a recent dispute among a group of people who stand in the background.[56] Further in the background can be seen a kiln alight with fires that symbolise the envy she has created, fire was seen as a destructive emblem at this time. Her breasts, similar to Dürer's imagery are hanging, phallic-like with hardened nipples to highlight the preternatural appearance of womanhood. Again, we can see the connection to Lucan's Erictho, who was described as similarly clutching at live vipers, and equally hideous and grotesque.

Dürer and Dolendo's images were driven by an innate fear of witches at this time, which shall be addressed in the final chapter, and even though this superstitious fear subsided by the end of the seventeenth century, the hag-like image of the witch persisted in art, sometimes as a reflection of social and political disorder, such as in Goya's over stylised and almost satirical imaginings in his *Black Paintings*, or at other times, as a lamentation for the pursuit of 'romantic excess and 'Gothic' horror'.[57]

The hag-witch seemed to be very much embedded in the artistic imagination beyond the seventeenth century. Thus, we have John Hamilton Mortimer's rendition of Erictho herself in his painting entitled 'Sextus Pompeius consulting Erichtho before the Battle of Pharsalia', c. eighteenth century (image 15). This painting was later engraved by Robert John Dunkarton, also c. eighteenth century (image 16). Both artists portray Erictho as baring her skin where we get a glimpse at her wizened body, the right breast appearing to sag in the same fashion as Dürer's witch; her dishevelled hair with snakes entwining it is reminiscent of the necromantic scene where Sextus seeks her out. She eagerly grasps the live vipers, her main weapon to use to whip the lifeless corpse as she threatens the world below if they do not do her bidding. The corpse lies by her foot and Sextus and his soldiers turn away in total fear and disgust. It is fair to surmise that the artistic imagination in early modern history successfully reanimated the harridan witch of Roman literature.

Erictho's hideous hag-like nature will persevere into the twentieth and twenty-first centuries and will not, as with the case of Hecate and Circe, become a more forgiving representation. As we saw at the start of this chapter, Baum's Wicked Witch of the West, exudes nefarious evilness and is very much the epitome of the witch that dominates our childhoods, despite the recent re-emergence of the feminist rendition of this character. The hag makes her appearance similarly in Disney's version of *Snow White and the Seven Dwarves* in the form of the classic stock character of the wicked stepmother. Additionally, there is Disney's 'Mad' Madam Mim, a dark hag-witch, who competes with Merlin in a crazed shape-shifting contest in the *Sword in the Stone*. Much later in the twentieth century, Roald Dahl's dark fantasy *Witches*, features the vile Grand High Witch, a book itself which was a target of complaints concerning misogyny.[58] Finally, the hag becomes an emblem of the cult horror film in more recent decades with a minor appearance of a hag-witch in such films as the final instalment of the *Evil Dead* series, as well as the 2013 horror version of *Hansel and Gretel*. The reason for this persistent and unnerving representation will be discussed in the following chapter, for now, it is evident that Erictho, Rome's most grotesque literary construct, is the first ever Wicked Witch of the West, an antagonist who is still very much within the imagination of our own contemporary culture.

Chapter Five

The Legacy of the Greek and Roman Witch

'You don't seem to understand that witches are not actually women at all. They look like women. They talk like women. And they are able to act like women. But in actual fact, they are totally different animals. They are demons in human shape with claws, and bald heads and strange nostrils and peculiar eyes... '.

Roald Dahl, *The Witches*
(London: Penguin, 1983), 37–38.

Why Is a Classical World Legacy Important?

Classicists the world over will stress the importance of studying and having knowledge of Greek and Roman culture. Fundamentally this is due to the immense impact these cultures have had upon the Western world, and in extension parts of Eastern Europe, from philosophical thinking, architecture, entertainment, education, politics and art; the list is quite endless. The stereotype of the witch also finds herself within this list. Whilst we are inclined to believe the hag-witch emerged during the medieval period and especially reached its zenith with the onset of the witch hunts, the previous chapters have revealed an evolutionary development of the witch starting with the ancient Greeks and culminating with the Roman hag-witch extraordinaire, the latter harbouring characteristics that prevail long after the fall of Rome in the West.

The answer to the dramatic shift in the image of the witch from the Greeks to the Romans has been analysed. The conclusions for this marked change could be due in part to the decline of moral behaviour within Roman women more generally, and, therefore, a need to make women adhere to more conventional roles within the domestic sphere, or an innate fear of emasculation amongst Roman men. The hag-witch, therefore, served as a pre-warning for what happens when women have power.[1] In essence, though, and aside from the political and societal reasons for promoting the hag-witch, this witch figure became an established literary stereotype that could be used to add a dark ominous feel to a piece of writing, providing a certain amount of horror that, as we shall see, appeals universally to our human imagination.

Firstly, let us summarise how the Romans regarded their witches. They were old, withered and, aside from Apuleius' witches, they were generally physically disgusting. Horace's Canidia is described as filthy, dishevelled with false teeth, implying they were rotten so have fallen out.[2] Lucan's Erictho similarly has wayward hair wrapped in live vipers.[3] They are often seen as having a countenance that is pale, and pallid, almost signifying death and decay. They are bestial as they claw at dirt and animals with their nails and teeth.[4] The nails are often described as untrimmed, again stressing a lack of care for personal hygiene. In Horace's *Epode* 5.47–48, he describes Canidia as 'gnawing at her untrimmed thumb'. What is more, Propertius similarly draws attention to witches' nails. His *Elegy* 4.5.16 focuses upon Acanthis, a procuress, who offers advice to his girlfriend to cultivate rich lovers and avoid the poet who offers only verses. We have seen how the bawd or procuress was a stereotype typically associated with witches.[5] In Propertius' vivid description of Acanthis, we are told that 'she digs out the innocent eyes of crows with her nail'.[6] The trope of eye-gorging with long nails is vividly portrayed in the character of Erictho too when she desecrated corpses by 'gleefully' digging out 'dead eyeballs'.[7] Eye-gorging will feature in later witches outside of the Roman Empire.

Roman witches also possess moral turpitude. This takes many forms from violating the male domain of the home, agonisingly prolonging pregnancy, raising spirits to haunt and terrify others and, most, disturbingly, killing, devouring or simply stealing infants. The latter, as we saw in the previous chapter, could represent a moral message against abortion, which although was not illegal until the third century AD, was still a practice that was very much frowned upon.[8] It has also been pointed out that the sudden rise in nefarious witches in the Roman literature of the first century BC – first century AD, coincided with 'a major advance in the care for women in pregnancy and their confinement with the emergence of midwives or obstetrics'.[9] Midwives would aid the woman both in care for her pregnancy but also with termination.[10] They were also regarded as being older women.[11] The witch literary construct could, therefore, be a warning against using midwives who would remove the foetus from the womb during the practice of abortion or offer certain herbs in early pregnancy to ensure the foetus dies *in utero*. Witches, abortion and infanticide more generally will be key characteristics of later, medieval witches. Finally, as Chapter Three discussed, Roman witches lived in the periphery, the liminal point between civilised society and the primitive, untrodden countryside, often in dark forests or marshy quagmires.

We must not neglect the impact of the Greek witch who has similarly left her mark upon the Western world. Greek witches are attractive, with the ability to lure those to them. They have a duality whereby on one hand they are hospitable by nature but on the other hand, hostile. Circe, as discussed in Chapter Two, demonstrates her remarkable transformative powers, the use of her wand, combined with knowledge of *pharmaka*, but serves as a hospitable guide for Odysseus and his achievement of his *nostos*. Likewise, Hecate, as seen in Chapter One, was a beneficial and much-needed protector of gateways and the transition between life and death, but later became a patron of witches and their craft, a conduit necessary to perform necromancy and to ensure the potency of a witch's potion. All these characteristics will similarly be seen in later witches as a result of the major impact that witches in Greece and Rome have had upon the modern world.

And this impact was indeed extraordinary. This chapter will explore the influence of this Greek and Roman literary construct. Witches from other cultures, including fairy tales will be examined as having some key similarities to the Roman hag, as well as the beautiful Greek witch. James I and his witch hunts will also be discussed and how the hag image prevailed during this dark part of British history, and finally the tenacity of the Greek and Roman witch will be addressed, particularly in their ability to prevail even in our own contemporary world.

Baba Yaga and Other Fairytale Witches

Baba Yaga is a popular East Slavic witch who has many folk tales attributed to her throughout the countries of Russia, Ukraine and Belarus. All of the tales seem to attribute the same characteristics to her: she resides in a forest in a hut which stands or turns on chicken legs;[12] she travels in a mortar, using a pestle to move herself along in the air and she carries the epithet 'Baba Yaga Bony Leg', perfectly encapsulated by artist Ivan Bilibin in image 17.

Most heroes or heroines that encounter Baba Yaga are invited into her hut where the witch's grotesque features astound her guests as she is able to stretch her body from one corner of the hut to the other, with her oversized nose touching the ceiling, her sagging breasts hang over her rod and her large nose can poke the coals in her hearth. She often comments on the distinct 'Russian scent' of her guests which has led some scholars to believe that Baba Yaga must be a foreign import, able to recognise the scent of the natives as something different to her own, who treat her as a social pariah, ostracising her to the forest due to her unusual and frightening appearance.[13]

Baba Yaga's first literary appearance is in the eighteenth century. Whilst her appearance may harbour qualities that make her uniquely Slavic – Andreas Johns for instance claims she possesses traditional characteristics that may have made her appealing to the peasant population[14] – she does, nonetheless, represent a complex witch that draws upon other traditions. Firstly, she is ambiguous, she can either help or hinder within her mythology.[15] This is somewhat reminiscent of Circe who hindered Odysseus with her transformation of his men into pigs but then became a helpful guide. In one version involving Baba Yaga, she threatens to 'gobble and eat…up' her visitor before conceding to her guest's request for food: 'The old woman set the table and fed the fine young fellow.'[16] Aside from her 'donor' qualities, she is also portrayed as a hideous and threatening witch. According to the poet Nikolai Nekrasov her appearance, as well as her actions are horrifying: she has fangs, long nostril hair that falls to her breasts, unusually large ears, horns and holes instead of eyes.[17] Nekrasov explains that her intentions are only evil, and she serves as a consort for the Devil, as such, she has transformative powers and changes a man called Bulat who had rejected her amorous advances into a statue. In a more gruesome tale, she delights in gouging out a man's eyes and even threatens castration.[18]

One further tale is extremely reminiscent of Odysseus' encounter with the Cyclops Polyphemus. In Kretov's and Kabashnikaw's version, a hero travels to Baba Yaga's hut in the hope of discovering the meaning behind grief and misfortune. Baba Yaga imprisons the man after slicing off his hand. He eventually escapes by cutting open a sheep and hiding in its belly. Kabashnikaw adds that the hero stabs one of Baba Yaga's eyes before he flees.[19] Whilst this story is remarkable in its closeness to Book 9 of Homer's *Odyssey* and does not draw upon the witch Circe, it serves to demonstrate the influence that classical myth has had upon the construction of this old woman, the cyclops is a symbol of uncivilised barbarity as is Baba Yaga.[20]

In combination with these attributes and tales, Baba Yaga has been associated with ravens and owls that circle her courtyard.[21] She has been viewed as the embodiment of life and death with her ability to hold a key to both heaven and hell; she is sometimes described as a snatcher of souls, especially with her ability to form storm clouds that enable her to carry out her perverse acts, and lastly, she has even been classed as a lunar witch.[22]

Connections between Baba Yaga and the Roman and Greek perception of a witch abound from the aforementioned details. She is like Circe with her transformative powers and her tales of help and hindrance. She represents Apuleius' Meroë with her threats of castration. The eye-gorging motif is also present in her tales as it is with Roman witches. What is more, she harbours some qualities of Hecate in her connection to the night, the moon and the boundaries between life and death. And she is generally grotesque in appearance, a product of the Roman hag-witch, coupled with her living in a liminal environment which is commonplace for witches in both Greek and Roman literature. Indeed, scholars have themselves made connections between Baba Yaga and classical mythology. Matthew Guthrie draws close correlations between Greek and Russian folklore, even equating Baba Yaga to Persephone, whilst Lomonosov links Roman deities with Russian and Slavic ones.[23]

Alongside these similarities, discussions concerning why Baba Yaga is portrayed in this way are very similar to the arguments as to why the Romans wished to create a hag-witch stereotype. Andreas Johns describes Baba Yaga as a 'phallic woman'. In other words, she possesses distinct masculine qualities through her symbolic use of the pestle, a phallic emblem, but also in her aggressive and dominant nature.

This, he believes, makes her a 'cautionary figure, a negative example of what a woman should not be'. Baba Yaga, therefore, is a threat to 'social order and harmony', an inversion of all that is natural.[24] She similarly serves, like Roman witches, to highlight the male fear of emasculation, or from a psychological perspective, the male castration anxiety. Baba Yaga's antagonistic qualities which very much dominated the eighteenth century, when she was first recorded, were certainly due to a pertinacious patriarchy that persisted not just in the Western world but also in the East. However, the Greek and Roman influence concerning witches must also play a part in this continual negative portrayal.

Folklore and fairy tales abound with representations of antagonistic characters. These can range from the predominantly masculine giant, ogre or troll, to the feminine witch and wicked stepmother. Often the last two can be merged together with the stepmother resorting to witchcraft in order to enact her plans. All four of these characters share the commonality of evilness, combined with desires to eat human flesh, and generally cause mayhem and anxiety before order is restored, often in the form of a heroine being rescued by a knight in shining armour or the abused daughter of the stepmother finding solace with her biological father.

The witch and the wicked stepmother play prominent roles in these stories and are a particular favourite of stalwart folklorists and writers that form the fairytale canon, namely the Brothers Grimm, Charles Perrault and Hans Christian Andersen. However, this is not to say that male characters are exempt from nefarious deeds. Take, for example, Perrault's dark tale entitled *Bluebeard*, a rather grisly story that relates the betrothal of a young woman to the tale's namesake. Despite Bluebeard's previous six wives mysteriously disappearing, he appears polite and affable and invites the young woman to reside in his palace prior to the marriage but she is forbidden to enter one chamber that remains out of bounds. On having to leave the palace, Bluebeard entrusts the young woman with a key to the chamber but once again reiterates that the chamber must remain closed at all times. Curiosity gets the better of her, leading her to open the room only to discover the murdered corpses of his previous six wives and copious amounts of blood. The tale, despite the unappetising content, ends happily, if rather gorily, with the murderer Bluebeard slaughtered by the young woman's sister and brothers, leaving the young woman inheriting the palace and his fortune.[25]

Maria Tatar explains that, on the whole, both male and female characters within fairytales exhibit equal amounts of horror in the form of physical or mental abuse upon their unsuspecting victims.[26] From a male perspective, this can take the form of either paternal or fraternal cruelty, such as in the tale of Rumpelstiltskin when the father boasts to the king that his daughter can spin straw into gold, leaving her to be unjustly imprisoned to carry out the seemingly impossible task in one night.[27] Nonetheless, it is the stepmother and her closely related counterpart, the witch, that remains the principal antagonist.[28]

The stepmother-cum-witch can take many forms. Maria Tatar argues that the evil female protagonist within the world of fairy tale is often maternal, whether they are the mother-in-law, stepmother and witch.[29] Indeed, witches are at first maternal in their dealings with their victims, luring them into their abode until they are able to unleash terror upon them. It must also be noted that all three of these maternal figures – mother-in-law, stepmother and witch – are also intrinsically linked as all exhibit a penchant for cannibalism, spell making, poison, curses and so on.

For instance, in one of Grimm's lesser-known tales entitled aptly as 'Mother-in-law', the king of the land leaves his wife and children under the care of his mother as he goes to war. After a few days, the mother demands the flesh of one of her grandsons. The story is unfortunately incomplete but the basis of a horrific figure in the mother-in-law is clearly apparent. Similarly, Perrault's famous 'Sleeping Beauty', which harbours the evil fairy-cum-witch figure that curses Sleeping Beauty, also contains an evil cannibalistic mother-in-law who later threatens to consume Sleeping Beauty's daughter, who she has had with her knight in shining armour. The cannibalistic theme continues in Grimm's horrific tale called 'The Juniper Tree', where the stepmother first decapitates her stepson and then serves his flesh in a stew to her husband. The most famous witches are found in the 'Hansel and Gretel' story and in 'Snow White' (or *Sneewittchen*). The former has both the evil stepmother and the witch. The stepmother in this story berates her husband to such an extent about their impoverished condition that he concedes to her plan of abandoning his children in the middle of the woods. In the woods, the children find a house made of delicacies thus luring them to it where they are met with a 'friendly' old woman who welcomes them as shown in image 19, feeding them milk and pancakes before revealing her desire to fatten them up and eventually consume them.

In 'Snow White', a story that has had many metamorphoses,[30] the most popular version consists of the stepmother, who incidentally practices witchcraft, described as being so jealous of her stepdaughter with her skin as white as snow, hair as black as ebony, and lips as red as blood, that she actively plans her death. This is planned through the use of a huntsman who was meant to kill her but could not go through with the task, presenting a boar's heart to the queen as evidence of the deed. When discovering this failed attempt, the stepmother resorts to witchcraft by transforming herself into an old peddler and then an elderly farmer's wife who offers Snow White a poisoned apple leaving her in a deep coma after biting into it.

What is the significance of these dark female characters? It is important firstly to remember, as stated above, that the stepmother, mother-in-law, or witch are in fact different titles to describe one villainous female who dominates the narrative in a threatening and horrifying manner, they share characteristics, motives and uses of magic. There have been many explanations for why this stock character is so persistent. For instance, the irresistible craving for human flesh has been explained in relation to historical famine whereby tales concerning cannibalism are seen as quite popular when villages, or society in general are suffering episodes of severe starvation. Secondly, and from a more psychoanalytic viewpoint, fairy tales exhibiting an evil stepmother have been seen as exploring Oedipal conflicts. The daughter who is on the receiving end of jealousy and abuse from the stepmother will, in turn, desperately try to seek and secure the total love of her father. Often these fairytales will end with the daughter happily receiving the desired love from the father figure.[31]

Bruno Bettelheim further states that fairy tales function as a stimulus for children's identity.[32] Most of the fairy tales, Bettelheim believes, suggest, by their symbolic meanings, how a child should behave in order to solve their concerns and integrate their characteristics into the wider environment of society.[33] There may well be some deeper psychological impact within these stories: for instance, we know that the Brothers Grimm initially wanted their collection of nursery and household tales to be aimed mostly at scholars, and not just children, therefore, they might have developed deep-rooted tales that explored the intricacies of familial relationships. However, the trope of the evil woman, especially in the role of stepmother and witch is an ancient one, and many of the aforementioned tales find their basis in the Greek and Roman world. This should not be surprising as it is common knowledge that all fairytales harbour aspects of tales from other cultures. Indeed, the Brothers Grimm, despite their desire to collate tales specific to German culture and traditions, in fact, draw upon a wide breadth of both European and Oriental folklore, as do other writers in this literary canon.[34]

It has been argued that during the early imperial era of ancient Rome, there were many accusations of *artes magicae* (magical arts) which involved the use of magic or sorcery, referred to in a myriad ways such as *maleficium*, *veneficium*, *carmina*, and *venena*.[35] These accusations were often levelled at the women of the imperial household or at other female or male rivals living outside of it. These accusations were, more often than not, made by the dominant matriarch within the palace. M. Douglas argues that these accusations helped remove rival factions or an internal enemy.[36] A case involving Fabia Numantina in 24 AD serves as a classic instance of how magic could be used as a way of committing someone of murder. Fabia Numantina was charged with *carmina* and *veneficium*[37] after her ex-husband, Plautius Silvanus, was arrested under suspicion of murdering his current wife. The charge against Numantina focused on her skills with herbs that could, when ingested, reignite her former husband's love for her. These herbs apparently drove Silvanus insane leading him to murder his current wife in order to live again with Numantina. According to Tacitus, Livia, the current matriarch of the imperial household and mother to the emperor Tiberius was very much involved in this affair, having just had Calpurnius Piso charged with keeping possession of *venenum* which he used to kill Germanicus.[38] Whilst Livia helped Numantina get acquitted of the charges, and encouraged the death of Silvanus, a rival, it demonstrates how the climate of magic accusations was rife amongst imperial women and was especially driven by the matriarch Livia.[39]

Another famous matriarch within the imperial household was Agrippina the Younger, mother of Nero and fourth wife to the emperor Claudius. Almost a generation after Livia's machinations and accusations of magic, Agrippina employed the same technique to rid herself of a rival called Lollia Paulina. Lollia was the former wife of Caligula but had become a rival to Agrippina as Claudius sought a new wife. Agrippina, therefore, resorted to charges of witchcraft against her, accusing her of seeking knowledge from *magi*. Lollia was eventually forced to commit suicide.[40] Graf argues that the idea of the evil mother and mother-in-law is prevalent in both Greece and Rome, with both societies seeing the wife and her mother as 'dangerous intruders' that may disrupt the patrilineal line of the household, thus these women were accused of malevolent behaviour in the form of witchcraft.[41]

What is evident from these cases of female rivalry and accusations of witchcraft is that the imperial women, namely the dominant matriarchs, are seen as stereotypical evil mothers within their histories. It is of no surprise, as has previously been argued, that during this time the image of the witch becomes a dominant and sinister imagining in the Roman literary world as a way to remedy the situation and to warn others of powerful female manipulators. Thus, the evil maternal figure may well have been born.

Furthermore, as we have seen, the stories of witches at this time are rife with cannibalism, infant snatching, murder, male oppression and general supernatural mayhem, all classic tropes evident in the world of fairy tale. What is more, even during the golden age of Augustan imperialism, stories abound with female dominance, use of magic and evil wives and mothers. The Ovidian tale of Procne and Philomela being one of the most grotesque: Procne is married to the tyrant Tereus of Thrace who harbours an insatiable appetite for lust leading him to brutally rape Procne's sister Philomela. To prevent Philomela from revealing the crime, he slices out her tongue and imprisons her. Through her ingenuity of weaving, however, Philomela weaves a tapestry portraying her crime that is sent to her sister. On seeing the tapestry, Procne seeks bitter vengeance and kills her son whom she has had with Tereus, serving his flesh to her husband to eat at his next meal.[42] This particular story rivals that of the Grimm's grisly tales of murder, vengeance and cannibalism, minus supernatural intervention, but nonetheless serves to accentuate the impact that Roman literature must have had upon the developing Western literary constructs. In fact, if we follow Maria Tatar's argument that any evil woman – be they ones that commit kin killings, partake in or encourage cannibalism, or the ones that dabble with witchcraft – can serve to represent and symbolise one particular character, that of the antagonistic maternal female, Procne's cannibalistic tale, therefore, falls within this category.

Although the idea of the evil maternal figure may have originated in ancient Rome, in the Greek world, we similarly see stories, both factual and fictional, relating to this malevolent stereotype. Antiphon, an ancient Greek orator from the fifth century BC, relates a speech for the prosecution in which a deceased man's son from his first marriage accuses his stepmother of poisoning his father.[43] Throughout the speech, the woman is only referred to as 'stepmother' thus stressing the son's disconnection with her biologically. The administration of the poison was carried out by a carefully crafted ruse by the stepmother who approached the concubine of her husband's friend. The concubine was a slave who was about to be disposed to a brothel. Playing upon her love for her master, the stepmother, claimed that she had a love potion that could reignite love if poured into his cup. The stepmother told the slave to do this when the slave's lover was dining with the stepmother's husband. She was to administer the potion to both her master and also the stepmother's husband as his love for her had also waned. The slave carried out the task and both men were found dead.

Throughout the speech, the stepmother is consistently presented as a scheming, immoral villain who is demonised with an association to Clytemnestra from Greek myth who famously plotted the murder of her husband Agamemnon when he returned from the Trojan War, although the speech has also been linked to Medean style manipulation and deceit.[44] The defence speech is unknown, as is the outcome of the trial, with most scholars believing that the prosecution speech is extremely weak given that it was made many years after the event and perhaps was only brought to trial due to a dispute concerning a recent inheritance claim.[45] Nonetheless, the speech itself demonstrates a lack of trust for the maternal figure, in this instance the stepmother who used the classic weapon of choice for female murderers – poison. Fictionally, we have the likes of the witch Medea, who famously kills her own children out of vengeance, and the previously mentioned Clytemnestra who kills her husband.

It is evident that wicked women are quite prolific in both the Greek and Roman worlds, whether they be mothers, wives, or stepmothers. Most are associated with witchcraft in some form or are linked to this practice with the use of poison and potions. Thus, we have the emergence of the evil maternal stereotype which is so dominant in the world of fairytale. Of course, from a visual viewpoint, the Roman hag-witch with her grotesque, unkempt and elderly appearance relates to the likes of the *Hansel and Gretel* witch and the hag that becomes the persona of the demoness in *Snow White*. These particular maternal figures represent the inversion of the matriarch, in other words how the mother should not act, and in turn, the female sex more generally. This was a dominant message for the stark patriarchy of the Greek and Roman eras, but likewise for the steadfast patriarchal world of the Georgian and Victorian periods when fairytales became more widespread.

James I and the Witch Hunts

Historically, witches dominated the fifteenth–seventeenth centuries in the form of the witch hunts that dramatically took hold of Europe. The seventeenth century, in particular, was one of the darkest periods for these hunts driven by the fervent zealot James I of England. Much of James I's youth was marked by a series of disturbances which may account for his bloody history as king. His mother, Mary, Queen of Scots, was largely absent from his childhood being held captive by Elizabeth I, it is believed that this absence increased a somewhat unsavoury dislike for women in general, especially as Mary was perceived to be promiscuous as well.[46] He also endured several assassination plots, one led by the Earl of Mar who apparently consulted with witches to shorten James' life.[47] As a result, James I's fascination, and repulsion, with witches grew further when he claimed to have been sent a vision of his mother's decapitated head before her execution, believing this to be a witch's prophecy. His misogynistic views concerning the female sex may well have been exasperated after this incident.

His interest in witches reached its height during the period of his betrothal to Anne of Denmark in 1589 which was thwarted by tempestuous weather preventing Anne from arriving safely to her betrothed. In a mark of chivalry, James set sail to Denmark himself in the hope of retrieving her and was subsequently exposed to an ardent belief in witchcraft that lay at the heart of Anne's country.[48] He was particularly fascinated with an astronomer called Tycho Brahe who spoke freely about the dangers of witchcraft prevalent in Denmark. This was coupled with the witch hunts that Denmark itself took part in and the belief that witches actively made pacts with demons. This no doubt furthered James' already established belief in the art of witchery and after suffering another tempest on the way back to Scotland, he set about targeting those witches he believed to be responsible for disrupting Anne and his sojourn across the ocean.

This witch hunt resulted in the much-publicised North Berwick trials which set forth the torture and execution of thousands of women, and to a lesser extent men, throughout one of the bloodiest periods in Scottish history.

The reasoning behind this deadly period has been richly examined and several theories have been postulated. Firstly, it is important to be aware that fundamentally the hunts were driven by religious persecution against those who were believed to be in consort with the devil.[49] Thus, a biblical and, so a Christian belief, form the basis for what it meant to be a witch during this period, this essentially was driven by the idea that these women were slaves of the Devil and so practiced his dark arts through curses, spells, poison and general deception by the power of manipulation.

The ideas surrounding witches, including their practices, their magical powers and the harm that the Jacobean peoples thought they suffered by having contact with witches are not too dissimilar to the beliefs that have been examined in relation to the Greek and Roman world. What is more, as stated in the introduction, biblical references are somewhat sparse when it comes to the practice and appearance of the witch per se, aside from the obvious 'thou shalt not suffer a witch to live'.[50] Ronald Hutton states that from the Middle Ages to the modern era, the Christian religion grew more fervently against witchcraft due to the 'transmission of texts copied by the literate elite' which exposed them to the beliefs and ideas of the ancient world.[51] Thus, the modern witch trials were, as Ronald Hutton believes, 'combined [with a] whole range of ancient traditions' from Mesopotamia, Persia, and the Graeco-Roman world, including, significantly, 'the Roman images of the evil witch'.[52]

What is more, the Roman Empire enacted severe laws against the functioning of witchcraft from the burning of books related to magic to even burning witches at the stake.[53] This hostility towards magic and witches no doubt would have impacted the early Christians who themselves were in close contact with the Romans.[54] Even though the miracles that the Christians attributed to their Messiah were thought to be carried out by magicians, a charge levelled at them during the Roman persecution of their religion, they made the distinction between themselves and the magicians and witches by claiming that their miracles were performed in the name of Jesus and the Bible and not through the acts of dark demonic power. This distinction became even more apparent with the rise of Augustine of Hippo in the fourth century AD who set in stone the miraculous wonders of Jesus as something holy and divine, and the ones performed by magicians and witches as something wholly wicked and contemptuous.[55]

These views persisted long into the Middle Ages and beyond and were significantly formulated against the backdrop of the Graeco-Roman world. Thus, when James I published his *Demonologie* which he based upon the biblical concept 'thou shalt not suffer a witch to live', he added many other already established anxieties regarding witches which we see embedded in the Greek and Roman literature. James I's *Demonologie*, a dissertation published not long after the North Berwick trials, was his tour de force in encouraging people to rise up against witches by endorsing the need for witch hunts. The first section of this treatise focuses on Saul's consultation with the Witch of Endor which leads to a detailed discussion of the art of necromancy and its obvious connections to witchcraft.[56] In the treatise, which is written in the form of a dialogue involving Philomathes doubting Epistemon's belief in witches, Epistemon provides what he believes to be clear evidence that witches exist. Epistemon refers to the witch of Endor's necromantic spirit as 'vnclean' and the practice of necromancy as a sin against God, and one that 'allures' both sorcerers and witches alike. The idea of magic itself is traced to the ancient Greeks who are described as 'importing all these kindes of vnlawfull artes'. Epistemon explains what witches are capable of with special attention to how the witch is able to transport herself from one place to the next, their use of parts of corpses to make their potions, how they make images of people they wish to bewitch with wax and clay, and how they can make men and women love and hate each other.[57] Whilst much of the *Demonologie* is laden with the idea that these women can only partake in such villainous crimes due to the aid of the Devil, the ultimate antithesis to God Himself, it is clear that the general belief in witchcraft and what they could do is no different to the Greek and Roman literature that has been under close analysis. The idea of necromancy, the use of wax figurines, body parts to make potions, and creating emotions in humans, even the ability to transform into nocturnal birds and fly are all classic tropes developed in the evolution of the literary construct of the witch from the Greek and Roman times.

However, this was also a period marked by severe disparity in wealth with stark austerity in some parts of Europe. A period, furthermore, that was sometimes dominated by disease and plague, and combined with this were many rural and isolated villages that were already breeding grounds for superstitious attitudes, especially towards those that were perceived different.[58] Keith Thomas sees the rise in accusations of witchcraft as a direct result of these social anxieties and especially sees the witch hunts as more related to death, disease and general misfortune as a result of poverty than anything else.[59] Women, he believes, were targeted due to their propensity to be more verbally aggressive, their bad language often misconstrued as cursing. Women, therefore, were not targeted due to some misogynistic crusade led by an embittered king but merely because of misfortune in what is now considered a severely socially and economically challenging period of history.[60]

Connected to this are those scholars that argue that witch hunts were local, dominating rural communities and driven not by a desire to tear down the female sex but arose out of conflicts between neighbours, mainly due to economic hardships and a need to eradicate a rival who appeared to be doing well.[61] Conversely, poorer women tended to be accused of witchcraft as they were easy targets and served as scapegoats to help villagers understand any sudden onset of mortality. Kimberly Stratton is a firm believer, however, that gender did indeed drive the witch hunts inspired by strong beliefs in 'women's moral weakness and proclivity';[62] a misogynistic need to attack women, which she argues, laid at the very heart of the portrayal of the witch in the ancient world. To support this argument, she draws upon Christina Larner's hypothesis that the Scottish witch hunts in particular were spurred on by the Aristotelian view that women are flawed and weaker than their male counterparts.[63] This, coupled with the idea of Eve committing the first sin in the Old Testament, was enough to inspire men to target the weaker sex, instil morality and prevent any women from acting with further concupiscence.

All of these arguments have been seen in relation to the representation of the witch in the classical world, whether the representation was driven by pure misogyny or by social factors particularly in the late republic and early imperial era, as a desire to instil morality due to an increase in more dominant and liberally minded women. Thus, the stereotype of the witch as a woman symbolic of immorality inspired the classical world writings and subsequently bled heavily into the modern world mentality, leading to widespread female persecution.

The Legacy of the Classical Witch in the Modern World

The witch as a negative literary construct established firm roots in the consciousness of humans from the fall of the Roman Empire in the West and certainly persisted well into the twentieth century with the rise of the motion picture. The idealised evil hag-witch finds its place in many well-known motion pictures from the 1939 version of *The Wizard of Oz* with the classic green-skinned Wicked Witch of the West, together with her hooked nose and cackle sending shivers down every child's spine, and the evil queen-cum-wizened stepmother in Disney's 1937 rendition of *Snow White* (see image 20), as well as their aptly named Maleficent in the 1959 *Sleeping Beauty*.

The witch, of course, has undergone much-needed feminisation since the 1960s and the rise of the religion Wicca has seen more people inclined to view witches as 'white witches' and, therefore, not a threat. These again have been set to the screen with such programmes as the 1990s *Charmed* which focuses upon three sisters inheriting their witch-like powers to bring down the Source of all Evil and any demon that dares to disrupt the world. Modernisations of such characters as Maleficent and, as we saw in Chapter Two, Madeleine Miller's *Circe* help to redeem the once demonised witch and reveal a much tamer and more beneficial female which laid at the heart of the Homeric epic the *Odyssey*. Nonetheless, the hag-witch extraordinaire, made so villainous by the first century BC and AD writers of the Roman world, still holds firm.

The witch with her unsavoury appearance, sadistic spells and general antagonistic characteristics has become the perfect stereotype for the genre of horror, fantasy and sword and sorcery, the latter of which can harbour both horror and fantasy simultaneously. Evil witches have made their appearance in iconic film horror classics such as the *Evil Dead* series, *Hansel and Gretel: Witch Hunters*, *The Blair Witch Project*, *Black Sunday*, *Mark of the Devil* and *Night of the Eagle*. The witches in these classics are generally perceived to be perilous and malignant, with the ability to cast spells, conjure evil and serve as an overriding juxtaposition to the hero. The 1960 Italian Gothic horror film *Black Sunday* is a perfect example of a resurrected vampiric witch seeking vengeance for her mutilation centuries before whereby she wreaks havoc upon two unsuspecting medical doctors. Such horrific scenes within the film see the witch draining a girl of her youth and threatening to drink blood before being thrown into a death pit where the witch meets her end by being torched, thus restoring civilised order. Fantasy and sword and sorcery films which often blend elements of horror within their storylines, are also susceptible to having witches as their antagonists.

The 1982 *Conan the Barbarian* sees an attractive witch in the same vein as ancient Greeks ones, luring Conan to her hut where she dines him before sexually seducing him, whilst foretelling his future and then attempting to suck his blood. *The Beastmaster* made in the same year as *Conan the Barbarian*, has three antagonistic witches serving the nefarious Maax, the Beastmaster's nemesis. These particular witches clearly have Shakespearean undertones but their grotesque appearance, prophetic powers, and ability to transform themselves into birds at will harbour many classical world tropes. Likewise, the 1980s fantasy film *Willow* has the antagonist in the form of Queen Bavmorda, a powerful and dangerous sorceress, who in one memorable scene transforms her opponents into pigs, a clear homage to Circe herself.

Thus, the witch is a key horrific character within such movies, finding her place alongside other antagonists like poltergeists, werewolves, vampires and the bogeyman. What is the appeal of seeing the witch characterised in this way given that some of these films have been made after the rise of the feminist movement of the 1960s? English literature professor Darryl Jones has recently analysed this dilemma in his work dedicated to the fascination of horror throughout history, postulating many theories as to why we as humans are drawn to the macabre.[64] We may have an insatiable appetite for our primal origins which involved ritualistic chanting, spell making and general belief in monsters and, therefore, a need to tell apotropaic tales.[65] Hence, Jones claims that this is why horror is open to the possibilities of magic and the supernatural, with ghost stories particularly seen as a way of warding off unwanted malevolence.[66]

This may be why horror and fantasy films make sequels as part of a franchise, all of which are very similar in tone, plot outline and outcome as that enables them to satisfy our ritualistic desires. This also means that antagonists will serve similar purposes of causing harm, and providing a certain horror, before being destroyed, the very reason why rituals have to be adhered to. Darryl Jones even considers political and social reasons as to why horror appeals to the masses.[67] This argument enables us to understand further why the Romans used the evil hag-witch as an example of how women should not act by trying to instil much-needed morality upon an ever-growing liberal female sex. Horror films, Jones argues, are undeniably conservative and used as a way of implementing morality in society.[68] By portraying orgiastic, female devil worshippers in some horror films who eventually are demonised and further ostracised, there can be no better way of controlling overt sexual behaviour through use of film. But fundamentally, if we follow fantasy and horror writer H P Lovecraft's analysis, humans are intrinsically drawn to but also greatly afraid of the unknown.[69] The witch who lives on the fringes of society and dabbles with taboos, such as digging away at corpses, raising dead spirits, casting spells that can transform us from our true selves, has become a creature that we fear, with powers that remain horrific but ultimately unknown to us which is, possibly, why she secures her place alongside some of the most fearful horror adversaries. Nonetheless, the wicked witch within these films is always portrayed as a stereotype: she is manipulative, dangerous and harbours destructive powers. Therefore, she is the witch found in the Greek and Roman texts, a legacy that will no doubt hold firm for many more centuries.

Conclusion

This chapter opened with a vivid description from Roald Dahl's controversial children's story *The Witches*. The witches are seen as ugly, animalistic, primal and just plain demonic. Although Roald Dahl has dehumanised his witches by referring to them as 'not actually women at all', no doubt he was influenced by the vivid portrayals of female demonic witches as illustrated by Albrecht Dürer.[70] But the inhuman description of these creatures could also find its place in Horatian poetry as a rival for the eye-gorging Canidia or Lucan's viper-wearing Erictho. The influence of the Roman writers upon our modern imaginings concerning the wicked witch is profound, to say the least. We have travelled from the depths of folkloric culture to the darkness of the witch hunts in the Jacobean world and ended with the modern-day horror movie spectacle and in doing so, we have encountered the Roman hag-witch and in all her goriness. She lives on in our dark thoughts, reigniting our inner most fears. Maybe as a lasting stronghold of misogyny and how the female should not act, or simply as a symbol of what we fear the most - the cannibalistic pariah. Amidst the doom, though, there is light, and the early Greek beneficial goddess-cum-witch is making a slow and steady resurrection in the likes of Circe who is now seen as an empathetic but strong female who we can all relate to, inspiring further feminisation of those classical mythological women that have for too long been cast onto the sidelines.

Conclusion

The Western witch found her origins in the Homeric world. She may well have been formed from the remnants of prehistorical mother goddess figures who, in their iconography, were often flanked by wild animals and birds, and whose mythologies placed them firmly in the realms of the living and the dead. Certainly, though, it is Homer's Circe that harbours the necessary characteristics we have long come to associate with the witch: from her use of the wand, powers of metamorphosis, to her residence within a forest, a place of isolation, and lacking contact with civilisation. Alongside Circe, Hecate, with her liminal associations and iconographical symbolism as a torch bearer, accompanied by hell hounds made her the forerunner for the mistress of the night and ultimate consort for the witch and her demonic activities. The Greeks were the first to develop the idea of a witch and the capabilities of her powers.

But it was the Romans, as we have seen, that morphed the divine image of witchcraft into the very emblem of the hideous, malevolent hag. Due to societal pressures, misogyny or just gender power play within these centuries, the hag began to dominate Western Roman literature from the first century BC. From Canidia, Dipsas, Meröe, Pamphile and Erictho, these witches form the basis of what it means for us to perceive the witch with all her goriness. So profound was the impact of Roman literature that the hag became a strong stereotype lasting beyond the fall of Rome in the West and embedding herself firmly into the minds of the Christians and the modern witch hunts. Even in our world of gender equality, the evil hag-witch is seen in horror and fantasy films and TV programs in much the same vein as she was seen 2,000 years ago.

The feminisation of Hecate and Circe may serve to demonstrate that these characters have long been misunderstood and that the femme fatale imagery of the former can slowly be eroded to reveal the true meaning behind Circean magic. There are also many people who embrace Wiccan beliefs, people who honour ancient paganism, whilst worshipping the greatness of nature and their own triple goddess that harbours all aspects of womanhood from youth, adulthood, and old age.[1] This new religion allows the old pagan ways to live on and to be seen with fresh eyes. However, it is unlikely that the Wiccan religion and the feminisation of mythological witch-like deities such as Circe will eradicate the devilish hags of Rome. They will remain a vestige of the misogyny of the West and a symbol of instilling conservatism upon immorality through the process of creating undesirable, frightening, and in this instance, female antagonists.

Appendix A

The Witch of Endor and Her Similarities to Lucan's Erictho

When the woman came to Saul and saw that he was greatly shaken, she said, 'Look, your servant has obeyed you. I took my life in my hands and did what you told me to do. Now please listen to your servant and let me give you some food so you may eat and have the strength to go on your way.'

1 *Samuel*, 21–22

Lucan's necromantic scene in his *Civil War* in which Erictho is called upon to prophesise the outcome of the war between Pompey and Julius Caesar has some resemblance to Saul meeting the Witch of Endor in the Hebrew Bible, 1 Samuel 28. During the oppression of the Philistines upon Israel, and after the death of the prophet Samuel, who had declared Saul as Israel's first king, Saul sought the Witch of Endor after God had failed to answer him in his dreams before the onset of battle. Prophets in the form of spiritualists and witches had been banned at that time but Saul still demanded of her to conjure the spirit of Samuel. Samuel, like Erictho's reanimated corpse, foretells a negative future for Saul, who, as a consequence of not obeying God, will be killed, together with his sons.

The similarities between this and Lucan's scene are twofold: firstly, the need to conjure a ghost who can foretell the future occurs during a period of war and oppression. Secondly, the person seeking the portent is seen in unworthy terms, therefore, it is of no surprise that their prophecies are of a foreboding nature. However, even though the Deuteronomistic history, from where this story derives, is thought to have been compiled in its entirety by the sixth century BC, it is more likely that Lucan drew upon necromantic scenes already familiar to a Greek and Roman audience, such as the classic scene in Book 11 of Homer's *Odyssey*. This epic, as we have seen, is thought to predate Deuteronomy by at least a couple of centuries. The necromancy in Book 11 of Homer's *Odyssey* is far more graphic in tone than the biblical version.[1] Given that Lucan's necromancy is grotesque, vivid and overly dramatic, he appears to be elaborating upon the already established Homeric tradition, which involved an intricate ritual of spilling of blood, incantations and rising spirits that make Odysseus trepidatious. Some ghosts are even more pessimistic in their portents than others – for instance, Agamemnon is more judgemental of wives given his murder by his own spouse.

It should be noted that the Witch of Endor is remarkably tame in appearance and behaviour than those of her Roman counterparts. After the conjuring, she leads Saul and his men to her house where she 'fattened a calf…which she butchered at once. She took some flour, kneaded it and baked bread without yeast. Then she set it before Saul and his men, and they ate' (1 Samuel 24–25). This hospitable scene is in juxtaposition to Roman witches, however it does have a connection to Circe's own friendliness when she transforms Odysseus' men back into human beings, and then allows them to reside with her for up to a year. Whatever the influences between the Circean witch and that found in the Hebrew bible, Lucan no doubt builds upon the unpleasantness found at the start of Book 11 of the *Odyssey*, transforming it into something commanded by his own unique antisocial witch. It was common practice for portents to be sought before the onset of battle, this took many forms in the classical world from consultation of the Delphic oracle, augury and even astrologers. Thus, Lucan uses an already established ancient tradition and, therefore, does not deliberately draw upon a biblical story that he may, or may not, have been exposed to.[2]

Appendix B

Common Tropes Associated with Witchcraft

'Thou shalt not suffer a witch to live'
Exodus 22:18

We have travelled through centuries of misogyny and have seen an evolutionary development as to how we perceive the witch, from a once benign goddess figure to the quintessential evil hag, the latter of which is still seen today. Along the way, the classical world also set in motion several motifs and symbols that have become associated with witchcraft, the most common of which is assessed here.

Castration

The threat of castration as a form of emasculation was made by Apuleius' witches, along with other forms of emasculation such as domineering the bedroom, leaving male occupants cowering under the bed, and having total control over the mind and body of men, even by physically removing their hearts. Castration was, indeed, a common form of masculine deprivation in the ancient world, the idea linked to the potency of the phallus with which the all-important heirs are made. Reducing the virility of the phallus, therefore, reduces the validity of the man and his ability to procreate. Much later, political mutilation in the Byzantine world, for instance, often involved castration as a means of rendering a man, who often was a political rival, as 'half-dead', leaving him with no ability to have an heir.[1] The witch threatening this form of mutilation was, therefore, seen as having total control over man, reducing him to a lesser entity within culture. The idea of castration is seen in later witches such as in the folklore associated with Baba Yaga.[2] Other forms of mutilation are evident in fairy tales whereby stepmothers resort to killing their stepchildren and even feeding them to their fathers, such as in Grimm's *Juniper Tree*.

Eye Gouging

As we saw with the witches Canidia and Erictho, eye gouging is another form of mutilation that has a similar impact to castration. Blinding a male victim leaves him severely disfigured and unable to live the life that was expected of him, such as being a leader of a state or an army, as sight was a symbol of being able to control a city. Part of the reasoning behind the self-inflicted blinding that Oedipus resorts to in Sophocles' *Tyrannus Rex* was a way of making himself incapable as a king and leader of his city for the pollution that he cast upon his state through his familial crimes of patricide and incest. Similarly, the political mutilation that occurred in medieval Byzantium followed the same principle; that blinding an opponent would render the man incapable of leading an army into battle and thus lay claim to a kingdom.[3] By having the witch remove the eyes of their victims, it demonstrated the terror that they could inflict upon the men targeted, further showing why witches needed to be ostracised, particularly as they had the potential to subvert the natural order of male rulership. We see this trope also played out in the likes of Baba Yaga, her folklore harbouring many fears related to the power and terror surrounding the capabilities of the witch. Moreover, Horace has his Canidia scrape out eyes with her clawed nails, enhancing her feral, animalistic attributes – another reason why the witch is associated with the wild peripheries of cities and towns and more likely to be seen in the dark woods.[4]

The Apple

The apple as a symbol of sin is a commonly used motif, with its most famous appearance in the Garden of Eden, picked by Eve the seductress who was easily manipulated by the serpent and who, similarly, went on to cajole Adam to take a bite. But the apple as a symbol of conflict is evident elsewhere in the ancient world. The Apple of Discord story, for instance, found in Greek mythology is the ultimate origin of the Trojan War. Eris, the goddess of discord and strife, is so incensed at not being invited to the wedding of Peleus and Thetis when all the other Olympian gods were present, that she seeks bitter vengeance by placing a golden apple amongst the goddesses Athena, Hera and Aphrodite, which bares the words 'to the fairest'. Believing themselves to be worthy of this title, the goddesses seek out Paris, the Trojan prince, to decide who should be gifted the apple. Each goddess tries to bribe Paris to choose her but the bribe that persuades him the most is Aphrodite's gift of the most beautiful woman in the world. This happens to be Helen who is married to Menelaus, king of Sparta. Paris abducts Helen, thus starting the conflict between the Trojans and the Greeks.

Whilst this may not involve a witch per se, the idea of the apple associated with conflict and disruption, is gradually used as an emblem of witchcraft in later tales. Most famously the stepmother-cum-witch of the Snow White story uses the apple as her chosen weapon, whilst disguised as an old crone, to lure Snow White to her. Modern artwork likewise played upon the themes that arise in the apple of discord story with artist Melchior Kusel portraying Eris symbolically as a witch in his rendition of the myth. In this artwork, Eris is seen as a cadaverous old hag with snake-infested hair, hanging breasts with hardened nipples. She holds a bellows as a symbol of igniting further conflict and strife amongst humans. She is the archetypal witch, illustrated in the same fashion as Albrecht Durer's witches, which was common iconography from the fourteenth–seventeenth century.[5]

Flying

Flying is probably the most common attribute related to witches. Most of us envision the witch flying on her broomstick in the thick of night and is an image closely related to a Jacobean audience as it is to a modern one with our perception of the witch at Halloween or even in Julia Donaldson's childhood classic *Room on a Broom.* But we also see flying witches in the classical world and it was probably a trope that was developed and built upon over the centuries. We saw in Chapter

Three that the Romans were believers in a type of witch called the *striga*, deriving from the Latin word 'strix' meaning screech owl. It was believed that these witches could morph into the screech owl in the dead of night and use their power of flight to seek out infants who they snatched for the purposes of draining their blood. Flight, therefore, gave them power to move from one place to the next to feast upon their next victim. No surprise that this trope moves beyond the Roman era and is found in medieval as well as Jacobean texts describing women as flying from one area to the next using the fat of young children. Whilst they no longer morph into birds, they still use the child as a reason for their flight.

Withered Appearance and the Number Three

The appearance of the Roman hag-witch has been vividly discussed in the last few chapters. Canidia with her unkempt hair and overgrown nails and Erictho with similar attire but with snakes writhing through her dishevelled hair are enough to create feelings of grotesqueness within the reader. Modern imaginings of witches from the fourteenth century onwards have adopted the same countenance. Albrecht Dürer's sixteenth-century image of *Invidia* shows a cadaverous old woman with long wayward hair, masculine muscles, and skinny hanging breasts, almost emblematic of the Roman hag-witch herself. Shakespeare's *Macbeth* likewise refers to the Weird Sisters with their 'choppy finger[s]', 'skinny lips' and beards spouting from their chins, the very inversion of the pretty feminine woman.[6] The hagged appearance of the old hag that has become so synonymous with the word 'witch' finds its origins within Roman literature. An influence that has remained steadfast and will likely do so for many more years.

The number three is also a number that has become linked to elements of witchcraft and even the occult. The idea being that it has some mysterious relationship to the dark arts. It is no coincidence that Shakespeare chose three witches as his most antagonistic females within his play. The number three itself is present in the ancient Greek and Roman world but not necessarily related to witches. It was three goddesses that dominated the Apple of Discord story. It was three Fates who, as soon as a human was born, began to weave the web of their inescapable destiny: Clotho would spin the thread of the person's life, Lachesis would measure out how long or short the thread would be and Atropos would snip the thread when the person was due to die. Significantly, Hecate, the goddess of witchcraft, as we saw in Chapter One, was iconographically portrayed with three faces each one linked to a specific direction: sky, earth and the underworld. Whilst the idea of three was later demonised, it has had a resurgence within the religion of Wicca or Neopaganism whereby the young maiden, mother and crone have become representative of the three stages of womanhood, perhaps pertaining to the dominance and influence of the original representation of Hecate herself or indeed of the Fates who symbolised life's all-important stages. The idea of three, therefore, can be seen to have arisen within the world of the Greeks and Romans.

The Loom and the Spindle

A woman seated at her loom is a quintessential image of feminality. It demonstrates her ability to weave beauty into fabrics for the purposes of special occasions or simply as a means to clothe those that she cares for on a daily basis. But the loom and ability to weave is so much more than diurnal preoccupation. For much of the ancient world it served to highlight the ingenuity of the female: her wits, wisdom, and, even at times, it was her weapon against others. For the Homeric Penelope, it was her way of warding off the suitors from their persistent demands for marriage. What better way of keeping irritants at bay than informing them that a man will be chosen once her weaving has been completed and then sneakily unpicking the work in the darkness of night so creating a seemingly never-ending task? Circe was also seated at her loom and singing when Odysseus' men felt inspired to knock at her door, taken in by her calm and tame outer appearance. She used the loom and all the feminality associated with it as a means to lure men to her, entrapping them and then subsequently showing her dominance over them with her transformative powers. The loom within the *Odyssey* may equally be a symbol of female manipulation highlighting their powers to weave lies or trick others. Both Helen and Calypso are similarly portrayed as being at their looms to stress their manipulation over men, with Helen having her work-basket with her which included her spindle. Helen's dealings with drugs in Book 4 of the *Odyssey* similarly places her alongside Circe. What is more, Helen is described as acquiring her drugs from Egypt, a place well known for its dabbling with sorcery and magic.[7]

In Ovid's Procne and Philomela tale, albeit a rather disturbing story, the loom becomes an emblem of female enfranchisement, when the violated and mutilated Philomela uses the loom to weave the story of her violent attack made upon her by her sister's husband which resulted in her rape and muting after he slices out her tongue rendering it impossible for her to speak yet still able to weave and retell his heinous crime.

Later, in more modern fairytales, the loom and the spindle were used as physical weapons to harm others. Sleeping Beauty, for instance, is lured to the spindle by the evil fairy-cum-witch who, after pricking her finger upon it, falls into a deep sleep. These tales focus upon the evilness of folkloric and mythological women, drawing upon the manipulation of the loom, and in this context the spindle, as a way of showcasing the danger of the female even when sat participating in a seemingly innocent pastime. The spindle, too, can be seen as emblematic of a phallus and that the female can wield it against others, using a distinct masculine object as a means to dominate and, in turn, render the male impotent.

From the above, it is clear that the loom and spindle is a symbol of the witch with many of the women mentioned associated with witchcraft. Those who are not witches tend to use the imagery of weaving for the greater good, but these are generally women who are juxtaposed with the nefarious hag.

Appendix C

Gagool: The Forgotten Victorian Witch

I observed the wizened monkey-like figure creeping from the shadow of the hut. It crept on all fours, but when it reached the place where the king sat it rose upon its feet, and throwing the furry covering from its face, revealed a most extraordinary and weird countenance. Apparently, it was that of a woman of great age so shrunken that in size it seemed no larger than the face of a year-old child, although made up of a number of deep and yellow wrinkles. Set in these wrinkles was a sunken slit, that represented the mouth, beneath which the chin curved outwards to a point. There was no nose to speak of; indeed, the visage might have been taken for that of a sun-dried corpse had it not been for a pair of large black eyes, still full of fire and intelligence, which gleamed and played under the snow-white eyebrows, and the projecting parchment-coloured skull, like jewels in a charnel-house. As for the head itself, it was perfectly bare, and yellow in hue, while its wrinkled scalp moved and contracted like the hood of a cobra.

The figure to which this fearful countenance belonged, a countenance so fearful indeed that it caused a shiver of fear to pass through us as we gazed on it, stood still for a moment. Then suddenly it projected a skinny claw armed with nails nearly an inch long, and laying it on the shoulder of Twala the king, began to speak in a thin and piercing voice.

H.R. Haggard's *King Solomon's Mines* (1885).

King Solomon's Mines is a swashbuckling story exploring the exploits of its narrator, Allan Quatermain. As the title suggests, the book takes us into the world of colonial Africa on an intrepid search for the fabled mines of Solomon and all the treasures these may hold. But the book has many subplots such as the need to find a lost brother, and at its heart, the reestablishment of the rightful heir to the tribe of the Kukuanas. It is the latter subplot that drives Quatermain and his intrepid men to the devilish witch Gagool.

Haggard's book has come under attack in recent years for his blatant misogyny and often racist comments. It is a book very much of its time. Women have no place in the actual novel and those that do are either the wicked Gagool or the mild and subservient Foulata. It is for this reason that many screen adaptations of this novel have decided to have a female protagonist alongside Quatermain and to dispense with the strong ideals of a brotherhood that dominates the entirety of the story. Gagool, though, remains a firm favourite as an antagonist. The description of her appearance and her prophetic powers are extraordinary, to say the least and harbour many classical world tropes.

Gagool is fittingly animalistic for an evil witch with her comparison to a monkey and her hands seen as claws. The simile of the cobra reminds us of her hypnotic nature and powers to control, manipulate and use poison. Haggard emphasises her age in great detail with the use of synonymous language related to age and death from wrinkles, wizened, corpse, yellow and charnel-house. She harbours prophetic powers, with the ability to foresee the dangers of the 'white men' within her community and at several moments tries to have them slaughtered by the hands of the king she controls, Twala.

This witch is seemingly long forgotten in the canon of literary antagonists, but her features and actions follow the tropes that this book has been exploring. You would be mistaken for reading the above extract as an excerpt from Lucan's *Civil War* or indeed Horace's *Epodes*. Gagool, the Victorian witch, serves, yet again, to demonstrate the profound influence that the Roman cadaverous, harridan hag has had upon the Western consciousness.

Notes

Introduction

1. The Hecate referred to here is the same one found in ancient Greek culture, the goddess of witchcraft. She will be discussed at length in this book.
2. Shakespeare, *Macbeth*, Act 4, Scene 1, lines 5.
3. In Shakespeare, *Macbeth*, Act 1, Scene 3, Banquo is astonished by their appearances, he stares aghast at one of the witch's 'choppy finger[s]' and 'skinny lips' and is also amazed at the presence of their 'beards': lines 42–44.
4. Marked references to the tempestuous nature of the weather that seems to surround the witches can be seen at the beginning of the play when they meet during 'thunder, lightning…rain': act 1 scene 1, line 2. The night of King Duncan's murder was also an 'unruly one' due to the nature of the weather: Act 2, Scene 3, line 49. The witches themselves are often linked to the death as the masterminds behind Macbeth's idea to commit regicide; the raven appears in Lady Macbeth's speech before she calls upon the witches to aid her in her manipulation of her husband to commit murder (Act 1, scene 5, line 37), and the screech owl can be heard just after the act of murder at the start of Act 2, Scene 2. Both birds are seen as harbingers of doom and are typically associated with witchcraft; the screech owl, in particular, has an ancient origin which will be discussed in this book.
5. The reasons for the tragedy of *Macbeth* are varied, but certainly the play upholds the idea that believing or even dabbling with witchcraft, and so the dark arts, can have disastrous consequences.

6. G. Gifford, *A Discourse of the Subtill Practises of Devilles by Witches and Sorcerers* (London, 1587), sig. B2.
7. W. West, *Simboleography* (London, 1615). See also R. Hart, *Witchcraft* (London, 1971).
8. Cf. T. Borman, *Witches: James I and the English Witch-Hunts* (London: Vintage Books, 2014), xv.
9. Ibid. See Also Ronald Hutton who claims that the Anglo-Saxon word 'wiccecraeft' is the ancestor for our word 'witchcraft' which combines 'craeft' with the female word 'wicce' from where our word 'witch' derives. R. Hutton, *The Witch: A History of Fear from Ancient Times to the Present* (New Haven: Yale University Press, 2017), 158.
10. Rodney Needham explains that a witch is essentially 'someone who causes harm to others by mystical means'. R. Needham, *Primordial Characters* (Charlottesville: 1978), 26. Ronald Hutton also confirms this view by explaining that witches 'have been regarded with loathing and horror and associated with generally antisocial attitudes'. Hutton, *The Witch*, 21.
11. James I republished his *Daemonologie* in 1603 (a dissertation that explained the dangers of practices such as necromancy, divination and black magic, and how witches themselves practiced these). The year 1603 was also the time that James I brought in the Witchcraft Act which was enforced by Matthew Hopkins, the Witchfinder General that sparked the onslaught of the witch hunts.
12. This image varies in the ancient Greek and Roman literature, but she ultimately becomes a *quaedam anus*, 'some old woman' from the Roman imperial times.
13. Tracy Borman states quite boldly that 'The Bible contains many references to witches, sorcerers, necromancers and other practitioners of dark arts', but then proceeds to list the ones that are mentioned in the introduction here, which, in itself, is comprised of a decidedly small amount of detail: Borman, *Witches*, 39–40. Moreover, medieval scholar, Richard Kieckhefer, does not deny the 'classical inheritance' of magic upon the Middle Ages and beyond. See Chapter Two in Kieckhefer, *Magic in the Middle Ages* (Cambridge: Cambridge University Press, 1989).
14. Exodus, 7.

15. G. Luck, 'Witches and Sorcerers in Classical Literature', in *Witchcraft and Magic in Europe* (Philadelphia: University of Pennsylvania Press, 1999), 115.
16. Josephus, *Antiquitates Judaciae*, 2.284.
17. *The Penguin Book of Witches*, ed. Katherine Howe (London, 2014), 3.
18. See Chapter Four and the Appendix.
19. Hutton, *The Witch*, 52. Ronald Hutton also reiterates that 'the Hebrew Bible does not spend much time on magic'.
20. Ibid, 55, and W.M. Dickie, *Magic and Magicians in the Greco-Roman World* (Woodbridge: Routledge, 2001), 12.
21. P.M. Teitel, *Canidia: Rome's First Witch* (London, Bloomsbury, 2017), 7–8.
22. Hutton, *The Witch*, 60. See also F. Graf, 'Victimology: or How to Deal with Untimely Death', in *Daughters of Hecate: Women and Magic in the Ancient World*, ed. K.B. Stratton and D.S. Kalleres (Oxford: Oxford University Press, 2014), 391.
23. Ibid, 61.
24. D. Ogden, *Magic, Witchcraft and Ghosts in the Greek and Roman Worlds* (Oxford: Oxford University Press, 2009), 333.
25. Ibid.
26. Ibid, 334.
27. Ibid, 283–84.
28. Suetonius, 'Augustus', in *The Twelve Caesars*, translated by Robert Graves (London: Penguin Classics, 2007), 31.
29. Cato, *De Agricultura*, clx.
30. See especially: W.B. McDaniel, 'A Sempiternal Superstition', *The Classical Journal* 45 (1950), 171–76.
31. Plato, *Republic*, 364b-e.
32. See especially Graf, 'Victimology'.
33. Ibid, 390.
34. Ibid.
35. Ibid, 395.
36. Ibid.
37. Ibid, 402.
38. Mary Douglas for instance draws upon the anthropological model of close-knit communities where witchcraft is more likely to exist due to the restricted nature that such communities have with the outside

world, leaving an environment where superstition can flourish. For Graf, this fits the model for Roman household accusations of witchcraft, an environment that was more than likely to suffer from social stress due to the strict nature of hierarchy and the fear of rivals, perhaps causing issues for those trying to maintain their reputation and status quo. Resorting to witchcraft and superstition was a way of ousting unnecessary individuals: See Chapter Seven in M. Douglas, *Natural Symbols: Explorations in Cosmology* (London: Barrie and Rockliff, 1970).

39. K. Stratton, *Naming the Witch: Magic, Ideology, and Stereotype in the Ancient World* (New York: Columbia University Press, 2022), 79–96. Kimberly Stratton provides a convincing argument as to why the image of the witch was used to encourage idealised female behaviour.
40. In his *Theogony*, Hesiod refers to Medea as being the niece of Circe (956–692), whilst Diodorus Siculus in his *Bibliotheca historica,* 4.45-46, states that Medea is the daughter of Hecate. Diodorus Siculus, *Bibliotheca historica*, trans. John Skelton, Early English Text Society Original Series (London: 1963).
41. The dating of Ovid's *Heroides* is still a subject of debate, see the introduction of P.E. Knox (ed.), *Ovid*: *Heroides*: *Select Epistles* (Cambridge, 1995), for further discussion concerning dating.
42. Homer, *Iliad*, 11.738–41.
43. Ibid, 313.
44. Euripides, *Medea*, line 473.
45. Ibid, line 490.
46. Diodorus Siculus, *Bibliotheca historica*, 4.51.
47. Ibid.
48. Ovid, *Metamorphoses*, 7.179. Book VII contains the entire mythology of Medea.
49. For further discussion concerning Thessaly and the pulling down of the moon phenomenon, see Chapter Three.
50. Ibid.
51. Cf. D. Ogden, *Night's Black Agents: Witches, Wizards and the Dead in the Ancient World* (Hambledon: Continuum, 2008), 39.
52. See the beginning of the introduction to this book.
53. Vergil, *Aeneid*, Book 1. Venus intervenes to aid the hospitality of Dido by encouraging her son Cupid to shoot his love arrow into her so that she will love Aeneas and cause him no harm, line 712.

54. The 'Maeonian bonnet' is a reference to Phoenicia, Dido's original birthplace. The idea of wearing such a bonnet would have been seen as effeminate and a step away from the masculine culture of ancient Rome.
55. Vergil, *Aeneid*, 4.490.
56. Ogden, *Magic, Witchcraft and Ghosts in the Greek and Roman Worlds*, 102. See also M. Davies, 'Deianeira and Medea: A Footnote to the Prehistory of Two Myths', *Mnemosyne* 42 (1989), 469–72.
57. Adrienne Mayor, 'The Nessus Shirt in the New World: Smallpox Blankets in History and Legend', *The Journal of American Folklore* 108, no. 427 (Winter, 1995), 54–77.
58. Ibid.
59. There are other literary references to the Nessus shirt as a motif of destruction. In Shakespeare's *Antony and Cleopatra*, Antony claims that 'The shirt of Nessus is upon me!' when he realises that he has lost the battle against the Roman Octavian and his life is effectively over. He even refers to Cleopatra as a 'witch', believing her to have abandoned him, Act 4, Scene 12, lines 47–51. With regard to history, we may recall how James I was influenced by references to witches in literature and his own disturbing beliefs in it.
60. Erictho will be one of the main witches discussed in the following chapters.
61. Teitel, *Canidia: Rome's First Witch*, 1.
62. Horace, *Epode*, Book 5.

Chapter One

1. *The Oxford Classical Dictionary*, ed. Simon Hornblower and Antony Spawforth, 3rd ed. (Oxford: Oxford University Press, 1996), 671.
2. Ibid.
3. See Chapter Four in Sarah Johnston, *Hekate Soteira* (Atlanta: Scholars Press Atlanta, 1990).
4. Ibid, 21.
5. L. Farnell, *Cults of the Greek States*, vol. 2 (Oxford: Oxford University Press, 1896), 501.
6. Ibid, 504.

7. Johnston, *Hekate Soteira*, 27.
8. Farnell, *Cults of the Greek*, 504.
9. Ibid. *Catalogue of Women* is a fragmentary poem that has been attributed to Hesiod. It is still a matter of debate as to whether he actually composed it.
10. Farnell, *Cults of the Greek States*, 504.
11. E. Mitropoulou, *Triple Hecate in Ancient Greek Religion* (Horned Owl Publishing, 1978), 17; cf. Johnston, *Hekate Soteira*, 21; cf. S. Johnston, *Restless Dead: Encounters between the Living and the Dead in Ancient Greece* (California: University of California Press, 1999), 205.
12. T. Kraus, *Hecate* (Heidelberg, 1960), 47.
13. Johnston, *Restless Dead*, 206.
14. Ibid. There is also symbolic usage of the key seen in Greece as early as the Mycenaean times, which is referenced in the Linear B tablets.
15. See the introduction to Hesiod, *Theogony and Works and Days*, trans. M.L West (Oxford: Oxford University Press, 1988).
16. Kraus, *Hecate*, 47. It should be noted that scholars have described the Homeric world as reflecting either the Mycenaean Age, the Dark Age or the Archaic Period. This, therefore, makes it difficult to ascertain an exact date for the Homeric texts. A Mycenaean interpretation is found in J.B. Bury and R. Meiggs. *A History or Greece*, 4th ed. (New York: Palgrave Macmillian, 1975) and in I. Morris and B. Powell (eds), *A New Companion to Homer* (New York: Brill, 1997), 536. The Dark Age view dominates in M.I. Finley, *Aspects of Antiquity: Discoveries and Controversies*, 2nd ed. (London: Penguin, 1977). The Archaic Age interpretation is found in G.S. Kirk, *The Nature of Greek Myths* (Harmondsworth: Penguin, 1983). A.M. Snodgrass, on the other hand, believes that the Homeric epics in particular do not present a consistent picture of any given historical period but rather an accumulation of different periods, thus forming a 'patchwork' composition: *Early Greek Armour and Weapons: From the End of the Bronze Age to 600 BC* (Edinburgh: Edinburgh University Press, 1964). This book will follow more recent scholarship that places the composition of Homeric works firmly in the Archaic period, that is, the eighth century BC: see H. van Wees, 'Homer and Early Greece', in

Homer: Critical Assessments, Vol. II, ed. I.de Jong (Abingdon: Routledge, 1999).

17. Johnston, *Restless Dead*, 206.
18. All quotes relating to Hecate can be found in Hesiod, *Theogony*, 404–52.
19. Ibid.
20. Ibid.
21. Ibid.
22. In particular, see Farnell, *Cults of the Greek States*.
23. Hesiod, *Theogony*, 277.
24. See above note. Cf. H. Bowden, *Mystery Cults in the Ancient World* (London: Thames and Hudson, 2023), 15.
25. The Eleusinian Mysteries was a mystery cult honouring Persephone's descent to the underworld and her subsequent return to earth. It represented her return as a rebirth, recognising her descent as a Katabasis – see Chapter Two for more details concerning a katabasis. Her reascension was symbolically linked to the regrowth of spring flowers, a common trope found in other mystical rites in ancient agricultural societies. The hymn explains the mythological establishment of these mysteries when Demeter abandons her duties as a goddess, especially after the lack of aid provided by the other immortals, and after disguising herself as an old woman, she settles in Eleusis where she founds the cult. For a more detailed discussion concerning the Hymn and the Eleusinian Mysteries, see Bowden, *Mystery Cults in the Ancient World*, Chapter One.
26. Homer, *Hymn to Demeter*, 52.
27. Ibid, 440.
28. Johnston, *Hekate Soteira*, 23. There will be some similarities here to Circe who also acts as a spiritual guide for Odysseus as he departs to the underworld, thus demonstrating the benevolence of these deities in their early mythologies. Further, their connections to the underworld, will be one of the key factors in their subsequent vilification.
29. Ibid.
30. The Sibyl in Vergil's *Aeneid* also resides within a cavern before departing with Aeneas as he set off to Hades. See the opening lines of Vergil, *Aeneid*, Book 6.
31. Cf. Johnston, *Hekate Soteira*, 23.

32. Sarah Iles Johnston provides a detailed and academic analysis of Hecate's role within these oracles in *Hekate Soteira*. But see also E.R. Dodds, 'New Light on the Chaldaean Oracles', *Harvard Theological Review* 54 (Cambridge: 1961), 263–72 and E.R. Dodds, 'Theurgy and its Relation to Neoplatonism', *Journal of Roman Studies* 37 (Cambridge: 1947), 62–65. Also, R. Majerick, *The Chaldaean Oracles*, Studies in Greek and Roman Religion 5 (Leiden: Brill, 1989).
33. See introduction Johnston, *Hekate Soteira*. Stories arose concerning Julian and how he was a deciding factor in the battles that Marcus Aurelius won, such as the conjuring of a human clay mask that fired thunderbolts at the enemy when they were fighting the Dacians.
34. See Chapter Four in Ibid.
35. Ibid. There are some correlations here to other mystic cults arising at the same time. Gnosticism, for example, has the female Sophia who was seen as analogous to the human soul, representing the feminine side of God, in much the same vein as Hecate and her relationship with the paternal intellect.
36. Cf. Johnston, *Hekate Soteira*, 24. The Hermae were found at crossings and boundaries between lands, they were typically stone rectangles topped off with the head of Hermes and his genitals placed upon the rectangle, as such they are commonly referred to as *ithyphallic herms*. W. Burkert argues that this represents a primal instinct for the male of the group to exert their dominance by showing their erections, so showcasing their masculinity and that they are the ultimate protector of their tribe. W. Burkert, *Structure and History in Greek Myth and Ritual* (Berkeley: University of California Press, 1979), 40. However, as there were also boundary stones made of Hecate, albeit on a more domestic sphere, it is more likely that these served a collective apotropaic purpose.
37. In Rome's foundation myth, Romulus and Remus decide to build a city of their own by each standing upon a hill – the Palatine and Aventine respectively – and through the process of augury, the practice of observing the behaviour of birds, it was decided that Romulus should be the founder given that twelve vultures encircled the hill where he stood, outnumbering the amount his brother saw. Whilst building the boundary of the new city, which was to be called Rome, Remus mocks the boundary stones and in a fit of rage, Romulus kills his brother. Although this symbolises an act of

bloody aggression, it can also stress the meaning and significance of the boundary to a city and that mocking these stones in any way is an irreligious and sacrilegious act, potentially causing harm to the state. Further instances of Rome's seriousness with regard to the boundaries can be seen in Cicero's Philippic, 2.102 in which Cicero records Antony's illegal establishment of a colony in Casilinum for the purposes of placing veteran soldiers. The act itself was illegal on the grounds that he was establishing a settlement in an area that had already been developed as a colonial settlement by Caesar. Antony dispenses with protocol which was fully engrained in the cultural make-up of the Romans. In order for a new colony to be founded, auspices at the site had to be taken, the settlement had to have an official boundary wall surrounding it dug out by a traditional plough called *sulcus primigenius* (primeval furrow), followed by a ritual purification of the new inhabitants. As Antony did not fully abide by these distinct rules, Cicero highlights this as further proof of his unconstitutional acts – the main focus of his *Philippics*. It further serves to stress the importance placed upon the demarcation. Cf. Cicero, *Philippic*, 2: 44–50, 78–92, 100–19, 323.

38. It may also be noted that the Romans, more than any other ancient culture, had some significant liminal deities. Janus, whose role was not too dissimilar to Hecate, almost acts as her male counterpart in that he has a dual face and protects crossroads and new beginnings – the month January is named after him as a result of his latter role – but there was also Limentius and Lima, god and goddess of the threshold and Cardea, goddess of door hinges. Cf. Johnston, *Hekate Soteira*, 25.
39. Johnston, *Restless Dead*, 211.
40. Ibid.
41. W.H. Roshcer, 'Das von der 'kynanthropie' handelnde Fragment des Marcellus von Side', in *Abhandlungen der philologisch-historischen Classe der Konigl*, Sachsischen Gesellschaft der Wissenschaften 3 (Leipzig, 1896), 25–50.
42. See Hesiod, *Theogony*, 404–52; cf. ibidIbid and Johnston, *Restless Dead*, Johnston, S. *Restless Dead: Encounters between the Living and the Dead in Ancient Greece*, (University of California Press, 1999), 212.
43. Kraus, *Hecate*, 45–48.

44. Cf. Johnston, *Hekate Soteira*, 29.
45. Ibid, 32. Plutarch also speaks of Hecate, equating her with Anubis but also the moon which has mixed characteristics paralleling daemones due to its waxing and waning abilities.
46. Sarah Iles Johnston's valuable discussion concerning Hecate's connection to mysticism even states how Hecate brought salvation to theurgists and that the magic practiced by the theurgists was a form of white magic: Johnston, *Hekate Soteira*, 75, 77, 79.
47. Theocritus, *Pharmakeutria*, 2.10.
48. Ibid. This also demonstrates a transformation of Hecate into a more dreaded entity.
49. Vergil, *Aeneid*, 4.490.
50. Ovid *Metamorphoses* 7 which contains the entirety of Ovid's myths relating to Medea.
51. Euripides, *Medea*, 386–423. Hecate is also invoked in a similar fashion in Apuleius' *Metamorphoses* and Lucan's *Civil War* which will be discussed in Chapters Three and Four respectively.
52. See the reference at the start of this chapter.
53. Johnston, *Hekate Soteira*, 146.
54. Seneca, *Oedipus*, 2.568.
55. Apuleius, *Metamorphoses*, 11.2.
56. Johnston, *Restless Dead*, 210. Johnston points out that fear concerning unwanted spirits or the 'restless dead' emerging from their graves became a persistent preoccupation of the Greeks in the Archaic Age, leading to a more desired and happier afterlife.
57. It is significant that Hecate and Hermes have some key similarities. As has already been mentioned, they were both used as liminal protectors for the city-state and the domestic sphere, see discussion concerning the use of the *Hekataia* and *Hermae* respectively. Here, they are both acting as psychopomps. Significantly, Hecate's role with the latter becomes darker, more dangerous and attached to necromantic power. Whilst necromantic power had some advantages – see Chapter Two 'The Encounter with Circe in Books 10–12' for Circe's beneficial role in calling up the dead –, this power will eventually be a negative and frightening trope of the witch, especially when we come to the time of Lucan's *Civil War*, see Chapter Four. The reasons for this transformation will be addressed more fully in the next chapter.

58. Shealsohasconnectionswithdaemonicdogs,phantasms,apparitions; the bringing of bad dreams, illness or even madness.
59. Statius, *Silvae,* 3.1.152–60.
60. Cf. D. Magie, *Roman Rule in Asia Minor to the End of the Third Century after Christ*, Vol. I–II (Princeton: Princeton University Press, 1950), 962.
61. R. Graves, *I Claudius* (London: Folio Society, 1940), 205.
62. Much debate has arisen as to whether this scene was written by Shakespeare with a belief among modern scholars that it, and indeed the character of Hecate herself, are, in fact, later interpolations, perhaps inserted by the playwright Thomas Middleton who revised the play *Macbeth*. Middleton himself also produced his own play written between 1613–1616 called *The Witch*. See *Macbeth*, ed. S. Clark and P. Mason (London: The Arden Shakespeare, 2015). Despite the debate concerning authorship, the scene is still written during the Jacobean era and contains the current fears surrounding the witch and the practice of her craft, with Hecate portrayed as their patron.
63. William Blake wrote his own mythology which was formed as part of his prophetic books. The female character Enitharmon is one of the main characters. Her symbol is the moon, and her character exerts dominance over the female which drives men to fear women.
64. In many cultures, negative connotations are often associated with the left-hand side. The Greeks had three words for left: *aristeros*, *laios* and *skaios*. The last, *skaios*, can mean something 'awkward' or 'foolish'. Likewise, in Plato's *Phaedrus*, he claims the left-hand side of the body is 'improper'. In Latin, there are similarly three words for left: *laevus*, *scaevus* and *sinister*. The word *sinister* is thought to derive from the fold in the toga that covers the left hand, leaving the right hand free to greet people. It was also common practice in the Roman world to form alliances with the right hand (*dextra*) through a handshake (cf. Aeneas' alliance with Evander in Book 8 of Vergil's *Aeneid*). Typically, all three words for left in Latin can have these negative translations: perverse, immoral and unlucky. Indeed, the Latin word '*scaevitas*' means choosing the wrong course.
65. The scene is almost reminiscent of Shakespeare's *Macbeth* where at the start of Act 4, Scene 1, in which the three witches who are later accompanied by Hecate, place into their cauldron some unsavoury

items: 'Fillet of fenny snake…Eye of newt, and toe of dog, Adder's fork…Lizard's leg, and howlet's wing', thus, snakes, frogs and owls are animals linked to Hecate, as portrayed in Blake's artwork.
66. Porphyry, *On Images*.
67. See R. Graves, *The White Goddess* (London: Faber and Faber), 1999, Chapter 22.
68. The practice of Theurgy, i.e. in Neoplatonism, in particular connected Hecate with a form of white or benevolent magic: see Part II in Johnston, *Hekate Soteira*.
69. See Diodorus Siculus, *Bibliotheca historia*, 4.45–46, 48.

Chapter Two

1. Homer, *Odyssey*, 10.138–40.
2. Hutton, *The Witch*, 58.
3. Ibid. In fact, Ronald Hutton boldly states that the Greeks 'do not appear to have had a belief in a witch figure until the Roman period', 281.
4. Dickie, *Magic and Magicians in the Greco-Roman World*, 23.
5. Ibid.
6. J. Yarnall, *Transformations of Circe: The History of an Enchantress* (Chicago: University of Illinois Press, 1994), 1, 27.
7. Ibid.
8. J. Cauvin, *The Birth of the Gods and the Origins of Agriculture* (Cambridge: Cambridge University Press, 2000), 25.
9. Ibid.
10. Ibid, 31–33. See also Yarnall, *Transformations of Circe*, 27.
11. Ogden, *Night's Black Agents*, 13–14.
12. Ibid.
13. Ibid.
14. Yarnall, *Transformations of Circe*, 27.
15. Ibid.
16. G. Knight, *A History of White Magic* (Cheltenham: Skylight Press, 2011). See especially Chapter One.
17. Sarah Iles Johnston states that 'virtually all goddesses, especially those of Eastern origin, can be allied with the "Great Mother"', further dismantling the theory that Circe is unique in her ancient

Eastern/Anatolian origin: Johnston, *Hekate Soteira*, 22. Hugh Bowden likewise stresses the constant contact that the Greeks had with the east, even claiming that their myths may have originated elsewhere: Bowden, *Mystery Cults in the Ancient World*, 11.

18. Daniel Ogden similarly uses this index in his very convincing argument that Circe is indeed a witch. See Ogden, *Night's Black Agents*, 14 ff. See also S. Thompson, *Motif-Index of Folk Literature*, 6 vols, 2nd ed. (Bloomington: 1955-1958).
19. Homer, *Odyssey*, 9.408-409.
20. Homer, *Odyssey*, 10.240.
21. Ibid, 466.
22. Another explanation as to why Odysseus wishes to hear their song is due to their prophetic nature which may reveal some detail about his homecoming. As the Sirens themselves state: 'we know whatever happens on this fruitful earth'. Homer, *Odyssey*, 10.191–92
23. Ibid, 12.60.
24. Ibid, 150–51.
25. Ibid. In Book 22 of the *Odyssey*, amidst the battle between Odysseus and the suitors, Athene takes the shape of a swallow and perches herself on the beam of the hall to observe the battle below and offer aid and encouragement should Odysseus need it: 240.
26. Yarnell argues that as Homer is thought to have lived around the Anatolia region, he may well have come into contact with people who had knowledge of an ancient goddess worship: *Transformations of Circe: The History of an Enchantress* (Chicago: University of Illinois Press, 1994), 27.
27. Homer, *Odyssey*, 12.39–40.
28. Ogden, *Night's Black Agents*, 17.
29. Ibid.
30. Cf. Ogden, *Night's Black Agents*, 14.
31. Yarnall, *Transformations of Circe*, 46.
32. Germain, G. *Genese de l'Odyssee*, Paris, 1954: 131–32, 149–50.
33. Ogden, *Magic, Witchcraft and Ghosts in the Greek and Roman Worlds*, 98-99.
34. W.B. Stanford, "That Circe's Ῥάβδος ('Od'. 10, 238 Ff.) Was Not A Magic Wand." *Hermathena* 66 (1945): 69–71.
35. Homer, *Odyssey* Book 12.21–22; see also J. Campbell, *The Hero with a Thousand Faces*, 3rd ed. (New World Library: 2012). Campbell

argues effectively how all heroes in myth follow the same path: they have a call to adventure, are aided by something supernatural, will descend to an abyss where they undergo a rebirth and then will return to their homeland. Many well-known ancient heroes follow this course, including Gilgamesh. Odysseus seems to fit this pattern, and Circe as his aid enables him to be reborn.

36. Daniel Ogden suggests that Circe has powers of invisibility and that she can even 'teleport herself through space'. This is apparent, he believes, when she is able to leave black sheep by Odysseus' boat needed for the necromancy. She had done this without being seen by Odysseus and his men: 'she had slipped past us with ease'. Homer, *Odyssey*, 10.571–72. This would mean that she may well have accompanied him during his ghostly encounters. The power of invisibility is also a motif linked to the witch as stated in *Motif-Index of Folk Literature*. Cf. Ogden, *Magic, Witchcraft and Ghosts in the Greek and Roman Worlds*, 18. On the other hand, most deities of the *Odyssey* are able to render themselves 'invisible', with Odysseus frequently exclaiming that 'some god guided' them when on their travels, without the deity revealing their true form. This idea of invisibility, then, is more likely a power enacted by all the gods, and not just Circe herself.
37. The Greeks called this 'choe', from the Greek χεῦμα (cheuma), 'that which is poured'.
38. These are some sacrifices that will be made afterwards.
39. Diodorus, *Bibliotheca*, 4.45–46, 48.
40. Ibid.
41. The scholarly debate concerning the *Aeneid* is vast. It tends to fall into two categories: those scholars that follow a European school of thought process, whereby they view the poem as an exemplary example of Augustan propaganda, empire and Roman power and those scholars that are more negative in their appraisal who are classed as Harvard school scholars. Some examples of these would be K.W. Gransden who sees the protagonist Aeneas as a Messianic figure bringing peace and posterity to his people and R.D. Williams who likes to excuse the flaws within Aeneas' character. Contrastingly, Lyne, a Harvard scholar disparages the lack of emotion within Aeneas and draws upon some sound examples within the poem which stress the ineffectuality of his pietas. K.W. Gransden, *Virgil: The Aeneid*, 3rd ed. (Cambridge: Cambridge University Press,

2010); R.D. Williams, *Aeneas and the Roman Hero* (Bristol: Bristol Classical Press, 1973); R.O.A.M. Lyne, *Further Voices in Vergil's Aeneid* (Oxford: Clarendon Press, 1987).

42. See especially Gransden's *Virgil's Iliad: An Essay on Epic Narrative* (Cambridge: Cambridge University Press, 1984).
43. Again, like the aforementioned readings of the *Aeneid*, much has been debated concerning the way Aeneas leaves the underworld. There are two gates, one of ivory where only false dreams can leave and the other the Gate of Horn, where true shades depart. As Aeneas leaves through the former, this has led many to view Aeneas' exit as a subtle reminder to his audience of the falsehood of Roman dreams, and, therefore, Augustan propaganda. See E.L. Highbarger, *The Gates of Dreams: An Archaeological Examination of Vergil, Aeneid VI,* 893–899 (Baltimore: John Hopkins Press, 1940).
44. Vergil, *Aeneid*, 7.11.
45. Ibid.
46. This follows Ogden's argument that Circe was responsible for transforming men into all types of animals on the island, and not just into pigs: Ogden, *Night's Black Agents*, 17.
47. Ibid, lines 324.
48. Ibid.
49. Father/man of the household and father of the fatherland respectively.
50. See Williams, *Aeneas and the Roman Hero*.
51. Ovid, *Tristia*, 2.207.
52. Ovid, *Tristes e Pónticas*, trans. José González Vázquez (Madrid: Editorial Gredos, 1992), 10. Both scholars argue that *Ars Amatoria* may have been used as an excuse for the exile as Ovidian poetry was similar in tone to other love elegists, and that the reason for his exile may have been more personal.
53. Ovid, *Metamorphoses*, 1.690.
54. Ibid.
55. Ibid, 14.1.
56. Ibid.
57. Ibid, lines 310.
58. Ibid.
59. Ibid.
60. Ibid.
61. Ibid.

62. Incidentally, 'picus' in Latin means woodpecker.
63. Ingo Gildenhard and Andrew Zissos, eds., *Transformative Change in Western Thought: A History of Metamorphosis from Homer to Hollywood* (Leeds: Maney Publishing, 2012), 100–1.
64. Ibid.
65. See introduction of this book.
66. J. Barsby, *Ovid Amores I* (Bristol: Bristol University Press, 1973).
67. M. Arthur, 'Liberated Women: The Classical Era', in *Becoming Visible*, ed. Renate Bridenthal and Claudia Koonz (Boston, 1977), 60–89.
68. Commonly referred to as the repeal of the Oppian Law found in Livy's *Ab Urbe Condita.*
69. Stratton, *Naming the Witch*, 79–96.
70. *Daughters of Hecate*, 155.
71. Ibid.
72. See Chapter Three in Yarnall's *Transformations of Circe.*
73. Ibid.
74. There are many different types of allegory concerning Circe from her being portrayed as a femme fatale, whore, deadly witch and sorceress.
75. C. Woods, *The Pre-Raphaelites* (New York: The Viking Press, 1981), 144.
76. See Chapter Six in Yarnall's *Transformations of Circe.*
77. M. Atwood, *You Are Happy* (Oxford: Oxford University Press, 1974).
78. The *Telegony* is a lost poem. We only have a summary of it by grammarian Proklos living in the second century AD. The story itself is supposed to follow directly from the end of the *Odyssey.*
79. M. Miller, *Circe* (London: Bloomsbury, 2018), 16.
80. Ibid, 76–77.
81. Ibid, 164–65.

Chapter Three

1. Ovid describes here Medea's foray into the Thessalian mountains to obtain the necessary herbs needed to rejuvenate Jason's father, Aeson. The Thessalian Tempe was a gorge located in Northern Thessaly, known

to the Byzantines as Λυκόστομο (Wolf's Throat). It was particularly referred to by Greek and Roman writers as a place of witchcraft.

2. Darryl Jones further analyses the shocking aspect of this film as a cinematic experience and concludes that having Jason travel to the region of Colchis, which would have been seen as the ends of the earths for the Greeks, he 'is also travelling back in time, to witness the origins of civilization in a region of magic, ritual and human sacrifice. Jason takes Medea back with him to Corinth, the city state of modernity…but Medea carries the primal world within her…and this enables her to summon up the appalling forces of vengeance…in order to kill her own children.' Thus, Medea is the very symbol of barbarity due to her immersion into the world of magic and witchcraft, which sets her far apart from the laws and procedures of the Greek world. cf. D. Jones, *Sleeping With The Lights On: The Unsettling Story of Horror* (Oxford: Oxford University Press, 2018). 3. Euripides likewise makes this a feature of his play when the chorus exclaim in horror at the notion that Medea will find refuge in Athens after her murderous exploits. They begin to bewail how Athens, a city of high culture and civilisation, dare welcome a woman so malicious for fear that her very presence will pollute the city state: 'How will Athens welcome you, the child-killer whose presence is pollution?' Euripides, *Medea,* 843.
3. See Ovid, *Amores*, 1.8.
4. Foreigners were generally classed as outsiders in the ancient Greek world. In Athens, they were specifically referred to as *metics* and, like women, were disenfranchised and had little role within the sphere of the city. Despite this, we know that mercenary soldiers were involved in the safeguarding of the city. Aristophanes mentions the use of a Scythian archer in his *Thesmophoriazusae* (*Women at Thesmophoria*) for instance.
5. H.D. Westlake, *Thessaly in the Fourth Century BC* (Groningen: Bouma's Boekhuis, 1969), 21.
6. Ibid, 37. According to Herodotus, an overall dislike for Thessaly arose in the fifth century BC when Aleuadae, the reigning family in Thessaly, assisted Xerxes in his invasion of Greece by allowing him passage and offering him support. This, therefore, encouraged the Greeks to view Thessaly as a treasonous area. Herodotus, *Histories*, 7.6.

7. One famous myth of note centres upon the *Centauromachy*, the battle between the Lapiths and Centaurs. The Lapiths were a tribe native to Thessaly and their king, Pirithous, invites the Centaurs who reside in the area to his wedding feast. At the feast, however, the Centaurs take advantage of the hospitality, proceeding to become inebriated, leading the Centaur Eurytion to try and abduct the bride. Eurytion is captured and his ears and nose are sliced off before being thrown from the palace. The *Centauromachy* begins at this moment and retells the vicious battle that took place as a result, highlighting the marked difference between barbarism (that is, the Centaurs) and civilised forces (the Lapiths who are aided by Theseus). The myth can be found in Homer's *Odyssey*, 21.292–304. It was also sculpted on the metopes of the Parthenon temple.
8. R. Buxton, *Imaginary Greece: The Context of Mythology* (Cambridge: Cambridge University Press, 1994), 82–92.
9. See Ovid's *Metamorphoses*, Book 7 for Medea's mythology and foray into the region of Thessaly.
10. R. Gordon, 'Aelian's Peony: The Location of Magic in Graeco-Roman Tradition', in *Comparative Criticism 9* (Cambridge: Cambridge University Press, 1987), 60.
11. Lucan, *Civil War*, 6.438–42.
12. D.E. Hill particularly believes this rather than the lunar eclipse theory, see D.E. Hill, 'The Thessalian Trick', *RhM*, 166 (1973), 221–37.
13. Aristophanes, *Clouds*, lines 749-752.
14. See also the introduction.
15. Cf. Ogden, *Night's Black Agents*, 43.
16. Hutton, *The Witch*, 62. Cf. D.S. Kalleres, 'Drunken Hags with Amulets and Prostitutes with Erotic Spells: The Re-Feminisation of Magic in Late Antique Christian Homilies', in *Daughters of Hecate*, ed. Stratton and Kalleres, 219. Kalleres states that during the early imperial period, 'Greco-Roman literature had constructed a deeply chiseled portrait of the witch – a harrowing image of a powerful, sexually voracious, female magical practitioner.'
17. See especially Vergil, *Eclogue*, 8.
18. Ogden, *Night's Black Agents*, 46.
19. These gardens are of historical importance, situated by the Esquiline Hill, an area once used as an open cemetery for the poor and where criminals were executed, and their bodies left to rot. Maecenas, a

close advisor of Augustus, acquired the land and transformed them into extensive gardens.

20. See Chapter One especially.
21. As discussed in Chapter One, the left hand was considered bad luck and associated with thievery.
22. Quote taken from *Satire*, 1.8, see Teitel, *Canidia: Rome's First Witch*, 24, for full translation of the poem.
23. Ibid, 32.
24. Cf. Ibid.
25. Ibid, 43. Maxwell provides a detailed explanation of the satire found within the poem.
26. Canidia's necromancy in the poem is very similar to the that of Odysseus' in Homer's *Odyssey*, Book 11. See Chapter Two. Likewise, there are similar elements of the rites Canidia performs to those of Theocritus' Simaetha and Vergil's witch in *Eclogue* 8, such as the use of dolls and incantations calling upon Hecate.
27. See Teitel, *Canidia: Rome's First Witch*. As the very title of Maxwell's work suggests, he certainly views Canidia as Rome's first literary witch construct.
28. For the full text of these stories see Petronius, *Satyricon*, 59–63.
29. Lycaon, wanting to test Zeus' omniscience, killed his own son and served him to the King of the Gods to see whether he would know he was eating human flesh. Disgusted by his actions, Zeus transformed Lycaon and all his sons into wolves. Another version of the tale can be found in Ovid's *Metamorphoses*, 1.199–243.
30. Cf. Ogden, *Night's Black Agents*, 57. Ogden also provides an interesting explanation as to why the clothes of the soldier turn to stone, 'a werewolf's recovery of the clothes he has disrobed himself of at the point of transformation may play a critical role in his return to human form', thus solidification of the clothes ensures that they will not be stolen and the human transformation will be complete.
31. Vergil, *Eclogue*, 8. The alternative title for this poem is *Pharmaceutria*, Sorceress. Essentially a bucolic poem in line with the rest of the *Eclogues*, this one stands alone in its referencing to magic and witchcraft and as mentioned earlier was clearly inspired by Theocritus' poetry.
32. The Lamia was a hideous child eating monster from Greek mythology and an unfortunate victim of Hera's wrath. She was

originally a beautiful woman who became one of Zeus' many affairs. Out of revenge for the liaison, Hera killed all of Lamia's children. In some accounts, Hera drove her mad to commit infanticide in much the same fashion as Herakles committing familicide. As a result of her children's deaths, Lamia morphed into a hideous creature, half woman, half serpent, who sought out other mothers to devour their children or babies. According to Aristotle in his *Nicomachean Ethics*, 7.5, Lamia was a monstrous woman who preferred to target pregnant women and eat their unborn foetuses. Hera even cursed Lamia with insomnia so that she was constantly mourning her children and destroying others. Zeus, being a god associated with justice, took pity on her and endowed her with the ability to remove her eyes so that she would have some respite.

33. See Hutton, *The Witch*, 69. Here Hutton describes the child killing demons found in Mesopotamia.
34. Samuel L. Macey provides a lengthy discussion concerning Saturn-Cronus in the classical world. See Chapter Two in *Patriarchs of Time: Dualism in Saturn-Cronus, Father Time, the Watchmaker God, and Father Christmas*, (Atlanta: University of Georgia Press, 2010).
35. Ibid, 28–36.
36. Diodorus of Sicily, 3.275–377. Vergil also adopts the argument that Saturn-Cronus is acknowledged mainly for his Golden Age. Vergil often correlates Saturn with Augustus who he argues from a propagandist viewpoint to be restoring a Golden Age in Rome similar to that carried out by Saturn in mythology. In 6.794 *Aeneid*, during the pageant of Roman heroes seen before the eyes of Aeneas, Augustus is the man who 'will bring back the golden years…once ruled over by Saturn'.
37. Plato, *Minos*, 8.397. Samuel L. Macey notes that there was one recorded instance of human sacrifice in Rome cited by Livy held when Hannibal reached Arno in 217 BC: 'Finally – the month was now December – victims were slain at the temple of Saturn in Rome…this time the senators administered the rite.' Livy, *Works*, 5.204–5; Macey, *Patriarchs of Time*, 32.
38. Juvenal, *Satire*, 6.603. The *lactoria columna*, the milk column, was an area in the Forum Holitroium where you could hire a wet nurse, bring your infant for milk, or abandon them. The *spurci lacus* was

a shallow pool in Rome that had legendary stories attached to it as retold by Livy. See Livy, *Works*, 1.13 and 6.6. During the imperial era, the lake or pool was used, according to Juvenal, to dispose of unwanted children.

39. Suetonius, 'Claudius', 27.
40. Other reasons for this kind of 'exposure' of infants could be linked to economy, illegitimacy, and even gender as females were more likely to be exposed than males given that the society was predominantly a patriarchy, where male heirs were preferred. There are also mythological examples of exposure: Oedipus is exposed due to the Delphic Oracle's prophecy that he would kill his own father and marry his mother; Romulus and Remus were left adrift in the River Tiber to prevent them from reclaiming their grandfather's kingdom; and Paris, prince of Troy, was similarly cast aside again due to a Delphic Oracle prophecy that stated he would bring destruction to the city of Troy. The practice, therefore, appears to be a well-established one predating the classical world.
41. Sophocles, *The Plays and Fragments*, ed. Lewis Campbell (Hildesheim, 1969), frag. 122 from *Andromeda*.
42. Incidentally, the Latin word 'strix' from where the strigae derive is itself translated as 'screech owl'.
43. Ovid, *Fasti*, 6.131–39. For other stories concerning the 'strix' see S.G. Oliphant, 'The Story of the Strix', *Transactions of the American Philological Association* 44 (1913), 133–49 and *TAPA* 45 (1914), 49–63. Also see C.M. McDonough, 'Carna, Proca and the Strix on the Kalends of June', *Transactions of the American Philological Association* 127 (1997), 315–44.
44. For further details, see McDonough, 'Carna, Proca and the Strix'. In his *Saturnalia*, Macrobius also attributes the origins of the goddess Carna with flesh and protection of vital organs in the human body. Macrobius, *Saturnalia*, 1.12.
45. Indeed, Ronald Hutton claims that the Anglo-Saxon word 'haegtis' meaning a 'malevolent old woman' is often equated in Early English glossaries with the Latin word 'striga' due to their nocturnal murderous pursuits. Hutton, *The Witch*, 159.
46. Sextus Pompeius Festus, *De Verborum Significatione*, 314.33.
47. Cf. O. Kolberg, *The People, Their Customs, Way of Life, Language*, vol. 15 (Krakow: Krakow Uniwersytet Jagiellonski, 1882), 24.

48. *Epitaph of Lucundus* (CIL VI.19747 = *ILS* 8522, Rome, c. AD 20). Cf. M.R. Lefkowitz and M.B. Fant, *Women's Life in Greece and Rome*, 3rd ed. (London: Bloomsbury, 2005), 294. Similar epitaphs related to witchcraft record the belief in spells that have been placed upon the dead victim leading to their demise. An epitaph from Lambaesis, Algeria records how a husband's wife was 'struck down by a spell, she lay dumb for a period, so that her spirit was torn out by force'. Epitaph erected by Aelius Proculinus, tribune of the legion III Augusta, *CIL VIII.2756.L.* With regard to epitaphs linked to children, Fritz Graf states that a surprising number of them highlight witchcraft and/or spells as a cause of death: Graf, 'Victimology', 396. This, of course, could be due to the untimely nature of the death of a child which has contributed to the parents' belief that foul play in the form of witchcraft was responsible, this also forms the basis of Graf's overall argument.
49. Cf. Introduction in: Apuleius, *The Golden Ass*, trans. P.G. Walsh (Oxford: Oxford University Press, 1994), xii.
50. Ibid, xiii.
51. Ibid.
52. Ibid.
53. Ibid.
54. Apuleius, *The Golden Ass*, 1.1.
55. Ovid's *Metamorphoses* covers a wide range of bestial as well as nature transformations from mythology. Ogden also points out the use of metaphorical transformations such as that of Aristomenes – see 'Apuleius' Witches' in this chapter for this story in Apuleius' novel – who compares himself to a tortoise as he cowers beneath a mattress when the witches enter his room. Ogden, *Night's Black Agents*, 65.
56. See 'Introduction' in: Apuleius, *The Golden Ass*, xix
57. Ibid.
58. Ogden actually refers to Photis as Pamphile's 'apprentice', conjuring up images of a sorcerer's apprentice. Ogden, *Night's Black Agents*, 65.
59. Apuleius, *The Golden Ass*, 1.7.
60. Ibid, 1.8.
61. The belief that beavers cut off their genitals appears to be an ancient one predating the Roman era and can be found as early as Ancient

Egypt. In the modern world, it has been observed that beavers secrete a liquid from their anal sacs called *castoreum* which helps to mark their territory. Historically, this *castoreum* was considered highly valuable and beavers were hunted for this liquid which was used medicinally and cosmetically. When hunting the animal, it would stop and appear to turn towards its genitals and nibble at them or, as has been mistakenly observed, bite them off. In actual fact, the beaver was getting ready to secrete the liquid. You would also be mistaken in thinking that the word 'castration' derives from *castoreum*, but the word 'castor' which is the name of the anal sac from where the beaver secretes the liquid is the word for beaver in Latin.

62. Interestingly, women's menstrual circle, a symbol of a female in her reproductive years, was thought to be linked to the phases of the moon, a celestial body which has connection to witchcraft and magic. Cf. previous chapter which discusses the connections of the moon and the witch goddess Hecate. See also R. Briffault, *The Mothers* (London: Allen & Unwin, 1959), 294–95.
63. Cf. Ogden, *Night's Black Agents*, 65.
64. J. Buxton, 'Mandari Witchcraft', in *Witchcraft and Sorcery in East Africa*, ed. J. Middleton and E.H. Winter (London:, 1963), 29–38. The idea of a pregnancy being controlled can also be seen in the mythology of Herakles when a disgruntled Hera, after she discovers the adultery her husband has committed with Alcmene, inverts her power as protector of childbirth to prolong the labour of Herakles' mother, Alcmene, in the hope that this would kill her baby. This act demonstrates that the power of Roman witches was as great and as potent as the gods themselves. Ogden further argues that Meroe is in fact using a binding magic with the pregnant woman, a form of magic that restricts the actions of an individual, this is shown with her ability to tie the baby to the womb and when she locks up the whole city in their houses. Ogden, *Night's Black Agents*, 66.
65. R. Firth, 'Reason and Unreason in Human Belief', in *Witchcraft and Sorcery*, ed. M. Marwick (London: 1982), 38–41.
66. D.W. Leinweber, 'Witchcraft and Lamiae in the Golden Ass', *Folklore* 105 (1994), 77–82.
67. Apuleius notes that she can 'black out the stars': *The Golden Ass*, 1.8.
68. Ogden points out that Apuleius uses the innkeeper motif, similar to Ovid's Dipsas in *Amores*, 1.8. Innkeepers seem to have been

associated with witchcraft in ancient Rome. Maybe, as Ogden claims, because they 'they serve as markers of the low life milieu favoured by the[se] tales'. Ogden, *Night's Black Agents*, 65.

69. Apuleius, *Golden Ass*, 2.36.
70. Barbette Stanley Spaeth points out that male practitioners of magic in the literature tend to be regarded in a far more positive light than their female counterparts. They are either learned men or philosophers who are called upon by high-ranking officials to provide valuable information through the reading of portents or spells. They are not hideous in appearance, terrifying, desiring personal gain or acting out of spite. 'From Goddess to Hag', in *Daughters of Hecate,* ed. Stratton and Kalleres, 52. The reasoning behind this disparity between female and male sorcerers will be discussed later in the chapter.
71. Ogden, *Night's Black Agents*, 69.
72. Apuleius, *The Golden Ass*, 2.5.
73. Romans used oil lamps, the oil serving as a fuel, the lamp would also contain a linen wick that would have been lit to provide the light. In the case of Pamphile, it appears she would use the flame of the lamp as a supernatural means of communicating with the spirits.
74. Ibid, 2.11.
75. Ibid, 3.21.
76. Ibid, 9.30.
77. See Chapter Two.
78. See Arthur, 'Liberated Women'.
79. See especially Elizabeth Ann Pollard's article 'Magic Accusations against Women in Tacitus' Annals', in *Daughters of Hecate: Women and Magic in the Ancient World*, ed. K.B. Stratton and D.S. Kalleres (Oxford: Oxford University Press, 2014), 183–218.
80. Ibid, 184.
81. Ibid, 183.
82. Book III of Tacitus' *Annals* covers the full account of Plancina's magical explorations.
83. Stratton, *Naming the Witch*, 96–105.
84. Barbette Stanley Spaeth, 'From the Goddess to Hag: The Greek and Roman Witch in Classical Literature', in *Daughters of Hecate*, ed. Stratton and Kalleres, 55.

85. Both the Greeks and the Romans considered guardianship of the home as one of the most important parts of manhood. For the Greeks, the male guardian was the *kurios*, who was responsible for the protection of the *oikos* (household), making sure the house was sufficiently run in his absence, this was through, according to the Socratic dialogue, vigorous training of the wife who held the economic and servile responsibilities of the domestic sphere: Socrates' student Xenophon records the dialogue between Socrates and Ischomachus, which describes Ischomachus' expert management of his wife, training her to keep charge of the domestic sphere like the 'leader bee' does within her hive: Xenophon 7.33 ff. For the Romans, this role was taken on by the *paterfamilias*, the male guardian who ensured that his house was a well-functioning entity, controlling such aspects as the birth of potential heirs, dinner parties and the salutations of clients. See also S. Dixon, *The Roman Family* (Baltimore: John Hopkins University Press, 1991).
86. Ibid, 56.
87. You may also note that Thelyphron refuses to return home due to his disfigurement so making himself a social outcast.
88. Spaeth, 'From the Goddess to Hag', 58.
89. Virgil, *Aeneid*, Book 4.
90. P. Ripat, 'Cheating Women: Curse Tablets and Roman Wives', in *Daughters of Hecate*, ed. Stratton and Kalleres, 340-364.
91. Ibid, 345.
92. Cf. Ibid, 346–47.
93. Ibid.
94. See Plautus, *Menaechmi*, 102.114–18. In this scene, the husband is angry due his wife's nagging and so dresses up his slave girl, with whom he is having an affair, as his wife states that she is 'compliant with his ways'. Cf. Ripat, 'Cheating Women', 346.
95. Ibid, 350.
96. Ibid, 352.
97. Artemidorus, *Oneirocritica*, 4.59. According to Artemidorus, one slave girl was driven by the intervention of her mistress and use of curses to have vivid fretful dreams of Andromache who was known to have been abused by her mistress in other sources.
98. Ripat, 'Cheating Women', 353.
99. Graf, 'Victimology', 386–417.

100. *Oikos* was the household in the ancient Greek world.
101. Graf, 'Victimology', 403.
102. Ibid.
103. Cf. Ibid, 403; Pliny, *Natural History*, 18.41–43.
104. Ibid, 402.
105. See Introduction, 'Witches in Ancient Greece and Rome'. Both Daniel Ogden and Ronald Hutton relate in detail the nature of the witch persecutions in the Roman times. See Ogden, *Magic, Witchcraft and Ghosts in the Greek and Roman Worlds* and Hutton, *The Witch.*
106. Ogden refers to the profound impact of Apuleius' Thessalian witches upon the villages in remote parts of Italy, claiming that these stories became the traditional folkloric tales told by villagers from the Roman world and beyond. He draws upon the modern memoir written by Carlo Levi, *Cristo si e fermato a Eboli* (Christ Stopped at Eboli, 1945), in which he records a village of witches who partake in spells and curses that are similar to Apuleius' *sagae*, thus highlighting the persistent hold that Roman witches have upon our imaginations. Ogden, *Night's Black Agents*, 71–75.

Chapter Four

1. G. Maguire, *Wicked: The Life and Times of the Wicked Witch of the West* (Headline Review, 2006).
2. Maguire derived the name Elphaba from Baum's initials: LFB; it should be noted that Baum's Wicked Witch of the West remains nameless.
3. It is only winged monkeys that make an appearance in the 1939 film.
4. Lucan, *Civil War*, Book 15.
5. Ibid.
6. Ibid, xvi
7. Ibid.
8. Ibid.
9. Ibid, xvii–xviii.
10. Nero in fact was forced to commit suicide. Suetonius explains that Nero lost his nerve and forced his private secretary, Epaphroditus, to perform the task. Suetonius, 'Nero', in *The Twelve Caesars*, 49.

11. The staunch conservatives (the Optimate faction in the senate house) refused to support the motion to provide land for Pompey's veterans; they also refused to grant a tax rebate for equestrian tax farmers, a motion raised by Crassus. Caesar opted for the consulship at this time over a triumph for his success in Spain as the two honours could not be given simultaneously. Prior to the consular election, the senate decided on provinces allocated to the consuls – Caesar was given administration of the forests and cattle tracks in Italy, a deliberate attempt to deprive him of an important post. This culminated in the forcible removal of his consular partner, Bibulus from the senate house in order to pass the motions for Pompey and Crassus and for Caesar to be allocated Gaul. Scullard claims that these measures put forward by these men 'were by no means outrageous' and the 'short-sighted reaction of the die-hard optimates' was 'uncompromising' and 'disrespectful'. H.H. Scullard, *From the Gracchi to Nero: A History of Rome 133 BC to AD 68*, 5th ed. (London: Routledge, 2000), 114.
12. Scholarly opinion on Caesar's stature as a stateman has always been hotly divided, with some feeling he did not have a viable vision for the Roman commonwealth beyond installing himself as a quasi-omnipotent dictator. See P. Marin, *Blood in the Forum: The Struggle for the Roman Republic* (New York: Continuum, 2009).
13. Lucan, *Civil War*, Book 19.
14. As we saw in Chapter Two, Vergil's works can sometimes be overbearing in their Augustan propaganda, such as with the grandiose display of Roman patriotism that comes through Jupiter's prophecy in *Aeneid*, Book 1, or the deliberate use of *ekphrasis* in Book 8. Both of these strengthen and heighten the glorious Roman history through the visual spectacle of success in battle with Augustus centre stage on Aeneas' newly forged shield, ready to bring down the aggressors of Mark Antony and Cleopatra, or the Lupercal scene, a reminder of their origins. Both events simultaneously stress how fratricidal strife, in the form of Romulus and Remus – itself serving as a metaphor for ruination – will come to an end with the ultimate unity and stability in the form of Augustus' successful reforms. For further use of ekphrasis in the Aeneid see M. Putnam, *Virgil's Epic Designs: Ekphrasis in the Aeneid* (New Haven: Yale University Press, 1998). Vergil

is also more subtly anti-Augustus, with his portrayal of a rather complex protagonist, who is meant to emulate Augustus himself, yet falls prey to *furor* (rage and anger), that leads to merciless acts – see Chapter Two for further details. Ovid, conversely, is much more outspoken of Augustus and his reforms, his *Amores* and *Ars Amatoria* are clearly an attack upon what Ovid would have deemed the unrealistic morality laws that Augustus had installed. However, his *Fasti*, contains an elaborately compiled compilation of all key festivals held in the Roman calendar, exuding piety and religious awe in some instances, very much in keeping with the *pietas* that Augustus wanted himself and his newly reformed state to embody. See Chapter Two for discussion concerning Ovid.

15. Susanna Braund, ed., 'Introduction', *Lucan*: *Civil War* (Oxford: Oxford University Press, 1992), xxv.
16. Lucan, *Civil War*, 3.10.
17. Ibid, 7.180–94.
18. The Sibyl is pivotal in convincing Charon, the ferryman, to carry Aeneas, a mortal who is not allowed to enter Dis, across to the entrance of the underworld despite Charon's obvious misgivings and forebodings. She refers to Aeneas as 'famous for his devotion', recognising his *pietas* (piety) and duty to his father for travelling to the depths to seek him out. She also drugs Cerberus, 'the huge monster', with soporific drugs, thus allowing Aeneas a safe pathway into the underworld: Vergil, *Aeneid*, 6.403 and 6.421 respectively.
19. Lucan, *Civil War*, 6.336.
20. Ibid.
21. Aloeus is a son of Poseidon and a Thessalian prince who, together with his sons, wage war upon the gods of Olympus, capturing Ares. His twin sons are eternally punished in Tartarus for their crimes by Rhadamanthus who delivered continual chastisement upon those who had gloated over their crimes in the upper world. Vergil, *Aeneid*, 6.570.
22. Lucan, *Civil War*, 6.336.
23. Ibid, 6.510.
24. Lucan, *Civil War*, 6.485
25. Ibid.
26. Ibid, 6.568.

27. Ibid, 620.
28. Ibid, 6.635.
29. Ibid.
30. Ibid, 6.653.
31. Ibid.
32. Ibid.
33. Ogden, *Night's Black Agents*, 51.
34. Please see 'Later Ericthos' for a discussion concerning the impact of this scene upon the modern world.
35. Lucan, *Civil War*, 6.763.
36. Ogden rather humorously refers to this as 'make-up', implying that Hecate makes up her face when she visits the other gods. Ogden, *Night's Black Agents*, 54.
37. Ibid. This is thought to be the Demogorgon, a demon that resided in the underworld.
38. Lucan's necromantic scene has some resemblance to Saul meeting the Witch of Endor in the Hebrew Bible, 1 *Samuel* 28 – see Appendix A.
39. Lucan's writing exudes with fitting mournful epithets to describe Erictho, combined with technical, almost surgical language to bring to life the actual reanimation: 'gloomy Erictho…fills the chest with boiling blood through new wounds that she opens, then washes out the bowels of putrefaction and liberally applies poison from the moon', Book 6.741–44. The added magical terms, such as 'poison' and 'moon', remind us of her true malevolent nature, despite her apparent medical adeptness at handling a dead body.
40. Women had a proactive role during funerary preparations from anointing the body to prepare it for burial, to providing lamentation for the deceased.
41. Blood sacrifices were the standard offering for a deity. The procedure would involve prayers to the particular god or goddess the sacrifice was held in honour of, combined with pipe music to create a solemn atmosphere. The animal chosen for sacrifice could be varied from pigs to bulls. The animal would be stunned by a stick, before its throat was cut, and its innards removed for examination.
42. Use of augury was a common practice in the ancient Roman world which observed the movement of birds and their behaviours. An approved action was known as *fas*, whereas an action seen

as a disapproval was a *nefas*, something deemed sacrilegious. According to Livy, the augur would veil their head and hold a bent staff called the *lituus* in his right hand which would be transferred to his left after prayers. He would pray to the gods for them to manifest signs for various occasions such as a confirmation of kingship. The auspices would then be read: Livy, *History of Rome* (or *Ab Urbe Condita*), 1.18.7–10.

43. See Chapter Two for further details.
44. Ronald Hutton argues that the early Germanic peoples had a stark belief in the magical ability of certain females who 'while their bodies lay in their beds at night…could go out as spirits through closed doors to join other women of the same kind. They would band together to kill people and cook and eat their organs'. Hutton, *The Witch*, 71. Hutton claims this was unique to their culture and serves as an early representation of the witches' sabbat. However, early Germanic peoples had connections with the Roman world, as attested by the contact between the two cultures that Julius Caesar and Tacitus mention at length, thus indicating at a possibility of shared ideas and shared superstitious beliefs. The Roman *strigae*, as discussed in the previous chapter, certainly seem very similar to the Germanic cannibalistic woman mentioned here by Hutton. See also Julius Caesar's *Gallic War* and Tacitus's *Germania*.
45. Cf. D. Petherbridge, *Witches and Wicked Bodies* (Edinburgh: National Galleries Scotland, 2013), 16.
46. Cf. Ibid, 14.
47. Cf. Ibid, 15.
48. Pregnancies in ancient Rome could be terminated if permitted by the husband, this could be due to social and economic purposes. Soranus even states that an abortion should be allowed if the uterus was considered too small, or if there was a risk to life for the mother. O. Temskin, *Soranus' Gynaecology* (Baltimore: John Hopkins Press, 1956), 63. However, if a woman aborted a child without her husband's permission, then this could be punished by the husband, in some cases through divorce. We are perhaps expected to see Erictho as an example of an 'illegal' terminator of pregnancies, who would act on the periphery of the city in secret and away from prying eyes. For further information concerning abortion in ancient Rome, see: J. Riddle, *Contraception and Abortion from*

the Ancient World to the Renaissance (Cambridge, MA: Harvard University Press, 1994), 62; and also D.A. Jones, *The Soul of the Embryo: An Enquiry into the Status of the Human Embryo in the Christian Tradition*, 2nd ed. (Continuum, 2005), 42. The latter covers an exploration of abortion in ancient Rome before moving onto the role and views of abortion in early Christianity.

49. *Malleus Malificarum*, Part 1. *Malleus Malificarum* (Hammer of Witches) was written by Dominican friars Jacob Sprenger and Heinrich Kramer and is deeply misogynistic.
50. Ibid.
51. Dante, *Inferno*, 9.25–30.
52. Dante draws on the popular belief, widespread in the Middle Ages, that Vergil himself possessed magical, prophetic powers. This arose from a variant upon his name – Virgil – which was believed to have derived from the Latin word 'virga', meaning wand.
53. Ogden, *Night's Black Agents*, 55–56.
54. Ibid.
55. M. Gaskill, 'The Fear and Loathing in Witches', in *Spellbound: Magic, Ritual and Witchcraft* (Oxford: Ashmolean Museum, 2018), 99.
56. Cf.D.Petherbridge, *WitchesandWickedBodies*(Edinburgh:National Galleries Scotland, 2013), 15.
57. Ibid, 18.
58. It was stated in an article issued by the *Times* that Roald Dahl's *Witches* was in fact banned in some libraries due to the encouragement of misogynistic views: 'Not in Front of the Censors', *The Times* 24 November 1986.

Chapter Five

1. Note also Pauline Ripat's arguments which centre upon the real-life concerns of upperclass females who felt inclined to use witchcraft as a way of regaining their status quo. See Chapter Three 'Conclusions' for more details; cf. Ripat, 'Cheating Women', 340-364.
2. Horace, *Epode*, 5.98 and 5.48.
3. See Chapter Four.

4. Horace, *Satire*, 1.8.23–28.
5. See Chapter Two.
6. Propertius, *Elegy*, 4.5.16.
7. Lucan, *Civil War*, 6.541–43.
8. See D. Todman, 'Childbirth in Ancient Rome: From Traditional Folklore to Obstetrics', *Australian and New Zealand Journal of Obstetrics and Gynaecology* 47 (2007), 82–85.
9. Ibid.
10. See Soranus, *Gynaecology*, 2.2.2–3 and P. Rieder, 'Pregnancy and Childbirth: Christian Women', in *Women and Gender in Medieval Europe: An Encyclopedia*, ed. Margaret Schaus (New York: Routledge, 2006), 667–68.
11. Plato for instance assumes it is common knowledge that midwives are beyond child- bearing age: *Theat*, 149b.
12. Cf. A. Johns, *Baba Yaga: The Ambiguous Mother and Witch of the Russian Folktale* (New York: Peter Lang, 2004), 2.
13. Ibid, 14. The idea of a fairytale villain being ostracised and serving as a threat to the hero is a common one, Jack and the Beanstalk being another classic example. Indeed, the idea of the 'Russian scent' may also habour vestiges to the 'fee fi fo fum' poem recited by the giant within the Jack and the Beanstalk story. See W.B. McCarthy, C. Oxford, and J.D. Sobol, *Jack in Two Worlds: Contemporary North American Tales and Their Tellers*, ed. W.B. McCarthy (North Carolina: University North Carolina Press, 1994), which relates details concerning the origin of the 'fee fi fo fum' poem, predating Baba Yaga by at least two centuries. See also M. Tatar, *The Hard Facts of the Grimms' Fairy Tales* (Princeton: Princeton University Press, 2019), 188, who discusses similar similarities. These stories of course contain elements of the Cyclopean encounter in Homer's *Odyssey* when Polyphemus consumes Odysseus' men and, in this way, serves as the classic hindrance to the hero.
14. Johns, *Baba Yaga,* 6.
15. Folktales often see adversaries as a mixture of a donor, helper or villain.
16. Johns, *Baba Yaga,* 157.
17. Ibid.
18. Ibid, 182.

19. Ibid.
20. The impact of Greek myth upon other tales must not be underestimated. Daniel Ogden similarly draws upon the influences of Greek myth in works such as *The Arabian Nights*, thought to be composed around 900 AD. The tales are rich in mythology and adventure and the Sinbad stories in particular reflect many Odyssean tropes such as Sinbad coming across a monstrous giant who devours Sinbad's crew. The monster is blinded by Sinbad before he and his men make their escape. See Ogden, *Night's Black Agents*, 17. See also S. Thompson, *Motif-Index of Folk Literature*, 6 vols., 2nd ed. (Bloomington: 1955-1958) which covers the wide variety of folktale motifs from cultures around the world.
21. Ibid, 13.
22. Ibid, 17 and 19.
23. Cf. Ibid, 228.
24. Ibid, 269.
25. Another grisly tale involving the luring of women to their deaths is Grimm's 'The Robber Bridegroom' which also involves cannibalistic tendencies of the bridegroom to consume the flesh of the woman he is betrothed to.
26. M. Tatar, *The Hard Facts of the Grimms' Fairy Tales* (Princeton: Princeton University Press, 2019), 141.
27. Cf. Ibid, 14.
28. Ibid, 141.
29. Ibid. See especially Chapter Six.
30. Ibid, 143.
31. Ibid, 151.
32. B. Bettelheim, *The Uses of Enchantment: The Meaning and Importance of Fairy Tales* (New York: Knopf, 1976).
33. Ibid.
34. Tatar, *The Hard Facts of the Grimms' Fairy Tales*, xiv. Thompson's *Motif-index of Folk Literature* also places together a wide variety of similarities between tales found in cultures worldwide.
35. Pollard, 'Magic Accusations against Women in Tacitus Annals', 183.
36. Cf. Ibid, 184. See also Mary Douglas' introduction to a collection of essays honouring Sir Edward Evans-Pritchard and Mary Douglas,

'Thirty Years after Witchcraft, Oracles and Magic', in *Witchcraft Confessions and Accusations*, ed. Mary Douglas (New York: Tavistock, 1970), xxv.

37. That is, incantations and poisoning through use of potions.
38. See Tacitus' *Annals* 2 and 3.
39. Ibid.
40. Ibid, 5.
41. Graf, 'Victimology'.
42. Ovid *Metamorphoses*, 6.
43. Antiphon, *Against the Stepmother for Poisoning*, *Φαρμακείας κατὰ τῆς μητρυιᾶς*. Cf. M. Gagarin, *Antiphon: The Speeches* (Cambridge: Cambridge University Press, 1997).
44. See E. Eidinow, *Envy, Poison, and Death: Women on Trial in Classical Athens* (Oxford: Oxford University Press, 2016).
45. See Gagarin, *Antiphon*.
46. Borman, *Witches*, 28.
47. Ibid.
48. Ibid. See especially Chapter Three.
49. Richard Kieckhefer claims that for a Christian, magic was seen as the worship of 'false gods', which they perceived to be demons. This, therefore, redefined magic, and so witchcraft, in the intense Christian world of the Middle Ages. Kieckhefer, *Magic in the Middle Ages*, 35–41.
50. Exodus, 22:18. See the introduction to 'Witches in Greece and Rome' for views concerning biblical references to witches and magic.
51. Hutton, *The Witch*, 147.
52. Ibid.
53. See Introduction, 'Witches in Greece and Rome'.
54. Cf. Hutton, *The Witch*, 148.
55. Cf. Ibid.
56. See Appendix A for more details concerning this encounter.
57. James I, *Demonologie*, 2.3, 5.
58. Tracy Borman provides an excellent discussion concerning village life at this time and how it was expected for 'great importance' to be 'placed upon harmony and conformity'. The rituals and festivals that the village partook in was of fundamental importance to the successful function of the village itself. 'Anyone who refused to

join in', Borman states, 'was immediately the subject of suspicion and hostility'. Borman, *Witches*, 1–2.

59. K. Thomas, *Religion and the Decline of Magic* (New York: Oxford University Press, 1971), 5.
60. Ibid.
61. B.K. Stratton, 'Interrogating the Magic-Gender Connection', in *Daughters of Hecate*, ed. Stratton and Kalleres, 7. On the other hand, there are some scholars who claim that wealthy, high-ranking women were equally targeted as witches. See especially, L. Yeoman, 'Hunting the Rich Witch in Scotland: High-Status Witchcraft Suspects and Their Persecutors, 1590–1650', in *The Scottish Witch-Hunt in Context*, ed. J. Goodare (Manchester: Manchester University Press, 2002).
62. Ibid, 8.
63. Ibid, 9.
64. Jones, *Sleeping with the Lights On*.
65. Ibid, 3.
66. Ibid, 74–75.
67. Ibid, 15.
68. Ibid.
69. H.P. Lovecraft, 'Supernatural Horror in Literature', a critical essay published in 1927.
70. See Chapter Four.

Conclusion

1. G.R. Varner, *The Dark Wind: Witches and the Concept of Evil: An Historical and Ethnographic Study of Witchcraft* (Lulu Press, 2007, 11). See also Chapter One, which also mentions the neo-pagan triple goddess.

Appendix A

1. See Chapter Two for more detail.
2. For further details concerning the Witch of Endor scene and, more specifically, the dating of the *Deuteronomy*. See Gwilym H. Jones,

'1 and 2 Samuel', in *The Oxford Bible Commentary*, eds. John Barton and John Muddiman (Oxford: Oxford University Press), 197 and Douglas A. Knight, 'Deuteronomy and the Deuteronomists', in *Old Testament Interpretation*, ed. James Luther Mays, David L. Petersen and Kent Harold Richards (Edinburgh: T&T Clark, 2008), 62. Darryl Jones actually places the origins of the Old Testament to around 800 BC which still coincides with the composition of the *Odyssey*. Jones. *Sleeping with the Lights On,* 75.

Appendix B

1. K. Ringrose, *The Perfect Servant: Eunuchs and the Social Construction of Gender in Byzantium* (Chicago: University of Chicago Press, 2003), 62.
2. See Chapter Five. With regard to emasculation, Daniel Ogden's theory concerning Circe and her transformation of men into animals could similarly be regarded as a form of control over the man, see Chapter Two for further details.
3. See Ringrose, *The Perfect Servant.* Ringrose provides an in-depth discussion concerning these mutilations.
4. See Chapter Four.
5. See especially Petherbridge, *Witches and Wicked Bodies*, 27.
6. Shakespeare, *Macbeth*, Act 1, Scene 3.
7. In Book 4, Telemachus visits Menelaus to find news of the whereabouts of his father. Helen greets Telemachus who is compared to Artemis with her distaff, whilst also being accompanied by her female attendants who carry her spindle. Later Helen pours drugs into the drinks of Menelaus and Telemachus after they become disconsolate when conversing about Odysseus as a way of allowing them to forget their woes. These drugs are ones she acquired from her time in Egypt and although she uses them here for beneficial means, this action is indicative of her dominance, as Jasper Griffin explains, 'her control is benign but complete'. Griffin, *Homer,* 82.

Bibliography

Primary Sources

Apuleius. *The Golden Ass*. Translated by P.G. Walsh (Oxford: Oxford University Press, 1994)

Aristophanes. *Thesmophoriazusae*. Translated by Stephen Halliwell (Oxford: Oxford University Press, 2016)

———. *Nephelai*. Translated by John Claughton (Cambridge: Cambridge University Press, 2012)

Aristotle. *Nicomachean Ethics*. Translated by Adam Beresford (London: Penguin Classics, 2020)

Artemidorus. *Oneirocritica*. Translated by Daniel E. Harris-McCoy (Oxford: Oxford University Press, 2012)

Cato. *De Agricultura*. Translated by Andrew Dalby (London: Prospect Books, 1998)

Cooper, T. *The Mystery of Witch-craft: Discovering the Truth, Nature, Occasions, Growth and Power Thereof* (London, 1617)

Dante. *The Divine Comedy: Inferno, Purgatorio, Paradiso*. Translated by Robin Kirkpatrick (London: Penguin Classics, 2012)

Diodorus of Sicily. Translated by C.H. Oldfather (Harvard: Loeb Classical Library, 1939)

———. *Bibliotheca historica*. Translated by John Skelton. Early English Text Society Original Series (Oxford: 1963)

Euripides. *Medea and Other Plays*. Translated by Philip Vellacott (London: Penguin Classics, 2002)

Gifford, G. *A Discourse of the Subtill Practises of Devilles by Witches and Sorcerers* (London, 1587)

Gildenhard, I. *Cicero: Philippic 2* (Cambridge: Open Book Publishers, 2018)

Gransden, K.W. (ed.) *Virgil: The Aeneid*. 3rd ed. (Cambridge: Cambridge University Press, 2010)

Griffin, J. *Homer* (London: Bloomsbury, 2001)

———. *Homer: The Odyssey*. 2nd ed. (Cambridge: Cambridge University Press, 2008)

Herodotus. *The Histories*. Translated by Robin Waterfield (Oxford: Oxford University Press, 2008)

Hesiod. *Theogony and Works and Days*. Translated by M.L West (Oxford: Oxford University Press, 1988)

Homer. *Hymns*. Translated by Susan Chadwick Shelmerdin (CreateSpace Independent Publishing Platform, 2018)

———. *Iliad*. Translated by Martin Hammond (London: Penguin Classics, 1987)

_____. *Odyssey*. Translated by E. V. Rieu (London: Penguin Classics, 2003)

Hopkins, M. *The Discovery of Witches: In Answer to Several Queries, lately Delivered to the Judges of Assize for the County of Norfolk* (London, 1647)

Horace. *Odes and Epodes*. Edited and translated by Niall Rudd (Harvard: Loeb Classical Library, 2004)

Kramer, H. and Sprenger, J. *The Malleus Maleficarum*. Translated by Montague Summers (New York: Dover Publications Inc., 2000)

Josephus. *Antiquitates Judaciae*: *The Antiquities of the Jews* (Independently Published, 2023)

Julius Caesar. *Gallic War*. Translated by Carolyn Hammond (Oxford: Oxford University Press, 2008)

Juvenal. *Satires*. Translated by Niall Rudd (Oxford: Oxford University Press, 2008)

Livy. *The Early History of Rome: Books I–V of the History of Rome from Its Foundation*. Translated by Aubrey De Sélincourt (London: Penguin, 2002)

Livy. *Works*. Translated by B.O. Foster (London, 1929)

Lucan. *Civil War*. Translated by Matthew Fox (London: Penguin Classics, 2012)

Macrobius. *Saturnalia*. Edited and translated by Robert A. Kaster (Harvard: Loeb Classical Library, 2010)

Ovid. *Amores I.* Edited and translated by John Barsby (London: Bloomsbury, 1991)
———. *Fasti*. Translated by Ann and Peter Wiseman (Oxford: Oxford University Press, 2013)
———. *Heroides*. Translated by Harold Isbell (London: Penguin Classics, 1990)
———. *Metamorphoses*. Translated by David Raeburn (London: Penguin Classics, 2004)
———.*Tristia*. Translated by José González Vázquez (Madrid: Editorial Gredos, 1992)
Petronius. *Satyricon*. Translated by P.G. Walsh (Oxford: Oxford University Press, 2009)
Plato. *Phaedrus*. Translated by Christopher Rowe (London: Penguin Classics, 2005)
———. *Theaetetus*. Translated by John Mcdowell (Oxford: Oxford University Press, 2014)
———. *Works*. Translated by W.R.M. Lamb (London, 1914)
Plautus. *Menaechmi*. Edited by A.S. Gratwick (Cambridge: Cambridge University Press, 2008)
Pliny the Elder. *Natural History: Books 17–19*. Translated by H. Rackham (Loeb Classical Library, 2008)
Propertius. *The Poems*. Translated by Guy Lee (Oxford: Oxford University Press, 2009)
Sextus Pompeius Festu. *De Verborum Significatione*. Edited by Wallace M. Lindsay (De Gruyter, 1997)
Shakespeare, William. *Antony and Cleopatra* (London: Bloomsbury, 1995)
———. *Macbeth* (Oxford: Oxford University Press, 2009)
———. *Macbeth*. Edited by S. Clark (London: Arden Shakespeare, 2015)
Sophocles. *Oedipus*. Translated by Damian Westfall (London: Recycled Shakespeare Books, 2019)
———. *The Plays and Fragments*. Edited by Lewis Campbell (Hildesheim, 1969)
Statius. *Silvae*. Translated by D.A. Slater (Leopold Classic Library, 2015)
Suetonius. *The Twelve Caesars*. Translated by Robert Graves (London: Penguin Classics, 2007)

Tacitus. *The Agricola and Germania*. Translated by J.B. Rives (London: Penguin Classics, 2010)
———. *Annals of Imperial Rome*. Translated by Michael Grant (London: Penguin Classics, 2003)
Theocritus. *Idylls*. Translated by Anthony Verity (Oxford: Oxford University Press, 2008)
Virgil. *Aeneid*. Translated by David West (London: Penguin Classics, 2003)
———. *The Eclogues and the Georgics*. Translated by C. Day Lewis (Oxford: Oxford University Press, 2009)
West, W. *Simboleography* (1594)
Xenophon. *Conversations of Socrates*. Translated by Robin Waterfield (London: Penguin Classics, 1990)

Secondary Sources

Allen, C. 'Ovid and Art'. In *The Cambridge Companion to Ovid*. Edited by Philip Hardie (Cambridge: Cambridge University Press, 2002): 336–67
Anderson, G. *Fairytale in the Ancient World* (London: Routledge, 2000)
Arens, W. *The Man-Eating Myth: Anthropology and Anthropophagy* (Oxford: Oxford University Press, 1979)
Arthur, M. 'Liberated Women: The Classical Era'. In *Becoming Visible*. Edited by Renate Bridenthal and Claudia Koonz (Boston: Houghton Mifflin, 1977): 60–89
Aune, D.E. 'Magic in Early Christianity'. *Aufstieg und Niedergang der romischen Welt ii* 23, no. 2 (1980): 1507–57
Atwood, M. *The Handmaid's Tale* (London: Vintage Classics, 2017)
———. *The Penelopiad* (Edinburgh: Canongate Canons, 2018)
———. *You Are Happy* (Oxford: Oxford University Press, 1974)
Baldwin, B. 'Executions, Trials and Punishment in the Reign of Nero.' *PP* 22 (1967): 425–39
———. 'Women in Tacitus'. *Prudentia* 4 (1972): 83–101
Barber, P. *Vampires, Burial, and Death: Folklore and Reality* (New Haven: Yale University Press, 1988)

Barrett, A.A. *Agrippina: Sex, Power and Politics in the Early Empire* (New Haven: Yale University Press, 1996)
———. *Livia: First Lady of Imperial Rome* (New Haven: Yale University Press, 2002)
Barsby, J. *Ovid Amores I* (Bristol: Bristol University Press, 1973)
Barstow, A.L. *Witchcraze: A New History of the European Witch Hunts* (San Francisco: Harper Collins, 1994)
Bartman, E. *Portraits of Livia: Imaging the Imperial Woman in Augustan Rome* (Cambridge: Cambridge University Press, 1998)
Barton, C. 'Being in the Eyes: Shame and Sight in Ancient Rome'. In *The Roman Gaze: Vision, Power, and the Body*. Edited by D. Fredrick (Baltimore: John Hopkins University Press, 2002): 216–35
Bartsch, S. *Ideology in Cold Blood: A Reading of Lucan's Civil War* (Cambridge, MA: Harvard University Press, 1998)
Baum, F. *The Wonderful Wizard of Oz* (London: Children's Classics, 1992)
Beagon, M. *Roman Nature* (Oxford: Oxford University Press, 1992)
Beard, M., J. North, and S. Price, S. *Religions of Rome Volume 1: A History*. 11th ed. (New York: Cambridge University Press, 2010)
Bettelheim. B. *The Uses of Enchantment: The Meaning and Importance of Fairy Tales* (New York: Knopf, 1976)
Bodel, J.P. 'Punishing Piso'. *American Journal of Philology* 120, no. 1 (1999): 43-63
Borman, T. *Witches: James I and the English Witch-Hunts* (London: Vintage Books, 2014)
Boulton, R. *A Compleat History of Magick: Sorcery and Witchcraft*. 2 vols. (London: Gale ECCO Print Editions, 1975)
Bovenschen, S. 'The Contemporary Witch, he Historical Witch, and the Witch Myth'. *New German Critique* 15 (1978): 83–119
Bowden, H. *Mystery Cults in the Ancient World* (London: Thames and Hudson, 2023)
Boyer, P. and S. Nissenbaum. *Salem Possessed: The Social Origins of Witchcraft* (Cambridge MA: Harvard University Press, 1974)
Braund, S. (ed.). *Lucan: Civil War*. Oxford World's Classics (Oxford: Oxford University Press, 1992)
———. 'Lucan 6.715'. *CQ* 39 (1989): 275–76
Briffault, R. *The Mothers* (London, 1959)

Briggs, R. *Witches and Neighbours: The Social and Cultural Context of European Witchcraft*. 2nd ed. (Malden: Blackwell, 2002)

Burkert, W. 'Itinerant Diviners and Magicians: A Neglected Element in Cultural Contacts'. In *The Greek Renaissance of the Eighth Century BC: Tradition and Innovation*. Edited by R. Hagg (Stockholm, 1983): 115–19

———. 'Oriental and Greek Mythology: The Meeting of Parallels'. In *Interpretations of Greek Mythology*. Edited by J. Bremmer, J. (London: 1987): 10–40

———. *Structure and History in Greek Myth and Ritual* (Berkeley: University of California Press, 1979)

———. 'The Poetics of the Magical Charm'. In *Magic and Ritual in the Ancient World*. Edited by P. Mirecki and M. Mayer. Religions in the Greco-Roman World, 141 (Leiden: Brill, 2002): 105-158

Bury, J.B and R. Meiggs. *A History or Greece*. 4th ed. (New York: Palgrave Macmillian, 1975)

Buxton, J. 'Mandari Witchcraft'. In *Witchcraft and Sorcery in East Africa*. Edited by J. Middleton and E.H. Winter (London: Routledge, 1963)

Buxton, R. *Imaginary Greece: The Context of Mythology* (Cambridge: Cambridge University Press, 1994)

Campbell, J. *The Hero with a Thousand Faces*. 3rd ed. (New World Library, 2012)

Caro Baroja, J. *The World of Witches* (Chicago: Orion, 1964)

Carpenter, R. *Folktales, Fiction and Saga in the Homeric Epics*, (Berkeley: Sather Classical Lecture, 1948)

Carson, A. 'Putting Her in Her Place: Woman, Dirt, and Desire'. In *Before Sexuality*. Edited by D.M. Halperin, J.J. Winkler, and F.I. Zeitlin (Princeton: Princeton University Press, 1990)

Castelli, E. 'Virginity and Its Meanings for Early Christian Women'. *Journal of Feminist Studies in Religion* 2, no.1, (1986): 61-88

Cauvin, J. *The Birth of the Gods and the Origins of Agriculture* (Cambridge: Cambridge University Press, 2000)

Clauss, J.J. and S. Johnston (ed.) *Medea: Essays on Medea in Myth, Literature, Philosophy, and Art* (Princeton: Princeton University Press, 1997)

Clerc, J. *Homines magici: Etude sur la sorcellerie et la magie dans la societe romaine imperiale* (Bern: University of Bern Press, 1995)

Cloke, G. *This Female Man of God: Women and Spiritual Power in the Patristic Age, AD 350–450* (New York: Routledge, 1995)
Cohn, N. *Europe's Inner Demons*. 2nd ed. (London: Pimlico, 1993)
Collon, D. *The Queen of the Night* (London: British Museum, 2005)
Cox, P. 'Origen and the Witch of Endor: Toward Iconoclastic Typology'. *Anglican Theological Review* 66, no. 2 (1984): 137–47
Dahl, R. *The Witches* (London: Penguin, 1983)
Davies, M. 'Deianeira and Medea: A Footnote to the Prehistory of Two Myths'. *Mnemosyne* 42 (1989): 469–72
Dickie, W. Matthew. 'The Learned Magician and the Collection and Transmission of Magical Lore'. In *Jordan et al* (1999): 163–94
________. *Magic and Magicians in the Greco-Roman World* (Woodbridge: Routledge, 2001)
________. 'Magic in Classical and Hellenistic Greece'. In *A Companion to Greek Religion*. Edited by D. Ogden (Oxford: Oxford University Press, 2007): 357–70
________ 'Who Practiced Love-magic in Classical Antiquity and in the Late Roman World?' *Classical Quarterly* 50 (2000): 563–83
Dillon, M. *Girls and Women in Classical Greek Religion* (London: Routledge, 2002)
Dingwall, E. *Ghosts and Spirits in the Ancient World* (London: Psyche Miniatures General Series, 1930)
Dixon, S. *The Roman Family* (Baltimore: John Hopkins University Press, 1991)
Dodds, E.R. *The Greeks and the Irrational*, Berkely, University of California Press, 1951
———. 'New Light on the Chaldaean Oracles'. *Harvard Theological Review* 54 (1961): 263–73
———. 'Theurgy and its Relation to Neoplatonism'. *Journal of Roman Studies* 37 (1947): 62–65
Doherty, L.E. 'Sirens, Muses, and Female Narrators in the Odyssey'. In *The Distaff Side: Representing the Female in Homer's Odyssey*. Edited by B. Cohen (Oxford: Oxford University Press, 1995): 81–92
Douglas, M. *Natural Symbols: Explorations in Cosmology* (London: Barrie and Rockliff, 1970)
———. 'Thirty Years after Witchcraft, Oracles and Magic'. In *Witchcraft Confessions and Accusations*. Edited by Mary Douglas (New York: Tavistock, 1970)

Dyck, A.R. 'On the Way to Colchis to Corinth: Medea in Book 4 of the Argonautica'. *Hermes* 117 (1989): 455–70
Eckels, R.P. 'Greek Wolf-Lore'. Dissertation, Philadelphia, 1937
Eidinow, E. *Envy, Poison, and Death: Women on Trial in Classical Athens* (Oxford: Oxford University Press, 2016)
_________. *Luck, Fate and Fortune: Antiquity and its Legacy* (Exeter: I.B. Tauris, 2010)
_________. *Oracles, Curses, and Risk Among the Ancient Greeks* (Oxford: Oxford University Press, 2013)
Eitrem, S. 'The Necromancy in the Persae of Aeschylus'. *Symbolae Osloenses* 6 (1928): 1–16
Faraone, C. 'The Wheel, The Whip, and Other Implements of Torture: Erotic Magic and Conditional Curses in the Earliest Inscribed Hexameters'. *Classical Antiquity* 15, no. 1 (1996): 76–112
Farnell, L. *Cults of the Greek States*. Vol. 2 (Oxford: Oxford University Press, 1896)
Feldherr, A. 'Metamorphosis in the Metamorphoses'. In *The Cambridge Companion to Ovid*. Edited by Philip Hardie (Cambridge: Cambridge University Press, 2002): 163–79
Felson, N. and L.M. Slatkin. 'Gender and Homeric Epic'. In *The Cambridge Companion to Homer*. Edited by R. Fowler (Cambridge: Cambridge University Press, 2004): 91–116
Felton, D. *Haunted Greece and Rome* (Austin: 1999)
Finley, M.I. *The Ancient Greeks* (London: Penguin, 1991)
———. *Aspects of Antiquity: Discoveries and Controversies*, 2nd ed. (London: Penguin, 1977)
———. *The Portable Greek Historians*. Edited by M.I. Finley (London: Penguin, 1977)
———. 'The Silent Women of Rome'. In *Sexuality and Gender in the Classical World: Readings and Sources*. Edited by Laura K. McClure (Oxford: Blackwell, 2002): 147–56
———. *The Use and Abuse of History* (London: Chatto and Windus, 1975)
———. *The World of Odysseus* (London: Chatto and Windus, 1977)
Firth, R. 'Reason and Unreason in Human Belief'. In *Witchcraft and Sorcery*. Edited by M. Marwick (London: Penguin, 1982): 38–41
Flint, V. 'The Demonization of Magic in Late Antiquity'. In *Witchcraft and Magic in Europe, Volume Two: Ancient Greece and Rome*.

Edited by B. Ankarloo and S. Clark (Princeton: Princeton University Press 1999)

Fowler, R. (ed.) *The Cambridge Companion to Homer* (Cambridge: Cambridge University Press, 2004)

Gagarin, M. *Antiphon: The Speeches* (Cambridge: Cambridge University Press, 1997)

Gaskill, M. 'The Fear and Loathing in Witches'. In *Spellbound: Magic, Ritual and Witchcraft* (Oxford: Ashmolean Museum, 2018)

———. *Witchfinders: A Seventeenth-Century English Tragedy* (London: John Murray Press, 2005)

Geertz, H. 'An Anthropology of Religion and Magic, I'. *JIH* 6 (1975): 71–89

Germain, G. *Genese de l'Odyssee* (Paris: 1954)

Gildenhard, I. and A. Zissos, ed. *Transformative Change in Western Thought: A History of Metamorphosis from Homer to Hollywood* (Leeds: Maney Publishing, 2012)

Girard, R. *Violence and the Sacred.* Translated by Patrick Gregory (London: Continuum, 2005)

Gordon, R. 'Aelian's Peony: The Location of Magic in Graeco-Roman Tradition'. In *Comparative Criticism 9* (Cambridge: Cambridge University Press, 1987)

Goode, W.J. 'Magic and Religion: A Continuum'. *Ethnos* 14 (1949): 172–82

Graf, F. *Magic in the Ancient World.* Translated by Franklin Philip. 6th ed. (Cambridge, MA: Harvard University Press, 2003)

______. 'Victimology or: How to Deal with Untimely Death'. In *Daughters of Hecate: Women and Magic in the Ancient World.* Edited by K.B. Stratton K.B. and D.S. Kalleres (Oxford: Oxford University Press, 2014): 386–417

Gransden, K.W. *Virgil's Iliad: An Essay on Epic Narrative* (Cambridge: Cambridge University Press, 1984)

Graves, R. *I Claudius* (London: Folio Society, 1994)

———. *The White Goddess* (London: Faber and Faber, 1999)

Greene, P. 'The Methods of Ancient Magic'. *Times Literary Supplement* 5168 (2002): 5-Gregoire, H. 'Thraces et Thessaliens, maitres de religion et de magie'. In *Homages a Joseph Bidez et a Franz Cumont*. Edited by J. Bidez and F. Cumont (Brussels): 375–78

Griffiths, F.T. 'Poetry as pharmakon in Theocritus' *Idyll 2*'. In *Arktouros*: *Hellenic Studies Presented to Bernard M.W. Knox on the Occasion of his Sixth-fifth Birthday*. Edited by G.W. Bowersock and W. Burkert (Berlind: Putman): 81–88
Grossfeld, B. 'Bible Translation'. In *Encyclopaedia Judaica*. 16 vols. (Jerusalem: Keter, 1972)
Habinek, T. 'Ovid and Empire'. In *The Cambridge Companion to Ovid*. Edited by Philip Hardie (Cambridge: Cambridge University Press, 2002): 46–61
Hall, E. *Inventing the Barbarian: Greek Self Definition Through Tragedy* (Oxford: Oxford University Press, 1989)
Halliday, W.R. *Greek Divination* (London, 1913)
Hardie, P. 'Virgil and Tragedy'. In *The Cambridge Companion to Virgil*. Edited by C. Martindale (Cambridge: Cambridge University Press, 1997): 315–26
________. *The Cambridge Companion to Ovid*. Cambridge: Cambridge University Press, 2002.
Hart, R. *Witchcraft* (London: Penguin, 1971)
Hester, M. *Lewd Women and Wicked Witches: A Study of the Dynamics of Male Domination* (London: Routledge, 1992)
Hickman, R. 'Ghostly Etiquette on the Classical Stage'. *Iowa Studies in Classical Philology 7* (Cedar Rapids, 1938)
Highbarger, E.L. *The Gates of Dreams: An Archaeological Examination of Vergil, Aeneid VI, 893–899* (Baltimore: John Hopkins University Press, 1940)
Hill, D.E. 'The Thessalian Trick'. *Rheinisches Museum für Philologie* 116 (3-4) (1973): 221–38
Holmes, C. 'Women and Witnesses'. *PaP* 140 (1993): 45–78
Hornblower, S. and A. Spawforth (ed.). *The Oxford Classical Dictionary*. 3rd ed. (Oxford: Oxford University Press, 1996)
Howe, K. (ed.), *The Penguin Book of Witches* (2014)
Hutton, R. 'The Global Context of the Scottish Witch-Hunt'. In *The Scottish Witch-Hunt in Context*, ed. Julian Goodare (Manchester: Manchester University Press, 2002)
———. *Pagan Britain* (New Haven: Yale University Press, 2013)
———. *The Witch: A History of Fear from Ancient Times to the Present* (New Haven: Yale University Press, 2017)

Johns, A. *Baba Yaga: The Ambiguous Mother and Witch of the Russian Folktale* (Peter Lang, 2004)

Jones, D. A. *The Soul of the Embryo: An Enquiry into the Status of the Human Embryo in the Christian Tradition*. 2nd ed. (New York: Continuum, 2005)

Jones, Gwilym H. '1 and 2 Samuel'. In *The Oxford Bible Commentary*. Edited by John Barton and John Muddiman (Oxford: Oxford University Press)

Kalleres, D.S. 'Drunken Hags with Amulets and Prostitutes with Erotic Spells: The Re-Feminisation of Magic in Late Antique Christian Homilies'. In *Daughters of Hecate: Women and Magic in the Ancient World*. Edited by K.B. Stratton with D.S. Kalleres (Oxford: Oxford University Press, 2014): 219–51

Kaplin, M. '*Agrippina Semper atrox*: A Study in Tacitus' Characterization of Women'. In *Studies in Latin Literature and Roman History*. Edited by C. Deroux. Vol. 1 (Brussels: Collection Latomus, 1978): 410–17

Kearns, E. 'The Gods in Homeric Epic'. In *The Cambridge Companion to Homer*. Edited by R. Fowler(Cambridge: Cambridge University Press, 2004): 59–73

Kieckhefer, R. 'Avenging the Blood of Children: Anxiety over Child Victims and the Origins of the European Witch Trials'. In *The Devil, Heresy and Witchcraft in the Middle Ages: Essays in Honor of Jeffrey B. Russell*. Edited by A. Ferreio (Leiden: Brill, 1998): 91–109

———. *Magic in the Middle Ages* (Cambridge: Cambridge University Press), 1989)

Kirk, G.S. *The Nature of Greek Myths* (Harmondsworth: Penguin, 1983)

Klaits, J. *Servants of Satan: The Age of the Witch Hunts* (Bloomington: Indiana University Press, 1985)

Knight, G. *A History of White Magic* (Cheltenham: Skylight Press, 2011)

Knust, J.W. *Abandoned to Lust: Sexual Slander and Early Christianity* (New York: Columbia University Press, 2003)

Kolenkow, A.B. 'Persons of Power and Their Communities'. In *Magic and Divination in the Ancient World*. Edited by L. Ciraolo and J. Seidel (Leiden: Brill, 2002): 133–44

———. 'A Problem of Power: How Miracle Doers Counter Charges of Magic in the Hellenistic World'. In *Society of Biblical Literature: 1976 Seminar Papers*. Edited by G. MacRae (Missoula: School Press, 1976): 105–10

Konstan, D. 'Premarital Sex, Illegitimacy, and Male Anxiety in Menander and Athens'. In *Athenian Identity and Civic Ideology*. Edited by A. Boegehold and A. Scafuro (Baltimore: John Hopkins University Press, 1994): 217–35

Kraus, T. *Hecate* (Heidelberg:, 1960)

Kugel, J. *The Bible as It Was* (Cambridge MA: Harvard University Press, 1999)

Janowitz, N. *Magic in the Roman World: Pagans, Jews and Christians* (London: Routledge, 2001)

Johnston S. 'Describing the Undefinable: New Books on Magic and Old Problems of Definition'. *HR* 43, no. 1(2003): 50–54

———. *Hekate Soteira* (Atlanta: Scholars Press, 1990)

———. *Restless Dead: Encounters between the Living and the Dead in Ancient Greece* (Los Angeles: University of California Press, 1999)

———. 'The Song of the Iynx: Magic and Rhetoric in Pythian 4'. *Transactions of the American Philological Association* 125 (1995): 177–206

Jones, D. *Sleeping with the Lights On: The Unsettling Story of Horror* (Oxford: Oxford University Press, 2018)

Kamensky, J. 'Female Speech and Other Demons: Witchcraft and Wordcraft in Early New England'. In *Spellbound: Women and Witchcraft in America*. Edited by Elizabeth Reis (Wilmington: Scholarly Resources, 1998)

Kieckhefer, R. *Magic in the Middle Ages* (Cambridge: Cambridge University Press, 1989)

Kolberg, O. *The People, Their Customs, Way of Life, Language*. Vol. 15 (Krakow: Krakow Uniwersytet Jagiellonski, 1882)

Laird, A. 'Approaching Characterisation in Virgil.' In *The Cambridge Companion to Virgil*. Edited by C. Martindale (Cambridge: Cambridge University Press, 1997): 282–93

Lefkowitz M.R. and Fant M.B. *Women's Life in Greece and Rome*. 3rd ed. (London: Bloomsbury, 2005)

Leinweber, D.W. 'Witchcraft and Lamiae in the Golden Ass'. *Folklore* 105(1994): 77–82

Levack, B.P. (ed.). *Witchcraft, Women, and Society.* Vol.10 of *Articles on Witchcraft, Magic, Demonology* (New York: Garland, 1992)
Lloyd, G.E.R. *Magic, Reason, and Experience: Studies in the Origin and Development of Greek Society*, (Cambridge: Cambridge University Press, 1979)
Lord, A.B. *The Singer of Tales* (Cambridge, MA: Harvard University Press, 1960)
Lovecraft, H.P. *Supernatural Horror in Literature and Other Literary Essays* (Baltimore: Wildside Press, 2011)
Luck. G. *Arcana Mundi: Magic and the Occult in the Greek and Roman Worlds*. 2nd ed. (Baltimore: 2006)
______. *Hexen and Zauberei in der romischen Dichtung* (Zurich: 1962)
______. 'Witches and Sorcerers in Classical Literature'. In *Witchcraft and Magic in Europe*. (Philadelphia: University of Pennsylvania Press, 1999)
Lyne, R.O.A.M. *Further Voices in Vergil's Aeneid* (Oxford: Clarendon Press, 1987)
MacCormack, C. and M. Strathern (eds.) *Nature, Culture and Gender* (Cambridge: Cambridge University Press, 1980)
Macey, S.L. *Patriarchs of Time: Dualism in Saturn-Cronus, Father Time, the Watchmaker God, and Father Christmas* (Atlanta: University of Georgia Press, 2010)
Macfarlane, A. *Witchcraft in Tudor and Stuart England: A Regional and Comparative Study* (London: Routledge, 1970)
Magie, D. *Roman Rule in Asia Minor to the End of the Third Century after Christ*. Vols. I-II (Princeton: Princeton University Press, 1950)
Maguire, G. *Wicked: The Life and Times of the Wicked Witch of the West* (London: Headline Review, 2006)
Mair, L. *Witchcraft* (London: World University Library, 1969)
Majerick, R. *The Chaldaean Oracles*. Studies in Greek and Roman Religion 5 (Leiden: Brill, 1989)
Mallory, J.P. and D.Q. Adams, *The Oxford Introduction to Proto-Indo-European and the Proto-Indo European World* (Oxford: Oxford University Press, 2006)
Malinowski, B. *Argonauts of the Western Pacific* (London: 1922)
Marin, P. *Blood in the Forum: The Struggle for the Roman Republic* (New York: Continuum, 2009)
Martin, M. *Magie et Magiciens dans le monde Greco-Romain* (Paris, 2005)

Martindale, C., ed. *The Cambridge Companion to Virgil* (Cambridge: Cambridge University Press, 1997)
Martinez, R.L. and R.M. Durling. *Introduction and Notes to Inferno by Dante Alighieri, Vol. 1 of the Divine Comedy of Dante Alighieri.* Translated by R.M. Durling (New York: Oxford University Press, 1996)
Matalene, C. 'Women as Witches'. In *Witchcraft, Women, and Society.* Edited by B.P. Levack. Vol. 10 of *Articles on Witchcraft, Magic, and Demonology* (New York: Garland, 1992): 51–66
Matyszak, P. *Ancient Magic in Greece and Rome: A Hands-On Guide* (London: Thames and Hudson, 2019)
Mauss, M. *A General Theory of Magic*. Translated by Robert Brain (London: Routledge, 1972)
Mayor, Adrienne. 'The Nessus Shirt in the New World: Smallpox Blankets in History and Legend'. *The Journal of American Folklore* 108, no. 427 (Winter, 1995): 57–77
McCarthy, W.B., C. Oxford, and J.D. Sobol. *Jack in Two Worlds: Contemporary North American Tales and Their Tellers*. Edited by W.B. McCarthy (Chapel Hill: University North Carolina Press, 1994)
McDaniel, W.B. 'A Sempiternal Superstition'. *The Classical Journal* 45 (1950)
McDonough, C.M. 'Carna, Proca and the Strix on the Kalends of June'. *Transactions of the American Philological Association* 127 (1997): 315–44
McDougall, J.I. 'Tacitus and the Portrayal of the Elder Agrippina'. *Echos du Monde Classique* 30 (1981): 104–8
McGinn, T.A.J. *The Economy of Prostitution in the Roman World: A Study of Social History and the Brothel* (Ann Arbor: University of Michigan Press, 2004)
McLachlan, H. and J.K. Swales. 'Witchcraft and the Status of Women: A Comment'. In *Witchcraft, Women, and Society*. Edited by B.P. Levack. Vol. 10 of *Articles on Witchcraft, Magic, and Demonology* (New York: Garland, 1992)
Meiggs, R. and D.A. Lewis. *A Selection of Greek Historical Inscriptions to the End of the Fifth Century BC* (Oxford: Clarendon Press, 1989)
Miller, M. *Circe* (London: Bloomsbury, 2018)
Miller, S. 'Evil and Fairy Tales: The Witch as Symbol of Evil in Fairytales'. PhD diss. California Institute of Integral Studies, 1984

Mitropoulou, E. *Triple Hecate in Ancient Greek Religion* (Horned Owl Publishing, 1978)

Morris, I. 'The Use and Abuse of Homer'. *CLANT* 5 (1986): 81–138

———, and B. Powell (ed.). *A New Companion to Homer* (New York: Brill, 1997)

Moss, L.W. and S.C. Cappannari. 'Folklore and Medicine in an Italian Village'. *The Journal of American Folklore 73* (1960): 95–102

Needham, R. *Primordial Characters* (Charlottesville: University of Virginia Press, 1978)

Newall, V. (ed.), *The Witch Figure: Folklore Essays by a Group of Scholars in England Honoring the 75th Birthday of Katherin M. Briggs* (London: Routledge, 1973)

Newlands, C.E. 'The Metamorphosis of Ovid's Medea'. In *Medea: Essays on Medea in Myth, Literature, Philosophy and Art*. Edited by J.J. Clauss and S.I. Johnston (Princeton: Princeton University Press, 1997): 178–208

Ogden, D. *Magic, Witchcraft and Ghosts in the Greek and Roman Worlds: A Sourcebook* (Oxford: Oxford University Press, 2009)

———. *Night's Black Agents: Witches, Wizards and the Dead in the Ancient World* (Hambledon: Continuum, 2008)

Oliphant, S.G. 'The Story of the Strix'. *Transactions of the American Philological Association* 44 (1913): 133-149 and 45 (1914), 49–63

Padel, R. 'Women: Model for Possession by Greek Daemons'. In *Images of Women in Antiquity*. Edited by A. Cameron and A. Kuhrt (Detroit: Wayne State University Press, 1983): 3–19

Pagan, V. *Conspiracy Narratives in Roman History* (Austin: University of Texas Press, 2004)

Patterson, C. 'The Case Against Neaira and the Public Ideology of the Athenian Family'. In *Athenian Identity and Civic Ideology*. Edited by A. Boegehold and A. Scafuro (Baltimore: John Hopkins University Press, 1994): 199–216

Pelling, C. 'Tacitus and Germanicus'. In *Tacitus and the Tacitean Tradition*. Edited by T.J. A.J. Woodman (Princeton: Princeton University Press, 1993): 59–85

Peters, E. *The Magician, The Witch, and The Law* (Philadelphia: University of Pennsylvania Press, 1978)

Petherbridge, D. *Witches and Wicked Bodies* (Edinburgh: National Galleries Scotland, 2013)

Phillips, C.R. 'The Sociology of Religious Knowledge in the Roman Empire to AD 284'. *ANRW* 16, no. 3, 2677–773

Phillips, O. 'The Witches' Thessaly'. In *Magic and Ritual in the Ancient World.* Edited by P. Mirecki and M. Mayer. Religions in the Greco-Roman World, 141 (Leiden: Brill, 2002): 378–85

Pollard, E.A. 'Magic Accusations against Women in Tacitus' Annals'. In *Daughters of Hecate: Women and Magic in the Ancient World.* Edited by K.B. Stratton and D.S. Kalleres (Oxford: Oxford University Press, 2014): 183–218

Pomeroy, S.B. *Goddesses, Whores, Wives and Slaves: Women in Classical Antiquity* (New York: Schocken Books, 1975)

Prusak, B.P. 'Woman: Seductive Siren and Source of Sin? Pseudepigraphal Myth and Christian Origins'. In *Religion and Sexism: Images of Women in the Jewish and Christian Tradition.* Edited by R.R. Ruether (New York: Wipf and Stock, 1974): 89–116

Putnam, M. *Virgil's Epic Designs: Ekphrasis in the Aeneid* (New Haven: Yale University Press, 1998)

Richlin, A. 'Approaches to the Sources on Adultery at Rome'. In *Reflections of Women in Antiquity*. Edited by H.P. Foley (New York: Gordon and Breach Science Publishers, 1981): 379–404

Riddle, J. *Contraception and Abortion from the Ancient World to the Renaissance* (New Haven: Harvard University Press, 1994)

Rieder, P. 'Pregnancy and Childbirth: Christian Women'. In *Women and Gender in Medieval Europe: An Encyclopedia*. Edited by Margaret Schaus (New York: Routledge, 2006): 667–68

Ripat, P. 'Cheating Women: Curse Tablets and Roman Wives'. In *Daughters of Hecate: Women and Magic in the Ancient World.* Edited by K.B. Stratton and D.S. Kalleres (Oxford: Oxford University Press, 2014): 340–64

Rogers, R.S. *Criminal Trials and Criminal Legislation under Tiberius* (American Philological Association, 1935)

Roper, L. *Oedipus and the Devil: Witchcraft, Sexuality and Religion in Early Modern Europe* (New York: Routledge, 1994)

Roshcer, W.H. 'Das von der 'kynanthropie' handelnde Fragment des Marcellus von Side'. *Abhandlungen der philologisch-historischen Classe der Konigl.* Sachsischen Gesellschaft der Wissenschaften 3 (Leipzig, 1896)

Sale, R. *Fairy Tales and After: From Snow White to E.B. White* (Cambridge, MA: Harvard University Press, 1978)

Santoro, F. 'Tacitus and Women's Usurpation of Power'. *Classical World* 88, no. 1 (1994): 5–25

———. *Tragedy, Rhetoric, and the Historiography of Tacitus' Annals* (Ann Arbor: University of Michigan Press, 2003)

Schmidt, M. 'Medeia'. *LIMCs* 1 (1992): 386–98

Schultz, C. *Women's Religious Activity in the Roman Republic* (Chapel Hill: University of North Carolina Press, 2006)

Scullard, H.H. *From the Gracchi to Nero: A History of Rome 133 BC to AD 68*. 5th ed. (London: Routledge, 2000)

Sharrock, A. 'Gender and Sexuality'. In *The Cambridge Companion to Ovid*. Edited b Philip Hardie (Cambridge: Cambridge University Press, 2002): 95–107

Shelley, M. *Frankenstein*. Revised ed. (London: Penguin Classics, 2003)

Smith, J.Z. *Map is Not Territory: Studies in the History of Religions* (Leiden: Brill, 1978)

Smith, K.F. 'An Historical Study of the Werewolf in Literature'. *Publications of the Modern Language Association of America* 9, no. 1 (1894): 1–42

Snell, B. *Scenes from Greek Dram*a (Berkeley: 1964)

Snodgrass, A.M. *Early Greek Armour and Weapons: From the End of the Bronze Age to 600 BC* (Edinburgh: Edinburgh University Press, 1964)

Spaeth, B.S. 'From Goddess to Hag: The Greek and Roman Witch in Classical Literature'. In *Daughters of Hecate: Women and Magic in the Ancient World*. Edited by K.B. Stratton and D.S. Kalleres (Oxford: Oxford University Press, 2014): 41–70

Spyros, N.T. 'Magic and the Devil: From the Old to the New Rome'. In *Greek Magic*. Edited by J.C.B. Petropoulos (London: Routledge, 2008): 44–52

Stanford, W.B. "That Circe's 'Ράβδος ('Od'. 10, 238 Ff.) Was Not A Magic Wand." *Hermathena* 66 (1945): 69–71

Staples, A. *From Good Goddess to Vestal Virgins: Sex and Category in Roman Religion*, London: Routledge, 1998

Stratton, K. *The Dark Age of Greece: An Archaeological Survey of the Eleventh to Eighth Centuries BC* (Edinburgh: Edinburgh University Press, 1971)

———. 'Interrogating the Magic-Gender Connection'. In *Daughters of Hecate: Women and Magic in the Ancient World*. Edited by K.B. Stratton K.B. and D.S. Kalleres (Oxford: Oxford University Press, 2014)

———. *Naming the Witch: Magic, Ideology, and Stereotype in the Ancient World* (New York: Columbia University Press, 2022)

———, and Kalleres S.D. (ed.). *Daughters of Hecate: Women and Magic in the Ancient World* (Oxford: Oxford University Press, 2014)

Syme, R. *The Roman Revolution* (London: Oxford University Press, 1939)

Tambiah, S.J. 'Form and Meaning of Magical Arts: A Point of View'. In *Modes of Thought: Essay on Thinking in Western and Non-Western Societies*. Edited by R. Horton and R. Finnegan (London: Faber, 1973): 199–229

———. *Magic, Science, and the Scope of Rationality* (Cambridge: Cambridge University Press, 1990)

———. 'The Magical Power of Words'. *Man* 3 (1986): 171–208

Tatar, M. *The Hard Facts of the Grimms' Fairy Tales* (Princeton: Princeton University Press, 2019)

Tatum, J. 'The Tales in Apuleius' Metamorphoses'. In *Oxford Readings in the Roman Novel*. Edited by S.J. Harrison (Oxford: Oxford University Press, 1999): 157–94

Tavenner, E. 'Canidia and Other Witches'. In *Witchcraft in the Ancient World and Middle Ages*. Vol.2 of *Articles on Witchcraft, Magic and Demonology*. Edited by B.P. Levack (New York: Garland, 1992): 38–39

———. 'Iynx and Rhombus'. *Transactions of the American Philological Association* 64 (1933): 109–27

———. *Studies in Magic from Latin Literature* (New York: Legare Street Press, 1916)

Teitel, P.M. *Canidia: Rome's First Witch* (London: Bloomsbury, 2017)

Thompson, S. *Motif-Index of Folk Literature*. 6 vols. 2nd ed. (Bloomington: 1955–1958)

Temskin, O. *Soranus' Gynaecology* (Baltimore: John Hopkins Press, 1956)

Thomas, K. *Religion and the Decline of Magic* (New York: Oxford University Press, 1971)

Thorndike, L. *A History of Magic and Experimental Science during the First Thirteen Centuries of Our Era*. Vol. 1 (New York: Columbia University Press, 1923)

Todman, D. 'Childbirth in Ancient Rome: From Traditional Folklore to Obstetrics'. *Australian and New Zealand Journal of Obstetrics and Gynaecology* 47 (2007): 82–85

Treggiari, G.B. *Roman Marriage: Lusti Coniuges from the Time of Cicero to the Time of Ulpian* (Oxford: Clarendon Press, 1991)

Tyson, D. *The Demonology of King James I* (Portland: Llewellyn Publications, 2011)

Varner, G.R. *The Dark Wind: Witches and the Concept of Evil: An Historical and Ethnographic Study of Witchcraft* (Lulu Press, 2007)

Viden, G. *Women in Roman Literature: Attitudes of Authors under the Early Empire*. Studia Graeca et Latina Gothoburgensia 57 (Goteborg: Acta Universitatis Gothobugensis, 1993)

Waite, G.K. *Heresy, Magic, and Witchcraft in Early Modern Europe* (Basingstoke: Palgrave Macmillan, 2003

Walcot, P. *Hesiod and the Near East*, (Cardiff: University of Wales Press, 1966)

Wallis, R.T. *Neoplatonism* (New York: Scribner, 1971)

Walters, J. 'Invading the Roman Body: Manliness and Impenetrability in Roman Thought'. In *Roman Sexualities*. Edited by J.P. Hallett, and M.B. Skinner (Princeton: Princeton University Press, 1997): 29–46

Ward, J.O. 'Women, Witchcraft and Social Patterning in the Later Roman Law Codes'. *Prudentia 13* (1981): 99–118

Wees, H.V. 'Homer and Early Greece'. In *Homer: Critical Assessments*, Vol.II. Edited by I.de Jong (London: Routledge, 1999)

Westlake, H.D. *Thessaly in the Fourth Century BC* (Groningen: Methuen and Company, 1969)

Williams, R.D. *Aeneas and the Roman Hero* (Bristol: Bristol Classical Press, 1973)

Willis, D. *Malevolent Nurture: Witch Hunting and Maternal Power in Early Modern England* (Ithaca: Cornell University Press, 1995)

Wills, G. *Witches and Jesuits: Shakespeare's Macbeth* (Oxford: Oxford University Press, 1995)

Winkler, J.J. *The Constraints of Desire: The Anthropology of Sex and Gender in Ancient Greece* (New York: Routledge, 1990)

Wiseman, J. 'Rethinking the Halls of Hades'. *Archaeology* 51, no. 3 (1998): 12–18

Wolfgang, B. *Witches and Witch-Hunts* (Cambridge: Cambridge University Press, 2004)

Woods, C. *The Pre-Raphaelites* (New York: The Viking Press, 1981)

Wortley, J. 'Some Light on Magic and Magicians in Late Antiquity'. *Greek, Roman and Studies* 20 (Brill: 2012): 31–57

Wright, T. *Narratives of Sorcery and Magic, From the Most Authentic Sources*. 2 vols. (London, 1851)

Wrightson, K. *English Society 1580–1680* (London: Routledge, 1982)

Yarnall, J. *Transformations of Circe: The History of an Enchantress* (Chicago: University of Illinois Press, 1994)

Yeoman, L. 'Hunting the Rich Witch in Scotland: High-Status Witchcraft Suspects and Their Persecutors, 1590–1650'. In *The Scottish Witch-Hunt in Context*. Edited by J. Goodare (Manchester: New York: Manchester University Press, 2002)

Zetzel, J.E.G. 'Rome and its Traditions'. In *The Cambridge Companion to Virgil*. Edited by C. Martindale (Cambridge: Cambridge University Press, 1997): 188–203

Zuntz, G. *Persephone* (Oxford: Oxford University Press, 1971)

Index